Perverts and Predators

Issues in Crime & Justice

Series Editor
Gregg Barak, Eastern Michigan University

As we embark upon the twentieth-first century, the meanings of crime continue to evolve and our approaches to justice are in flux. The contributions to this series focus their attention on crime and justice as well as on crime control and prevention in the context of a dynamically changing legal order. Across the series, there are books that consider the full range of crime and criminality and that engage a diverse set of topics related to the formal and informal workings of the administration of criminal justice. In an age of globalization, crime and criminality are no longer confined, if they ever were, to the boundaries of single nation-states. As a consequence, while many books in the series will address crime and justice in the United States, the scope of these books will accommodate a global perspective and they will consider such eminently global issues such as slavery, terrorism, or punishment. Books in the series are written to be used as supplements in standard undergraduate and graduate courses in criminology and criminal justice and related courses in sociology. Some of the standard courses in these areas include: introduction to criminal justice, introduction to law enforcement, introduction to corrections, juvenile justice, crime and delinquency, criminal law, white collar, corporate, and organized crime.

TITLES IN SERIES:

Effigy, By Allison Cotton

Perverts and Predators, By Laura J. Zilney and Lisa Anne Zilney

The Prisoners' World, By William Tregea and Marjorie Larmour

Racial Profiling, By Karen S. Glover

Perverts and Predators

The Making of
Sexual Offending Laws

Laura J. Zilney and Lisa Anne Zilney

ROWMAN & LITTLEFIELD PUBLISHERS, INC.
Lanham • Boulder • New York • Toronto • Plymouth, UK

ROWMAN & LITTLEFIELD PUBLISHERS, INC.

Published in the United States of America
by Rowman & Littlefield Publishers, Inc.
A wholly owned subsidiary of The Rowman & Littlefield Publishing Group, Inc.
4501 Forbes Boulevard, Suite 200, Lanham, Maryland 20706
www.rowmanlittlefield.com

Estover Road
Plymouth PL6 7PY
United Kingdom

British Library Cataloguing in Publication Information Available

Library of Congress Cataloging-in-Publication Data:

Zilney, Laura J.
  Perverts and predators : the making of sexual offending laws / Laura J. Zilney
and Lisa Anne Zilney.
    p. cm. — (Issues in crime & justice)
  Includes bibliographical references.
  ISBN 978-0-7425-6622-4 (cloth : alk. paper) — ISBN 978-0-7425-6623-1 (pbk. :
alk. paper) — ISBN 978-0-7425-6624-8 (electronic)
  1. Sex offenders—Legal status, laws, etc.— United States. 2. Sex offenders—
Psychology—United States. 3. Sex crimes—United States. 4. Sex crimes—
History—United States. 5. Sex crimes—Psychological aspects—United States.
6. Child molesters—Legal status, laws, etc.—United States. I. Zilney, Lisa Anne.
II. Title.
  KF9325.Z55 2009
  345.73'0253—dc22   2008049955

Printed in the United States of America

To my husband and son,
consummate sources of love and support.
L.J.

To my parents,
for a lifetime of support.
Lisa

Contents

Part II: The Crime and the Criminals

Part III: Learning Alternatives

Acknowledgments

We are grateful to Gregg Barak (Eastern Michigan University) for initiating the current project as part of his edited series. His interest and encouragement in our work bolstered our confidence, and his constructive feedback was extremely helpful in formulating this final project. We are grateful to our Rowman & Littlefield editor, Sarah Stanton, for seeing the manuscript through the production process. We are also thankful to Randall Greenman (Montclair State University) for providing valuable feedback from a student perspective. Despite all this input, any errors in interpretation remain our own.

Preface

An act that is contrary to the mores of one small group may be entirely in accord with the mores of another. . . . Thus, what is considered a casual inconsequential contact in one setting is an affront to the mores in another and a sex offense in still another.

—Gebhard, Gagnon, Pomeroy, and Christenson (1965)

There have been many books written about sex offending and sexual offenders, often with contradictory information. As such, it has become virtually impossible to distinguish fact from fiction. Added to this are terrifying news stories of kidnapped and sexually assaulted children and women being raped and viciously attacked. Then add the pontifications of politicians trying desperately to garner votes with their "get-tough" crime legislation. It is no wonder that people are fearful and fall victim to the misconceptions portrayed by the media. We ask that you read this book with an open mind: much of what you read will challenge your beliefs about sex crimes and sex offenders. This book is written from two unique perspectives: sexology and criminology. Consequently, there has been a conscious effort to avoid the use of labels such as deviant, pervert, and predator, as we recognize that labels stigmatize people and fail to address the underlying reasons for the problem. Sex offending is a somewhat unique crime, as it directly deals with one of society's most taboo topics—sex and sexuality.

Many people, perhaps fortunately, have no conception that their everyday sexual activities may, in actuality, be contrary to law. . . . In its attempt to protect itself from serious sex offenders, society has threatened the security of most of its members who are old enough to perform sexually.

—Kinsey, Pomeroy, Martin, and Gebhard (1953)

This book is written from the standpoint that nothing sexual is inherently deviant and that the fundamental issue defining a sex crime is lack of consent. As this book will demonstrate, sex crimes legislation has tended to be based on knee-jerk reactions of politicians (often at the pleading of the public) to highly violent and stranger-based sexual violations. However, statistics show that those close to the victims commit most crimes, and our current laws are neither designed nor capable of dealing with this aspect of sexual crime. This is coupled with the fact that the definition of sex crimes has changed dramatically over the years, and what is considered deviant today was common in yesteryears. This book is written from a sex-positive viewpoint, meaning that sex is good—and good for you—and that society must learn to deal with it in a more open, forthright manner. The problem of sexual offending will continue to exist so long as we, as a society, are secretive about all things sexual. Ask yourself why Americans are focused on crimes involving strangers when most sexual violations occur between people who are known or related to one another. The answer may lie in the fact that it is easier to demonize someone who is unknown. However, society cannot begin to deal with sexual offending until we recognize that abuse and exploitation have their home in the family unit.

Coupled with the familial source of sexual offending, it is equally challenging to understand how certain behaviors come to be defined as sex crimes in our society and others do not. Recently, people have been "doggin' it," meeting strangers online and arranging to meet for sex in public places. This is technically a sex crime but rarely results in charges or convictions because the participants are usually from the middle and upper classes. But how is "doggin' it" different than a man paying a sex worker for intercourse in a park? There is no difference—both involve the same behavior, but one involves a member of a demonized or marginalized group (the sex trade worker or prostitute). Most of us have participated in some sex activity that is illegal at some point in our lives: the difference between "us" and "them" is that we have not been caught. Urinating in public, exposing your breasts at a party or on the street while intoxicated (e.g., Mardi Gras), dating someone five or six years our junior or senior, staring at someone while they get changed in a change room, having oral sex, receiving sexual aids via mail order—all of these are or have been defined as sexually based crimes. Thus, when reading about sex crimes and criminals, analyze the information critically and ask yourself why the behavior is illegal, who is being charged and convicted, who are the victims, and who is benefiting from having certain sexual behaviors criminalized.

Part I of the book encompasses the history of sexual offending and sex crimes laws. Chapter 1 begins with an overview of how Judeo-Christianity has influenced the manner in which Americans view sex and sexuality. Although the Bible and Torah are overwhelmingly sex positive, the views expressed by Church leaders are surprisingly negative. The Church sought increasing control over its members by establishing complex rules about appropriate versus inappropriate sexual behavior and required members to describe, in minute detail, all their sexual encounters. The purpose was to ensure that followers were behaving according to their social status. The Church accomplished compliance by involving the legal community. Concepts developed by canonical law found their way into legislation, and it soon became the responsibility of the state to control the sexual behaviors of its citizens. Chapter 2 discusses the medical model and its role in controlling sexual behavior. With the Church playing a leading role in defining sexual transgressions and the legal establishment enforcing the rules of conduct, it was left to the medical community to diagnose and treat those deemed sexual deviates. Key figures in the fields of psychology, psychiatry, and sexology and their roles in diagnosing the "perversions" are outlined. Chapter 3 looks more closely at sexological and criminological theory and how theory can contribute to the explanation of sex offenses. The section ends with an overview of historical sex offending laws in chapter 4 and the various ways in which society has dealt with sex criminals. This chapter details the main legislation beginning in the 1930s and continuing through the reforms brought about by social movements of the 1960s, 1970s, and 1980s.

Part II focuses on the types of sex crimes that exist today and the people who commit these offenses. Chapter 5 is dedicated to outlining the myriad of federal and state laws that deal exclusively with sexual offending. It addresses how and why certain laws came into effect and the types of crimes the laws encompass. High-profile cases of the 1990s and beyond are discussed, as are the resulting legislation that was passed, including three-strikes laws, castration laws, Internet restrictions, and the death penalty. Chapter 6 examines the prevalence of sex crimes and who is charged and convicted. Moreover, it illustrates that the recidivism rates for sexually based crimes are significantly lower than for nonsexual crimes, and thus the fear instilled in the public about being assaulted is dramatically overstated. Chapter 7 provides an in-depth elaboration of community control of offenders, including discussions of community notification and management, residency restrictions, and civil commitment legislation. The last chapter of this section, chapter 8, discusses the victim's perspective and how treatment of sexual assault victims is still misogynistic by dichotomizing victims between the Madonna/whore continuum and forcing them to relive their assault numerous times in order to seek some semblance of justice in the criminal justice system.

Part III examines what Americans can learn about sexual offending from external sources. Chapter 9 outlines the findings of research on the effectiveness of sex offender treatment. Moreover, it outlines the various treatment modalities in existence and the advantages and disadvantages of each, including the lesser-known sexological treatment that boasts a truly remarkable success rate. The book concludes with chapter 10 and a discussion of how different countries address the issue of sexual offending. Three country case studies have been selected based on their location on a continuum from sex positive (Thailand) to sex neutral (Japan) to sex negative (Canada). The chapter asks the question of whether the United States can learn from how other countries deal with sex legally and culturally and how that could be translated to mesh with American mores.

This book weaves together an understanding of how religion, law, and medicine intersect to control what Americans do sexually. Contrary to popular belief, sex crimes are not just violent attacks by strangers against women and children. Sex crimes also include consensual activity, such as paying a sex worker, teens having intercourse, and in some states oral and anal coitus. American lawmakers have created a "war on sex crimes" that is eerily reminiscent of America's war on crime, war on drugs, and war on terror. In response to supposed dramatic increases in sexual assaults, huge establishments have been created to fight such "wars" at great expense to taxpayers. But have these enormous expenses resulted in any change? Is the idiom "once a sex offender, always a sex offender" correct? What this book demonstrates is that not all persons who commit sexual crimes are homogeneous, and most are nonviolent. Most of the legislation that has been passed has been in response to high-profile, very violent stranger assaults. The result has been the widespread support of legislation to severely restrict the movement and activities of sexual offenders. The unintended consequence is that this legislation has been applied to members of our communities who are engaged in minor violations of the law. We ask that as you read this book you remember that a person is worth more and is more valuable to our community than the worst thing they have done. If you or a family member were charged and convicted of a sexually based crime, would you want to have this one act ruin your life? After all, research has shown that most of us have done sexual things that are against the law. It is now up to you to sift through the information and ascertain fact from fiction. Only when we examine an issue objectively can we work to make society safe from sexual violence.

I

HISTORICAL PERSPECTIVES ON SEXUAL OFFENDING

1

The Role of Religion

Religion plays an integral role in defining appropriate sexuality, both historically and in current times. Although separation of Church and state is supposed to exist in developed countries such as the United States, this is not necessarily the case. Christianity forms the basis of the U.S. Constitution, and its moral codes are embedded throughout state and federal laws. Religion is especially relevant today as the world increasingly becomes a cultural mosaic. Christianity and Judaism have in common broad concepts of what is considered "deviant" sexual behavior. An analysis of religion and sexuality involves the consideration of many questions: Who decides what is and is not deviant in these religions? Have the definitions of deviancy changed throughout history to better align with changing social mores, or have they remained static for thousands of years? How are the concepts of two of the major world religions embedded into our laws and customs, and how does that impact how we treat those labeled sexual offenders? Each of these questions is challenging and requires a critical examination of our belief systems and who we let define our sexual expression.

Judeo-Christianity forms the basis of the social and legal normative systems in Western cultures. Although the scriptures, the Bible and the Torah, are overwhelmingly sex positive, the focus of religious leaders is on prohibiting behavior. Religious leaders have supplemented the scriptures with canonical law—Church doctrine outlining moral and immoral behaviors. Canonical law has tended to be a reactive response by the Church to a supposed social malaise, such as homosexuality, premarital sex, and abortion. The resulting list of prohibited behaviors the Church has created predominantly focus on sexual activities that do not lead to procreation within the confines of a heterosexual marriage. Thus, it is considered immoral and offensive to engage in homosexuality, adultery, and oral or anal intercourse. The Church is suspiciously silent on child sexual abuse, rape, exposure, and voyeurism. Too frequently, canonical law places ideology above reason, uses scientific findings in a misleading way, and reduces biblical arguments to quotations of scriptures without regard for the context of the moral lesson (Palmer and Haffner 2007). As a case in point, approximately thirty years ago, the Church and its congregations were in rigorous debate over the issues of divorce and the place of women in the faith community. Now, the debates surround homosexuality and the acceptance of persons who have offended sexually into congregations.

The Church has condemned not only sexual acts but also sexual desire, thus resulting in a blurring of the lines between body and soul, thought and action (Foucault 1978). This is not a new phenomenon and can be traced back to the seventeenth century when the Church espoused more stringent views on confessionals and the requirement of followers to disclose all their sexual thoughts and actions to the clergy. As described by Foucault (1978: 23), "Western man has been drawn for three centuries to the task of telling everything concerning his sex: that since the classical age there has been a constant optimization and an increasing valorization of the discourse on sex; and that thus carefully analytical discourse was meant to yield multiple effects of displacement, intensification, reorientation, and modification of desire itself." The Church had originally designed confession to have participants outline all the details of their sexual encounters and then shifted to having followers confess their sexual desires. The change in procedure coincided with changes in law where sex now became something to be managed and administered.

Slowly, there was a movement in the faiths to control all things sexual. This started with the development of canonical law, moved to the control of language and access to knowledge, and eventually shifted to the supposed secular government in the form of sex crimes laws. This control may be in part due to the need of the faith community to establish a strong sense of belonging among its members, but there are also other substantial factors that play a role in the control of sex and sexuality. Controlling the use of language ensured that there was a clear demarcation between believers and nonbelievers as well as between social classes. This was also the case for controlling access to knowledge, where the upper classes and clergy were allowed to conduct and read studies on sexuality that the lower and working classes were denied. In fact, the Vatican has several rooms adorned in sexual and erotic imagery—the same imagery that the clergy thought too provocative to allow converts to view.

Religion can have an enormous influence on social and legal life, as conveyed in a case from history:

> One day in 1867, a farm hand from the village of Lapcourt, who was some-what simple-minded, employed here then there, depending on the season, living hand-to-mouth from a little charity or in exchange for the worst sort of labor, sleeping in barns and stables, was turned in to the authorities. At the border of the field, he had obtained a few caresses from a little girl, just as he had done before and seen done by village urchins round about him; for, at the edge of the wood, or in the ditch by the road leading to Saint-Nicolas, they would play the familiar game called "curdled milk." So he was pointed out by the girl's parents to the mayor of the village, reported by the mayor to the gendarmes, led by the gendarmes to the judge, who indicted him and turned him over to the first doctors, then to two other experts who not only wrote their report but also had it published. What is the significant thing about this story? The pettiness of it all; the fact that this everyday occurrence in the life of village sexuality, these inconsequential bucolic pleasures, could become, from a certain time, the object not only of a collective intolerance but of a judicial action, a medical intervention, a careful clinical examination, and an entire theoretical elaboration. The thing to note is that they went so far as to measure the brainpan, study the facial bone structure, and inspect for possible signs of degenerescence the anatomy of this personage who up to that moment had been an integral part of village life; that they made him talk; that they questioned him concerning his thought, inclinations, habits, sensations, and opinions. And then, acquitting him of any crime, they decided finally to make him into a pure object of medicine and knowledge—an object to be shut away till the end of his life. (Foucault 1978: 31–32)

This example illustrates the shifting nature of sexual discourse in Western countries. Religion promoted an active policy that all things sexual must be openly discussed, analyzed, and repented for, which in turn was followed by the development of legal and medical establishments to support this structure. All told, religion formed the basis of the current legal and medical systems and the manner in which society deals with those deemed to be sexual offenders.

With such influence over secular institutions and the manner in which sex is dealt with in society, how has the Church handled sexual crises? Most people have read articles about Church sex scandals in both the Christian and the Jewish faiths. In fact, priests have come to be associated with pedophiles in the minds of much of the public. By being so repressive and secretive about sex and sexual knowledge, organized religion is now forced to grapple with the same issues confronting the rest of society. Faith communities are now being judged on their response to these sexual scandals. To add to the debate, Church congregations are vehemently discussing whether convicted sex offenders should be allowed to partake in services. Should the Church welcome persons who have committed sex crimes (including priests) back into the congregation as espoused in Isaiah 56:7, "My house shall be called a house of prayer for all peoples," or should it ostracize them? This debate rages and will likely not be settled anytime soon. However, it speaks to the much broader issue of how Christianity and Judaism are dealing with sex crimes, both in society in general and as a result of Church/Temple members' actions.

CHRISTIANITY

For many Christians, the answers to complicated questions, such as sexual ethics, are found in the Bible. However, it can be challenging for many Christians to deconstruct insights and guidance that can be useful to present day society from a literal biblical interpretation. Taking the Bible literally would result in society forbidding divorce, coitus during menstruation, and remarriage yet accepting polygamy, prostitution, and the treatment of women as property. Meanwhile, the Bible is fairly silent on such controversial issues as abortion, birth control, and masturbation. Moreover, it is silent on what we consider to be sexual crimes today, such as exhibitionism, child sexual abuse, rape, and voyeurism. Many of the behaviors we currently regard as sex offenses are deemed immoral by the Church not because they are prohibited in the Bible but because modern church theologians have made conscious decisions to select certain behaviors as examples of sin. People have not created new sexual acts since the Bible was recorded—in fact, activities now considered immoral or illegal have been in existence for thousands of years. Such behaviors become problematic only when they threaten the status quo or social order.

When the Bible was written, sexual relationships were based on rigid gender roles and the concept of power and dominance. Words like "sodomite" did not appear in any Bible until the King James Version in 1611, and "homosexual" was not a concept that was even developed until the late nineteenth century. It is more a reflection of the sexual mores of English society than religious teaching. Consequently, Church doctrine regarding homosexuality was developed in recent times and was not communicated to Christians from God. Moreover, there is some debate within the faith community as to the applicability of the Old Testament in relation to the New Testament. The Old Testament was written prior to the birth of Jesus Christ and contains several references to behaviors and activities that were later contradicted by the teachings of Jesus. The New Testament focuses on love, acceptance, and the healing powers of faith and specifically denounces only certain forms of sexual behaviors.

Marriage between a male and a female is only one recognized form of sexuality identified in the Bible. It also recognizes concubinage and levirate marriage (where a man must have sex and procreate with his dead brother's wife—a practice still in place in several Middle Eastern and African countries). It was in the fifth century that St. Augustine developed Church policy on sex that came to dominate Christianity. This policy focused on the acceptability of married, procreative sex, which became an idealized sexuality to which all Christians were to aspire (Morrison 2008). This policy was so popularized that it was brought to the American colonies during settlement times, and the Puritans established specific laws to prohibit what they considered to be alternative sexualities, such as sex outside the confines of marriage (Morrison 2008). Christianity espoused the belief that sexuality is a benchmark for the moral health of communities and nations. Historically, Puritans actively preached against the alternative sexualities and went so far as to call all people who engaged in "carnal excesses" sex offenders (Morrison 2008). Such persons were publicly named and ostracized—in much the same way current laws require those convicted of certain sexual crimes to register for life. It was believed that public notification of sexually unacceptable behavior would result in better group cohesion and a more faithful community.

Overall, the Bible is a sex-positive document. The Song of Songs celebrates loving, sexual relationships between unmarried adults and recognizes celibacy and singleness as legitimate sexual preferences. Passages that prohibit specific kinds of sexual activities represent less than 0.03 percent of the verses contained in the Hebrew and Christian testaments (Palmer and Haffner 2007). Sexual sin in the Bible is defined as the abuse or exploitation of sexuality. Thus, the Bible does not represent a sexual code of conduct. The prohibitions found in the Scriptures are mostly in the Old Testament, which is extremely difficult to contextualize today because of cultural and language changes (Palmer and Haffner 2007).

Sexual offending as we define it today is a relatively new concept for the Church. The Church has taken a stand against certain sexual transgressions in the past, identifying certain behaviors as deviant or sinful:

> First, Christianity's influence over American society is strong, whether the currents of influence flow one way or two. Second, Christianity's influence over societal norms is felt most strongly in the realm of sexuality, specifically in regards to establishing a dominant/normative sexuality as well as alternative, deviant sexualities that exist outside of the norm. It can scarcely be denied that biblical sexual prohibitions have had a major effect on Western law. It is largely by biblical precepts that society today condemns adultery, male homosexuality, bestiality, and incest. Moreover, many criminal laws have at least partly religious origins. No area of criminal law feels Christianity's influence more than that which regulates sexual activity. One need only

appreciate the language of morality inherent in sex crime statutes. Words and phrases such as "indecent," "lewd," "obscene," "immoral," and "the infamous crime against nature" indicate a normative morality and Christian history. (Morrison 2008: 14–15)

Morrison goes on to explain the linkage between the Church and the definition of sex crimes:

This view of sex offenders and its truth for a few offenders does, however, serve the American Christian need to create alternate sexualities as deviant and evil. Sex crimes law prohibits a few truly dangerous and incurable offenders from acting, but under the same "sex offense" category also outlaws homosexuality, public displays of nudity, obscenity (including porn), and risqué sexual proposals. Given society's pervasive religious foundation, it is not very hard to convince the public that all of these forms of sexuality are as bad under sex crimes law as was Kanka's rape and murder. Instead of targeting the truly dangerous individuals, therefore, sex crimes and the offenders who are caught in them range from the truly dangerous to the utterly harmless. (Morrison 2008: 33–34)

The changes to Church laws, social behavior, and state law ensured there was no distinction between transgressions such as rape, adultery, incest, or sodomy.

For Americans, the very concept of democracy is founded on Christian doctrine. Pope John Paul II said in 1997 that "the vast majority of Americans, regardless of their religious persuasion, are convinced that religious conviction and religiously informed moral argument have a vital role in public life" (Morrison 2008: 12). Thus, American laws meshed concepts of religion and morality and have used such principles to communicate their deepest beliefs about justice and how it should be delivered.

JUDAISM

The religious Scripture for those of the Jewish faith is the Torah, also referred to as Chumash, Pentateuch, or the Five Books of Moses. In the Torah, sex is not regarded as harmful, sinful, or obscene per se, but there is an underlying belief that sexual desire has to be controlled, channeled, and satisfied in a religiously appropriate manner to be engaged in at the proper time and place. There are warnings in the Torah about the potentially destructive and exploitative uses of sexuality. As early as A.D. 325, rabbis debated issues such as marriage eligibility, the suitability of sexual acts and sexual relationships, and the appropriate role for women and men in religious life. That is, rabbis were concerned with who should become religious leaders and what sexual restrictions would apply to those leaders (Palmer and Haffner 2007).

As with the Bible, the key to understanding and interpreting the Hebrew Scriptures is to garner insight and guidance from the writings but not to literally interpret passages. The Torah is as contextually relevant as the Bible: society is simply not as concerned with issues such as remarriage, sex during menstruation, and prostitution as people were thousands of years ago. Followers of Judaism, however, do take guidance from the Torah in reference to sexual enjoyment and concepts of modesty. The Torah contends that the only sex that is permissible is within the confines of marriage and forbids any sexual contact, from coitus to hand-holding, outside of marriage. Having sexual fantasies, masturbation, and mutual masturbation are also forbidden outside of marriage. However, unlike the Bible, there is no prohibition against oral or anal intercourse as long as a couple procreates. The Torah expressly forbids the use of sex as a weapon, by either men or women, and in this way speaks to the crime of rape. Like the Bible, the Torah condemns homosexuality, adultery, and certain forms of incest and bestiality, all of which are punishable by death. The Torah states,

{S} 6 None of you shall approach to any that is near of kin to him, to uncover their nakedness. I am the LORD. {S} 7 The nakedness of thy father, and the nakedness of thy mother, shalt thou not uncover: she is thy mother; thou shalt not uncover her nakedness. {S} 8 The nakedness of thy father's wife shalt thou not uncover: it is thy father's nakedness. {S} 9 The nakedness of thy sister, the daughter of thy father, or the daughter of thy mother, whether born at home, or born abroad, even their nakedness thou shalt not uncover. {S} 10 The nakedness of thy son's daughter, or of thy daughter's daughter, even their nakedness thou shalt not uncover; for theirs is thine own nakedness. {S} 11 The nakedness of thy father's wife's daughter, begotten of thy father, she is thy sister, thou shalt not uncover her nakedness. {S} 12 Thou shalt not uncover the nakedness of thy father's sister: she is thy father's near kinswoman. {S} 13 Thou shalt not uncover the nakedness of thy mother's sister; for she is thy mother's near kinswoman. {S} 14 Thou shalt not uncover the nakedness of thy father's brother, thou shalt not approach to his wife: she is thine aunt. {S} 15 Thou shalt not uncover the nakedness of thy daughter-in-law: she is thy son's wife; thou shalt not uncover her nakedness. {S} 16 Thou shalt not uncover the nakedness of thy brother's wife: it is thy brother's nakedness. {S} 17 Thou shalt not uncover the nakedness of a woman and her daughter; thou shalt not take her son's daughter, or her daughter's daughter, to uncover her nakedness: they are near kinswomen; it is lewdness. 18 And thou shalt not take a woman to her sister, to be a rival to her, to uncover her nakedness, beside the other in her lifetime. 19 And thou shalt not approach unto a woman to uncover her nakedness, as long as she is impure by her uncleanness. 20 And thou shalt not lie carnally with thy neighbour's wife, to defile thyself with her. 21 And thou shalt not give any of thy seed to set them apart to Molech, neither shalt thou profane the name of thy God: I am the LORD. 22 Thou shalt not lie with mankind, as with womankind; it is abomination. 23 And thou shalt not lie with any beast to defile thyself therewith;

neither shall any woman stand before a beast, to lie down thereto; it is perversion. **24** Defile not ye yourselves in any of these things; for in all these the nations are defiled, which I cast out from before you. **25** And the land was defiled, therefore I did visit the iniquity thereof upon it, and the land vomited out her inhabitants. **26** Ye therefore shall keep My statutes and Mine ordinances, and shall not do any of these abominations; neither the home-born, nor the stranger that sojourneth among you— **27** for all these abominations have the men of the land done, that were before you, and the land is defiled— **28** that the land vomit not you out also, when ye defile it, as it vomited out the nation that was before you. **29** For whosoever shall do any of these abominations, even the souls that do them shall be cut off from among their people. **30** Therefore shall ye keep My charge, that ye do not any of these abominable customs, which were done before you, and that ye defile not yourselves therein: I am the LORD your God. (Leviticus 18)

It is important to recognize that although religion is the foundation of modern-day American democracy, it does not specifically address current sex crimes. The Bible and the Torah are contextual documents designed to teach the word of God to followers by outlining a manner in which to live based on mutual respect and love. Church theologians have used sex and access to sexual knowledge to control followers and ensure an "us-versus-them" mentality. Thus, individuals who partake in alternative sexualities, not necessarily sex crimes, are labeled as outsiders who threaten the order of the Church. Slowly, as more and more alternative sexualities are becoming mainstream (e.g., homosexuality, bisexuality, divorce and remarriage, and serial monogamy), the Church has been forced to shift its position on sexuality. The focus has now moved to those who commit sexually based crimes.

But how can the Church reconcile the biblical and Torah principle of welcoming all into the house of God with the desire by some religious officials and followers to marginalize persons who have offended sexually? If past practice dictates future actions, then the Church will flow with the popular belief that once a sex offender, always a sex offender. The problem with this line of reasoning is that it is based on assumptions, misinformation, and bigotry. More important, it neglects the fact that sexual violations are systemic in American culture and that followers of religion are also the nation's political, medical, and judicial leaders. The Church plays a significant role in how society views sexually based crimes and the persons who commit them and could contribute to a more informed understanding of sexual crimes and aid in the successful reintegration of offenders into the community.

2

The Medical Model

Americans have traditionally dealt with persons who have offended sexually as though they are mentally diseased. Consequently, the medical model has prevailed as the favored sphere in which to provide treatment. The strong deference to medical personnel as more knowledgeable about the causes of sexual offending and more capable of providing solutions to this social issue has resulted in the creation and perpetuation of myths surrounding sexual offending and offenders. These myths include that there is a genetic basis to crime, that lifelong drug treatment is required for sexual offenders, and that permanent hospitalization or imprisonment is necessary because there is no "cure" for this type of criminal offending. These myths continue to hold weight today and influence the development of social policy. This chapter examines the medical model historically and how it is currently used as well as contributions of key figures in the field. A discussion around the creation and usage of the *Diagnostic and Statistical Manual of Mental Disorders* is elucidated, as is an examination of the various tests in existence that determine who is labeled a sexual offender.

THE MEDICAL MODEL

As discussed in chapter 1, historically the Church was actively involved in identifying and defining sexual transgressions. These definitions often found their way into the legal system, which was ill equipped to deal with the myriad of "dangerous" sexual behaviors. Consequently, the law often deferred to the medical establishment to "cure" people of their sexual ailments. This resulted in a blurring of lines between sickness and evil and between madness and badness (Petrunik 1994). Crimes tended to focus on certain segments of society that were deemed problematic, especially those that went against social mores and were politically or economically bothersome (e.g., vagrants). After World War II, society started to focus on sex crimes against children, and this quickly came to be viewed as one of society's most pressing social problems (Chenier 2003). At this time, sexual offenses were regarded as mental health problems, best dealt with through criminal sexual psychopath laws that were based on the notion that sex offenders are driven by uncontrollable impulses that can be stopped only by permanent incarceration and medical treatment (Chenier 2003). A mixture of medical and legal frameworks formed the laws, but ultimately the underlying premise was to eliminate sexual immorality, hence the focus on crimes against children and homosexual activity.

Thus, laws were based on religious notions of morality and were formed around medical treatment protocols. However, the medical establishment began defining sex offenders as perverts whose uncontrollable behavior would become increasingly violent without proper intervention (Chenier 2003). On the surface, it seems laudable that society was taking an interest in preventing and eliminating sexual violence; however, homosexuality, transgenderism, and intergenerational sexual contact were the targets. Assaults against adult women and intrafamilial abuse were virtually ignored as social harms. The notion of the dangerous sex offender refers more to the individual charged or suspected of crime than supposedly harmful sexual acts.

It is the responsibility of the medical establishment to provide a diagnosis, prognosis, and treatment for those regarded as sexually dangerous. Within the medical model, the view is toward the future by seeking to ascertain what predisposes a person to offend sexually and then alter that variable to render it harmless (Petrunik 1994). While the medical model has been inclined toward the use of drugs to treat sexual offending, the results have been questionable (refer to chapter 9 for a complete discussion of the various treatment options currently available). Indeed, there is a very low success rate for medically based treatment programs for sex offenders in general (Petrunik 1994). Medical science has created a system of treatment modalities and "expert" knowledge of offending that is reinforced by exclusive language and has ensured its continued supremacy in the realm of human sexuality (Cowburn 2005). For instance, forensic psychiatrists are regarded as experts on the identification and treatment of sexual "deviants" yet base their research on only those convicted of sex crimes, which are a minority of individuals who could be charged with breaking sexually based laws. The medical model asserts that it is based on objective scientific truth, yet critics contend that it merely serves to highlight discourse created by the socially and economically powerful (Cowburn 2005). Is it any wonder that the majority of persons charged and convicted of sex crimes are males from lower socioeconomic classes?

The entire basis of the medical model is on classification systems and typologies gathered from convicted offenders. Research has illustrated, though, that there is no difference between the sexual interests and responsiveness of "normal" males to coercive sexual activity (e.g., rape) as compared to sex offenders (Cowburn 2005). It can reasonably be concluded that the medical model is based on value judgments of what is and is not "normal" sexual behavior as opposed to what is spurious or socially unacceptable behavior (Cowburn 2005). The premise is that sex offenders are predatory strangers who escalate their behaviors and have some form of personality disorder or mental abnormality that can reliably be diagnosed (Petrunik 1994). Thus, the medical model was able to transform a societal harm into an individual pathology of a person convicted of a sex offense.

Other obvious concerns with the medical model include the circularity of its main ideas, whereby concepts are vaguely defined and then later regarded as the cause or predisposition of the offensive behaviors. For example, antisocial personality disorder and psychopathy are extremely vague concepts and are inferred to exist in sex offenders because of their sexually "deviant" behavior (Petrunik 1994). In addition, there is a low reliability of diagnoses for personality disorders commonly attributed to sex offenders and an inaccuracy in the predictors of violence (Petrunik 1994). In fact, medical professionals are wrong twice as many times as they are right in determining risk of reoffending (Petrunik 1994). The next section elaborates on prominent figures in the field.

KEY FIGURES IN MEDICINE

A discussion of how sex offenders are labeled would not be complete without delving into the backgrounds of key thinkers, both past and present. Within psychology and psychiatry it is obvious that Sigmund Freud has had great sway over how society views sex and sexuality. More currently, William Marshall has been providing substantive research on convicted sex offenders in Canada. In the field of sexology, several prominent figures have created theories and perspectives that have influenced how society perceives those who commit sexual crimes. Richard Freiherr von Krafft-Ebing, Havelock Ellis, Albert Moll, Iwan Bloch, and Alfred Kinsey are highlighted, as is the work on sex offenders by Wardell Pomeroy. It is worthy to note that there are few current sexological researchers focusing on this area of inquiry. Finally, a discussion of other intellectuals is included, as there are a handful of researchers who are not psychologists, psychiatrists, or sexologists who have contributed to this field, including Michel Foucault.

Psychology and Psychiatry

Sigmund Freud

Although Sigmund Freud (1856–1939) is best known as a psychoanalyst, he was also a sexologist and wrote extensively within the discipline. He was highly influenced by the writings of Albert Moll (a sexologist who is discussed later in the chapter) on childhood sexuality and developed extensive theories on the origins of sexual inclinations. Freud's work on deviancy, titled *Sexual Aberrations*, dealt with the variances of sexual instinct, including what Freud considered to be "perversions," as well as bestiality, scopophilia (viewing sexual scenes in preference over sexual activity), and exhibitionism. Freud believed that sexuality was expressed in childhood and thus contradicted a popularly held view that children are asexual and that sexuality emerged only in adolescence with the onset of puberty. A large segment of Freud's essay on sexual deviations was spent analyzing homosexuality, or inversion as it was referred to historically. This was a great social malaise of the time, as homosexuals were blamed for a variety of crimes, most frequently child sexual abuse. Bisexuality, thought to be closely linked to homosexuality, was also addressed in Freud's deviancy essay. Like other sexologists, Freud believed it necessary to understand the "normal" in order to analyze the "abnormal." He believed that the true aim of any sex was to have the genitals of a male and a female connect to relieve tension and temporarily extinguish an individual's innate sexual instinct (Freud 1962). While he recognized other sexual activities, he suggested that it was foreplay to coitus rather than ends in and of themselves. Thus, Freud considered any activity outside of penis–vagina sex abnormal.

Freud sought to add a new dimension into the discussion of sexual deviancy. He strongly believed that the notion of disgust was a key reason why society regarded certain activities as abhorrent. This argument was made for both oral and anal sex. For Freud, use of the mouth and anus in sex and people's fascination with them as adults stemmed from their childhood and the focus on food and defecation (Freud 1962). Moreover, as Freud aged, he became more liberal in his evaluations of sexuality and sexual deviancy. Freud was one of the first scholars to suggest that fetishism, whereby persons become sexually fixated on objects, was not harmful if the person was still able to have intercourse. This was remarkably liberal for the time period, as fetishism was often regarded as a gateway activity for violent sexual assaults. Importantly, Freud believed that all people could be considered sex offenders at some point:

> If circumstances favor such an occurrence, normal people too can substitute a perversion of this kind for the normal sexual aim for quite a time, or can find place for the one alongside the other. No healthy person, it appears, can fail to make some addition that might be called perverse to the normal sexual aim; and the universality of this finding is in itself enough to show how inappropriate it is to use the word perverse as a term of reproach. (Freud 1962: 26)

Freud contended that for an activity to be considered perverse, it had to be exclusive, meaning that it was the sole fixation of the person. How could a person be a sexual "deviant"? They must lack the necessary shame and disgust associated with certain behaviors. Moreover, Freud believed that sexual repression was a cause of "perversion," and this had to be tempered with knowledge of psychosexual development.

After Freud, little theoretical work was completed in the psychological and psychiatric fields in relation to sexual offending. The most significant work came decades later when William Marshall began conducting research studies on convicted sexual offenders.

William Marshall

William Marshall has been publishing in the area of theories and treatment modalities related to sexual offenders for decades. He is a trained psychologist, affiliated with a major university as well as the Canadian government, and he oversees a clinic for convicted sex offenders in Kingston, Ontario. His hypotheses regarding therapist traits, attachment and isolation, and denial have been integrated into treatment programs across North America. Marshall contends that the perceived behavior of a therapist by a sexual offender in treatment does more to determine the treatment outcome than what the therapist actually says or does (Marshall et al. 2003). That is, when offenders perceive their therapist as confrontational or judgmental, treatment outcomes are adversely impacted, regardless of how experienced the therapist may be in treating offenders (Wakeling, Webster, and Mann 2005). Thus, it has been demonstrated that those offenders in group therapy with supportive therapists have the greatest likelihood of succeeding, assuming that other group members are supportive, the group is of reasonably small size, and there are not a significant number of cultural differences among group members (Wakeling, Webster, and Mann 2005).

Marshall further hypothesized that insecure attachment styles increase a person's vulnerability to criminality. In other words, persons who have

offended sexually may have greater difficulty establishing close relationships with others, and this could be an etiological factor to their offending
(Ward, Hudson, and Marshall 1996). The bonds that people develop with
their parents or caregivers in early childhood teach valuable skills, provide the confidence to trust others, and provide the foundation necessary
to form lasting emotional commitments as adults (Mann 2004). Thus, sex
offenders may indirectly attempt to achieve intimacy through sex, even if
that means their partner is forced into participating (Mann 2004; Ward,
Hudson, and Marshall 1996). Insecure attachment then leads to "promiscuity" and increasing sexual "deviance." However, promiscuity is a
highly value-laden term, as is deviance, and both should be critically analyzed. What is promiscuous? Having three partners? Ten partners?
Twenty-five partners? One hundred partners over a lifetime? Does a person have to engage in coitus with all of these partners to be considered
promiscuous or just "make out"? Sexologists have a phrase they use when
addressing this issue: "promiscuous is someone who is having more sex,
in whatever form, than you." It becomes readily apparent how that definition changes between each person and within society. The same can be
said of the term "deviance." Deviance is socially constructed, and its definition changes according to a person's religion, ethics, family background, socioeconomic status, and education.

Marshall also hypothesized that attachment styles (or lack thereof) vary
according to the type of offender. For instance, rapists and child offenders
were markedly more insecure in their adult sexual relationships than
other types of offenders (Ward et al. 1996). Rapists were more dismissive
in their attachment styles and exhibited extreme aggression with others,
whereas child offenders were more fearful and preoccupied with gaining
the acceptance of others (Ward et al. 1996). Later theorists added to this
framework by suggesting that sexual arousal was intricately connected to
the underlying emotional states of sex offenders (Mann 2004). Thus, it is
believed that rapists express anger, humiliation, and loneliness when sexually aroused, heterosexual child offenders express loneliness and humiliation when sexually aroused, and homosexual child offenders express
loneliness when sexually aroused (Mann 2004). Psychologists have based
entire treatment programs on this attachment hypothesis. These programs are termed strength-based treatment and are a relatively new innovation that is designed to ensure that sex offenders are provided with
the capabilities to engage in personal and social experiences in a socially
acceptable manner. This treatment uses approach-oriented methods and
is intended to help manufacture a "new-me" attitude that is based within
the framework of relapse prevention (Mann 2004).

Attachment theory borrows heavily from the "intimacy anger" model
of partner abuse, suggesting a strong relationship between anger, attach-

ment, and anxiety. This model seeks to explain the anger of an offender in the context of sexual violence whereby frustrated or interrupted attachment is expressed by anger and affective instability, which may ultimately be risk factors for aggression toward persons who represent those to whom the person is insecurely attached (Lyn and Burton 2005). "Proving" this theory is difficult, however, as ascertaining the level of attachment offenders had with their parents is based solely on self-reports. If offenders believe that disclosing physical, emotional, or sexual abuse as a child will get them out of prison earlier or prevent jail time altogether, there is cause to question the validity of their self-reports. Moreover, some researchers believe that the skill deficits derived from insecure attachment may not be as strong as asserted in some studies. Several studies hypothesize that sex offenders have the knowledge and skills to manage their emotions but lack the capacity to implement the knowledge under certain situations, such as extreme interpersonal crises (Puglia, Stough, Carter, and Joseph 2005).

In 2005, William Marshall updated his concept of attachment by combining it with a new notion called hope theory. Hope theory is part of the new strength-based models and suggests that having offenders work toward positive goals (e.g., becoming gainfully employed or ending a tumultuous relationship), as opposed to avoidance goals (e.g., stop going to parks and community centers), will ensure longer-lasting success in treatment (Moulden and Marshall 2005). It is a metatheory that Marshall contends can apply to all psychological treatment, as it incorporates cognitive, affective, and behavioral experiences related to the evaluation of the sex offender's individual goals (Moulden and Marshall 2005). Hope theory relates to theories on attachment by suggesting that father figures are especially important to the development of coercive sexual behavior because if boys do not learn prosocial responses to sexual situations from their fathers, they will be unable to achieve their emotional goals within sexual relationships (Moulden and Marshall 2005).

Thus, the contributions of psychology and psychiatry are based on the assumptions that people offend sexually for one of three reasons: 1) motivational, 2) intrinsic, and 3) extrinsic. Motivationally, sex offenders lack insight into why they offend and why they have chosen their particular victims and lack the motivation to change their behavior. Intrinsic reasons include poor self-image, threats to self-esteem, and fear of being negatively evaluated by others. Extrinsic reasons include a lack of trust or a fear of negative consequences if one's true personality is displayed and a need to have power over or get attention from others (Cooper 2005). This theory was founded on a set of assumptions that are often value laden and reinforced by research conducted on a very small fraction of sexual offenders. There is an assumption that sex offenders come from poor backgrounds, socially, financially, and sexually, and this assumption has been "confirmed" by interviewing and treating offenders in prison who often self-report being previous victims of abuse. However, most sex offenders never get caught, are never charged, and do not go to prison. In fact, most offenders know their victims, either as relatives or as family friends, and most families are unwilling to disclose abusive behavior for fear of destroying the family unit. Consequently, what the medical community knows of offenders is highly skewed, and to base theories and treatment programs on such a small percentage of offenders is simply bad science.

Sexology

Richard Freiherr von Krafft-Ebing

Richard Freiherr von Krafft-Ebing (1840–1902) was the most significant medical writer on human sexuality during the latter part of the nineteenth century. He authored the first comprehensive description and classification of sexual disturbances in the classic *Psychopathia Sexualis*, which focused on "perversions" (Meyenburg and Sigusch 1977). His work, first published in 1906, was developed for the medical and legal professions to assist in dealing with individuals charged with what were considered to be sexual perversions. Krafft-Ebing succeeded in identifying and elaborating a wide range of sexual activities that had been previously ignored or regarded as inappropriate for social conversation. For Krafft-Ebing, it was imperative that the psychology and physiology of sex be understood so that "normal" sexual development would serve as the benchmark from which to measure deviance. Krafft-Ebing was and continues to be a highly controversial figure in the field of sexology, as he was responsible for notions of sexual deviancy and perversion, concepts that the field has shunned over the past seventy years.

Krafft-Ebing focused his efforts on sexual psychology and the causes and treatments of various sexological disorders (Lewandowski 1984–1985). He contended that pathology was intricately connected to neurology and psychology, and he developed a classification system for sexual mental diseases that he generally ascribed to the theory of degeneration (Haeberle 1983). For Krafft-Ebing, all sexual activities were considered to be pathological unless related to procreation. He was a product of his time and his environment and served to advance the popular notion of Victorian-era sexuality, whereby most forms of sexual activity were regarded as unnatural and a perversion of human sexual instinct (Haeberle 1983).

Psychopathia Sexualis was organized into sections on biology, physiology, and anthropology and provided a detailed discussion of various perversions. Krafft-Ebing contended that sexuality is biologically based and instinctive and that sexual feelings were the root of all ethics, aestheticism, and religion (Krafft-Ebing 1922). He claimed that the presence of shame in relation to sexuality was the foundation of morality and that if most of society felt shameful about an activity, then it became socially and religiously inappropriate. The book was very much a product of its social time, and the author broadly employed stereotypes in relation to gender, religion, and class. Krafft-Ebing contended that life was a constant struggle between animal instinct and morality. Importantly, he believed that sexual criminals had an abnormally high sexual desire that resulted in frequent and violent impulses to satisfy the need for gratification. Persons afflicted with hyperaesthesia (increased sexual desire) were identified as perpetrators of incest, adultery, child abuse, rape, and public masturbation (Krafft-Ebing 1922). Because he saw these behaviors as a result of biological degeneracy, Krafft-Ebing believed that criminal punishment was not appropriate or effective in dealing with this social problem. Moreover, he differentiated between the concepts of "perversion," which was considered a disease to be treated medically, and "perversity," which was a vice.

He made the controversial assertion that sexual instinct rests in the brain, as does sexual functioning. Because Krafft-Ebing believed that the brain was vital in sexuality, he also contended that sexual perversions stemmed from pathologies of thought due to heredity or preexisting mental disease (Krafft-Ebing 1922). He postulated that sexual disturbances or deviations were likely caused by a disruption in the evolution of psychosexual processes due predominantly to mental illness. He believed that people who participated in sexual activities not related to procreation, such as sadomasochism or anal sex, could function sexually only when engaged in such activities and could not be otherwise productive members of society. Krafft-Ebing speculated that mental illness and sexual pathology were the result of masturbation (Bullough 1994). He hypothesized that disease was caused by the physical nervous system and that hereditary defects in this system resulted from overstressing the system through activities such as masturbation (Bullough 1994). For Krafft-Ebing, some forms of homosexuality could be explained by his theory of disease etiology. He did, however, demarcate between innate and acquired perversions but still contended that both existed because of a weakness in the physical nervous system (Bullough 1994). Krafft-Ebing believed that homosexuality was defined on the basis of the feelings one had for the same sex as opposed to the activities in which one engaged (Krafft-Ebing 1922). He hypothesized various reasons for homosexuality and developed a rating system that was similar to what Kinsey reinvented in the 1940s.

Anthropologically, Krafft-Ebing linked the primary and secondary sexual characteristics with biological and anatomical aspects. He postulated that the basis of general pathology lay in the functional signs of degeneration and provided readers with a schedule of sexual neuroses. He suggested that the general sexual pathologies included such things as arousal without stimulation, absence of arousal, increased desire, perversion instinct, sadism, masochism, and fetishism (Krafft-Ebing 1922). In essence, the items listed by Krafft-Ebing formed the basis of the future *Diagnostic and Statistical Manual of Mental Disorders.* Unfortunately, he failed to elaborate on why these items were pathological but instead based his comments on the cultural mores of the time. Moreover, he linked highly charged issues, such as lust murder, with basic fetishes, such as interest in women's feet (Krafft-Ebing 1922). Of importance is that Krafft-Ebing noted that a clinical diagnosis of sexual perversion or perversity was exceedingly difficult, as the symptoms were highly subjective and dependent on the self-reports of patients (Krafft-Ebing 1922). Ideas for treatment often included various masturbation prevention activities, hypnotic suggestion, and the promotion of good hygiene.

One of the key features of this work is the belief that pathology is based on natural emotions that have been redirected to a sexual outlet. This concept is the premise for treatment programs today that deal with sex offenders, alcoholics, and drug abusers. Krafft-Ebing stated that perversity does not necessarily equate with perversion and distinguished between those who engaged in a sexual activity because no suitable outlet was available (e.g., homosexuality in prison) and those who participated in a sexual activity for pleasure.

Moreover, Krafft-Ebing related certain types of crime with low intelligence, as he believed that child offenders and zoophiles could not contain their sudden and violent urges for sexual satisfaction. He also placed conditions such as epilepsy, homosexuality, masturbation, and sadomasochism on the same level as rape, lust murder, the torture of animals, and bestiality (Krafft-Ebing 1922). Although his work is clearly a product of its time and expresses the social biases that existed in early 1900s America and Europe, it paved the way for the development of the sexological and psychological fields. The notion that social mores play a key role in defining what is and is not appropriate sexual behavior was a significant contribution to sex research. The fact that Krafft-Ebing made clear distinctions between those who participate in an activity because of situational factors and those who participate because they take pleasure in it is an idea that still permeates psychological and sociological research.

For critics, Krafft-Ebing represents a low point in the development of the field of sexology, as he portrayed all things sexual as a collection of loathsome diseases (Brecher 2000). Krafft-Ebing's goal was to describe how women and men differed from Victorian social mores, and in this way he weaved together a story that illustrated how the simplest and most harmless of sexual acts are related to aberrations and perversions (Brecher 2000). The most damaging critique is the lack of empirical evidence to support any of his claims, specifically his hypothesis that stated that masturbation was the source of all sexual deviations (Brecher 2000). He used examples of average citizens partaking in sexual activity that eventually led to deviance with the moral of the story being that sexuality is evil and uncontrollable. Despite the critiques, the work of Krafft-Ebing is extremely valuable, as it provides a glimpse into the historical foundation of the field of sexology as well as the continuing shame and guilt that are associated with all things sexual.

Havelock Ellis

Havelock Ellis (1859–1939) was a medical doctor who specialized in the study of human sexuality. He wrote four volumes titled *Studies in the Psychology of Sex*. Ellis believed it imperative that society understand common sexual practices in order to comprehend sexual pathologies. He based many of his claims about sexuality on the concept of modesty. Ellis contended that modesty, or the desire to conceal the body in some form, was instinctual for all societies and went so far as to define it as a secondary sexual characteristic (Ellis 1942). He traveled the world observing other cultures to ascertain if there were any universals in sexuality and believed that modesty was one. He cited examples in his research of various cultural understandings of modesty: natives in central Brazil who cover only a part of their genitals, the Nias in the Indian Ocean where women cover their breasts and nothing else because they believe it necessary to cover only what develops as an adult, and the history of undergarments in Europe.

Despite his understanding of the expression of sexuality in other cultures, Ellis was often bound by the Victorian ideas under which he was raised. He believed that women were innately modest and men naturally aggressive in terms of sexuality (Ellis 1942). Men were always the pursuer sexually and women always the pursued. It was believed that this became so ingrained in Western culture that men were socialized into finding coyness and extreme modesty as sexually exciting and something to be overcome, whether or not their advances were met with resistance. Ellis utilized the example of an African culture in which the women are taught to be flirtatious and encourage the interest of men but then refuse all sexual advances, whereas the men are taught to demand sex and take it whenever they choose (Ellis 1942). The result is a type of culturally sanctioned rape. In addition, Ellis made some advances in the sexological field by contending that although those afflicted with sexual pathologies were degenerates, it was on par with minor physiological annoyances, such as color blindness, and not something to be deemed vulgar or unmanageable (Ellis 1942). Thus, Ellis believed that those who committed sexual crimes were mentally ill, though not so ill that they would require hospitalization or institutionalization.

Albert Moll

Albert Moll (1862–1939) was a medical doctor and political conservative who was the founder of the International Society for Sex Research. Moll believed that early sexual experiences or activities were not correlated to the later development of perversions (Bullough 1994). Moreover, Moll criticized the notion that masturbation was dangerous and contended instead that mutual masturbation in childhood did not lead to homosexuality, as was being hypothesized by his colleagues. Importantly, Moll was one of the first individuals to differentiate between innate and acquired homosexuality and was the first to compare "normal" and "abnormal" sexual development (Bullough 1994).

Moll authored several important sexological books, including *Contrary Feelings* (1891), *Investigations Concerning the Libido Sexualis* (1897), and *The Sexual Life of the Child* (1909). Sigmund Freud relied significantly on Moll's writings concerning the development of concepts regarding childhood sexuality and the sexual fixations that can emerge during childhood and present themselves as pathologies during adulthood. Moll sought to destroy the notion that puberty causes sexual inclinations and interests and hypothesized that youth became sexualized at a much earlier age (Bullough 1994). Moll authored a monograph on homosexuality and the nature of sexual urges and edited the first sexological handbook, which succeeded in promoting sexology as a legitimate academic field of inquiry (Haeberle 1983).

Iwan Bloch

Iwan Bloch (1872–1922) was a famous dermatologist in Berlin who founded the field of sexology. He succeeded in legitimizing the study of sexual problems and sought to convey objective insight into sexuality. Bloch developed an international reputation as a medical historian for his sociocultural studies in human sexuality (Haeberle 1983). Bloch was unique in his approach to human sexuality in that he attacked and dismissed the concept of degeneracy utilized by previous scholars, such as Krafft-Ebing (Haeberle 1983). He believed that the source of all sexual perversions was the need for variety in sexual relations (Bloch 1930). Bloch created what he coined "basic ideas" about human sexuality that were designed to develop sexology into a comprehensive discipline

(Bloch 1930). He believed that sexuality should be considered a biological science, as the forms and effects are physical, psychological, individual, and social (Haeberle 1983). His views of sexuality encompassed history and anthropology, as Bloch understood that many behaviors considered pathological in Victorian society had always existed and continued to exist in other cultures. For Bloch, "sexual psychopathologies" were timeless, universal manifestations of humanity that could be correlated to socioeconomic level (Haeberle 1983).

Bloch believed that although society evolved from a state of "promiscuity" to expression of sexuality through marriage, he postulated that unrestricted sex was the natural state and that marriage was an artificial institution (Bloch 1930). His evidence was the increasing divorce rates in Europe as well as his belief that group marriage was the oldest form of social union (Bloch 1930). Bloch was optimistic and believed that the future of relationships would bring equal rights and responsibilities in marriage for women and men, easily obtained divorce, and individual freedom (Bloch 1930).

Alfred Kinsey

Alfred Kinsey's (1894–1956) *Sexual Behavior in the Human Male* (Kinsey et al. 1948) and *Sexual Behavior in the Human Female* (Kinsey et al. 1953) articulated the findings of research conducted over more than two decades through the use of sex interviews or sex histories. Although the books became popular with the general public, the intent of Kinsey and his coauthors was to outline the enormous variety of sexual activity in society to assist clinicians and law enforcement in becoming more tolerant of the diversity of behavior that exists. The overarching purpose of the research was to learn what people do sexually, the factors accounting for their behaviors, how their experiences have impacted their lives, and the social significance people have attached to each of their sexual behaviors. Kinsey and his team went to great lengths to highlight what they perceived to be the shortcomings of their research, including a lack of older respondents, a lack of youthful respondents, a lack of respondents who were visible minorities, a lack of working-class respondents, and an absence of varied religious groups (Kinsey et al. 1948).

One of the most important accomplishments of Kinsey's two volumes is the success in debunking sexual myths and misconceptions. Kinsey and his team challenged the most basic assumptions regarding sexual activity in the United States. The research brought to public notice many practices that were previously not discussed, such as animal contacts and homosexuality (Bullough 1998). The work caused great controversy when Kinsey challenged the belief that intergenerational sexual contact always causes harm to the minor, and in fact Kinsey was accused by many critics of being a pedophile for holding such beliefs (Bullough 1998). Kinsey and his team were trailblazers in the field of human sexuality and represented a small group of people who openly and willingly challenged the most basic of societal beliefs. Kinsey found that a large number of people engaged in behaviors that were viewed as socially unacceptable or illegal. Moreover, he contended that "poorly established distinctions between normality and abnormality led to the enactment of sexual psychopath laws which are unrealistic, unenforceable, and incapable of providing the protection which the social organization has been led to believe they can provide" (Kinsey et al. 1953: 8). Kinsey believed that the supposed increase in the number of sexual offenses had more to do with increased arrests than actual behaviors and that the fluctuations in crime rates were caused predominantly by changes in the activities of law enforcement (Kinsey et al. 1953). Kinsey's research revealed that less than 1 percent of those involved in sex crimes were ever apprehended, prosecuted, or convicted (Kinsey et al. 1953). Moreover, he hypothesized that other factors greatly influenced the charging practices of law enforcement, such as officer embarrassment over their own sexual behavior (Kinsey et al. 1953). Kinsey truly believed that a study of sex offenders could not be complete unless it compared and contrasted those convicted of sex crimes to those who engaged in the same behaviors but were never in contact with law enforcement.

A major critique of Kinsey's work is that he believed in the innate, fixed distribution of behavior and therefore did not question whether incidences of various behaviors were historically specific (Ericksen 1998). As the research was conducted over a twenty-year period, it is likely that behavior patterns changed as a result of social movements. Kinsey insisted that as the study progressed, the language of the questions should be changed according to who the interview participants were and what social classes they represented. Current research on survey methodology indicates that changing the wording or reordering the questions can have a significant impact on the responses received (Ericksen 1998). For example, prefacing a question with fact and permission giving increases the number of positive responses received. Although Kinsey's interview technique was revolutionary and engendered truthful responses, critics charge that it introduced bias into the findings, as interviewers were trained to reassure respondents that their behaviors were normal and provide information regarding proper sexual techniques if required (Ericksen 1998). Kinsey and his team did overlook and disregard some sexual activities that form part of the sexual spectrum: group sex, sadomasochism, voyeurism, and other activities were not incorporated into Kinsey's research (Bullough 1998). Unfortunately, his avoidance of these issues did a great disservice because the activities that were included became more normalized in society. By failing to include activities such as sado-masochism and fetishism, it appeared as though these activities were uncommon, unusual, and somehow deviant.

Kinsey's works provided comprehensive information about the incidence and frequency of various sexual events, thereby demystifying both sexual activity and sexual actors. Kinsey's research challenged lawmakers to justify why certain activities were illegal when clearly common in society. Kinsey's research was so powerful and influenced so many lives that its impacts reverberate throughout time. It helped to engender support for various social movements, such as gay liberation and the sexual revolution, that ultimately changed the nature of sexual interaction in America. Importantly, Kinsey demonstrated that laws are an ineffective method of dealing with sexual issues, as they enforce too much social control over the lives of citizens. According to Kinsey's research, most people engage in some form of illegal sexual activity, and the laws and law enforcement could never deal with all of these crimes. However, there appears to be a social and political agenda for Kinsey's work. He and his team went to great lengths to discuss how sexual variety was the norm. In his attempts to loosen the sexual restraints of the Victorian era, Kinsey likely biased his research findings by attempting to swing the pendulum in the opposite direction.

Overall, the volumes by Kinsey and his team are groundbreaking sexological studies that have yet to be replicated, verified, or enhanced. Kinsey was a trailblazer in his study of human sexual behavior, and despite the many controversies and criticisms confronting Kinsey the man and his work, the research remains invaluable to the social sciences. Without the insights provided by Kinsey, social scientists would not be studying sexuality as they do today and would be unable to ask the difficult questions in relation to sexual behavior. Kinsey's development of an interview technique can be held as a model for acquiring detailed, reliable, and forthright information about individuals' most personal sexual issues. Both of his previously mentioned works continue to be sources of valuable information with which to compare current research findings.

Wardell Pomeroy

Wardell Pomeroy (1913–2001) was the lead researcher for *Sex Offenders*, which was a comprehensive study on the sexual histories and behaviors of sex offenders in the United States in the 1960s. The research was undertaken and authored by scholars from the Institute for Sex Research, now called the Kinsey Institute, and utilized the format made famous by Kinsey. The researchers supplemented Kinsey's sex questionnaire by asking offense-specific information, thereby allowing comparisons to be made between and within groups of sex offenders. The researchers interviewed 1,500 sex offenders to ascertain if their histories, both sexual and socioeconomic, were different from nonsexual offenders (prison control group) as well as the general public (control group from Kinsey's original data) (Gebhard, Gagnon, Pomeroy, and Christenson 1965). The purpose of the research was to identify differences in order to assist with public policy and treatment efforts.

The researchers interviewed mostly white men who had committed more than one sex offense. The participants were inmates serving less than a year in Indiana State Farm, prisoners serving felony sentences in California prisons, and sexual offenders deemed psychopaths in need of civil commitment by the California Department of Mental Hygiene. After reviewing the legal, cultural, and psychiatric definitions of sex offenders and sexual offending, Pomeroy and his team concluded that current definitions were unsatisfactory for a variety of reasons (e.g., failure to account for differences in acceptable behavior between the socioeconomic classes) and developed their own "pragmatic and functional" definition that focused on the motivation of the offense (Gebhard et al. 1965). Interestingly, current sex researchers continue to use motivation in assessing the risk and likelihood of recidivism in offenders through the use of tools such as the Static-99 risk assessment.

The research team developed the following definition of sex offending: an act committed for "immediate sexual gratification" and contrary to the sexual mores in the society in which an offender lives, an act that is legally punishable, and an act that results in a legal conviction (Gebhard et al. 1965). It was unclear whether the social mores applied to society in general or the specific social class in which the offender resided. For instance, the authors use the example of a man grabbing a woman's buttocks and how that act has different meaning according to the actors and setting involved. The authors subdivided sex offenders into those who committed acts that were mildly taboo but common, acts that were uncommon and strongly taboo, acts between consenting adults sixteen years of age and older, occasional peeping, relations with minors and children, incest, forced relations, exhibitionism, and frequent peeping (Gebhard et al. 1965). In addition, three independent variables were used to classify the sex offenders: homosexual versus heterosexual, consensual versus threat, and minor versus adult. These three variables combined to create twelve types of offenses, which the authors reduced to nine, as they contended that force in homosexual activity, outside of prison, is rare (Gebhard et al. 1965).

Sex Offenders represented the first comprehensive research study in the United States to include data gathered from interviews and arrest records and could be used by clinicians in identifying the treatment model that would be most effective based on the socioeconomic status and sexual history of their clients. Importantly, this research is easily replicated, and the data gathered in repeating the research could be analyzed against data from the Kinsey Institute. However, there are several issues with the research that inhibit its usage. There is a clear bias, as the researchers evaluate the intelligence of participants based on their family income, upbringing, and personal impressions. The researchers further contend that women cannot be sex offenders because they lack the sex drive of men and that questionable sexual behavior from women is more tolerated socially. It is unfortunate that leading sex experts have such skewed views regarding the sexual functioning of women. Additionally, there is a bias in the research toward southern states with strong rural communities, which, as illustrated in Kinsey's work, engage in different types of sexual activities than do urban communities (Gebhard et al. 1965; Kinsey et al. 1953).

To reiterate, Krafft-Ebing introduced the concept of sexual perversion and how it should be classified, and his influence continues in the psychological and medical communities with regard to how the law deals with sexually based issues. Ellis brought to sexuality an international perspective and demonstrated that sexual customs and mores are not universal. Moll developed the notion of childhood sexuality and its impact on later sexual functioning that ultimately influenced the work of Sigmund Freud and other leading child experts. Bloch sought to make sexology a cohesive and rational field of inquiry and thus required researchers to be interdisciplinary in their analysis of sexual issues. Kinsey opened the door to more insightful and thought-provoking research on human sexuality. Finally, Pomeroy discovered an extraordinary amount about sex offenders, including that their behaviors and attitudes are not much different from "normal" males. In combination, these scholars laid the groundwork for the field of sexology as it is known today and continue to have significant influence over the social, political, and legal impacts of human sexuality.

Other Figures in the Study of Sex Offending and Sexuality

Michel Foucault

The History of Sexuality outlines Foucault's (1926–1984) treatise on how the experience of and framework for understanding sexuality has changed throughout the centuries. Foucault's work is essential for illustrating how various class groups and genders experience sexuality differently and the systemic nature of the suppression and repression of sex and sexuality. Foucault suggested that sexuality had gone from a subject frankly discussed to a Victorian attitude in which it was medicalized and marginalized.

Foucault demonstrated that throughout the ages, the language used to conceptualize sexuality had been "cleaned" and placed within established professions, such as religion and medicine, in order for it to be discussed legitimately (Foucault 1978). He contended that the pendulum had swung so far to the right that children were regarded as not having a sexuality and being in need of constant protection and monitoring to ensure that they were not corrupted by the behaviors of adults.

This famous work describes how certain sexual behaviors have become marginalized, what Foucault terms the "other Victorians," and confined to brothels and mental institutions. Foucault contended that around the same point in history, the use of language became very important. For the lower class, speaking of sex acted as a transgression against the upper class. Alongside this change, speaking of sex became professionalized so that only qualified individuals were given the knowledge and permission to relay sexual information. Foucault claimed that this change coincided with increasing capitalism, whereby the upper class was seeking to control the knowledge and sexual activity of the working classes in order to ensure continued production of goods and services (Foucault 1978).

The History of Sexuality is a theoretical and historical overview of how politics, economics, religion, and gender all interact to change the manner in which society thinks, feels, and acts about sex. It is a foundational work for all fields analyzing sex and sexuality, as it illustrates that the only constant in sexuality is that the state/powerful class controls what is done, who is allowed to do it, what is learned, and who makes up the professional class (Foucault 1978). It clearly articulates how what is now considered immoral or illegal is classified that way only as a result of shifts in Church and state policy—shifts that were often the result of the upper class trying to gain more control of the working classes.

Karl Hanson

Karl Hanson is best known as the co-creator of the Static-99, an actuarial risk assessment instrument used by law enforcement and clinicians dealing with sexual offenders. Hanson is also a leading researcher in the field of sexual crime and has conducted significant meta-analyses of studies that have resulted in the development of treatment programs. He was one of the first scholars to contend that there was no association between victim empathy and sexual recidivism, and in so doing the landscape of offender treatment made a marked turn in direction. As a result, programs do not necessarily incorporate components on empathy (Hanson 2003). In addition, Hanson contends that the skill that offenders need to learn is perspective taking, whereby many offenders have distrust for their preferred victim group and a general inability to identify stress cues from their victims (Hanson 2003). In other words, a rapist may perceive a woman saying "no" as merely a weak form of resistance because she does not want to appear to be "easy" and may not see the woman's physical and mental anxiety over being confronted for sex.

Another important finding in Hanson's research relates to the role of shame. It is hypothesized that shame is an effective treatment goal because it can force offenders to confront the harm to their victims and not resort to guilt, which has proven only temporarily effective in reducing recidivism (Hanson 2003). Hanson has worked to identify factors he believes influence the sympathetic responses of offenders to their victims, such as the relationship between the offender and the victim, perspective-taking ability, the mechanisms the offender has for dealing with distress, and the emotional reactions resulting from distress (Hanson 2003).

Many scholars have contributed to the study of sexual violence and sex offenders, with each study focusing on a new and different element. The result has been a convoluted collection of findings and fields of thought that often contradict one another. Many questions have remained unanswered: Is shame a more important factor than skill deficit in the etiology of a sex offender? What role does sex and sexuality play? If an act is acceptable in another culture, such as intergenerational sex, how can it be morally wrong? Moreover, how do we go about eradicating unacceptable behaviors? Perhaps more important, should we eliminate behaviors that some in society consider inappropriate? It was not long ago that women were considered property under the law. What if society had created "treatment" programs for women who failed to follow appropriate societal norms? Could this be likened to creating "treatment" programs for voyeurs or persons convicted of intergenerational sex (which in other countries is legal)? It may be difficult to fathom at this historical and cultural moment in time, but what if the law changes in a few decades and the age of consent is lowered to fourteen or twelve years? All the people society has tried to "cure" will have been subjected to medical interventions that were unnecessary—just like society has done historically with homosexuals, the transgendered, and cross-dressers. Even the greatest thinkers and theorists cannot predict changing social mores, so society must proceed cautiously in the realm of "appropriate" and "inappropriate" sexual behavior.

DIAGNOSTIC AND STATISTICAL MANUAL OF MENTAL DISORDERS

A major contribution of the medical field has been the *Diagnostic and Statistical Manual of Mental Disorders* (*DSM*), which is the cornerstone of the psychiatric profession and is used by virtually all mental health professionals in diagnosing problematic behaviors. Historically, there has been minimal agreement as to which disorders should be classified and what level of emphasis should be placed on phenomenology, etiology, and defining features. Thousands of instruments have been developed to identify and define alleged mental diseases, and all have differed according to whether their purpose was clinical, research, or statistical (American Psychiatric Association [APA] 2008).

Therapists and mental health professionals working with sex offenders utilize terms stemming from the *DSM*. Terminology from this manual is used to establish legitimacy for the fields of sex therapy, psychology, and psychiatry and ensure that they are recognized as scientific/medical specializations that are capable of identifying and treating various pathologies. The terms used emphasize "abnormality" in adult male sexual desire for persons under the age of eighteen years yet fail to distinguish between what is abnormal and what is socially unacceptable (Cowburn 2005). For example, the APA and the *DSM* assume that because intergenerational sex is socially unacceptable, it occurs infrequently and is therefore abnormal. Consequently, this behavior, which is actually fairly common throughout American society and is consistent with dominant male sexual practices historically (e.g., individual power and potency), is pathologized.

Prior to 1939, the American scientific community was interested in collecting statistics on mental disorders; however, a classification system was needed to make the information usable. Very basic categorization of a select few mental illnesses took place prior to the 1900s. More standardization developed in the early 1900s because of input from the APA; however, the classification system was still not comprehensive. After 1944, the U.S. Army developed a more substantial nomenclature in order to address the mental health issues of soldiers returning home from World War II, and the World Health Organization included a section on mental disorders in the sixth edition of the *International Classification of Diseases* (*ICD*) (APA 2008). The APA used the *ICD* as the foundation for the first *DSM*, published in 1952. The underlying assumption of the first edition of the *DSM* was that mental disorders stem from reactions of the individual to psychological, social, and biological factors (APA 2008). There were serious flaws in this version in that reliable definitions for disorders were lacking, making clinical diagnoses near impossible. The second edition of the *DSM* remained unchanged from the first edition, except for the elimination of the focus on reaction (APA 2008).

The APA published the third edition of the *DSM* (*DSM-III*) in 1980, and it represented a substantial shift in direction, including explicit diagnostic criteria, a decentralized system, and a descriptive approach in order to avoid supporting any particular theory of disease etiology (APA 2008). However, the *DSM-III* was not without its controversy in the medical field. Many clinicians were dissatisfied with the inconsistencies present in the classification system and the fact that defining criteria were not always clearly articulated (APA 2008). As a result, revisions were undertaken. The fourth edition of the *DSM* (*DSM-IV*) was published in 1994 and was the result of more than 1,000 medical professionals providing input into the types of disorders that should be added, deleted, and reorganized (APA 2008). Included but controversial was a classification for "psychopath." This is frequently a differential diagnosis for sex offenders, although medical professionals fail to agree on defining characteristics, the etiology is completely unknown, there are few empirical studies on its treatment, and even fewer studies have involved follow-up with individuals categorized as psychopaths (Craig, Browne, Stringer, and Beech 2005).

The *DSM-IV* contains more than forty sexual behaviors considered to be psychiatric in nature and covers everything from bisexuality to fetishism and transvestitism. However, the extent of the behaviors covered is subject to change based on current psychological and psychiatric research and the political perspectives of its creators. For instance, the gay rights movement in the 1960s and 1970s sought to have homosexuality delisted as a mental health disorder in the *DSM*. Through advocacy and education, proponents were successful in lobbying for its removal. This is just one example of the manner in which identified sexual behaviors are socially constructed. The significance of having a disorder placed in the *DSM* cannot be overstated; when a person is diagnosed with a *DSM*-identified illness, insurance, employment, and security clearances can be denied, and the person is forced to contend with the stigma of having a mental disorder. Table 2.1 lists the sexually based disorders present in the *DSM-III* and *DSM-IV*. For each of the "disorders" in the table, note that persons can be diagnosed if they have participated *or* fantasized about the behavior for a period of six months.

In reviewing the table, it becomes evident that noncriminal behaviors, such as cross-dressing and homosexuality, are included in the *DSM*, whereas illegal behaviors, such as rape, are not explicitly listed. This is a leading criticism of the *DSM* among sexual health professionals. Moreover, it is problematic to label all people who have a *DSM*-listed disorder as mentally ill when not all individuals are distressed or dissatisfied about their behavior. How can consensual sexual activity be considered a mental disorder that requires medical intervention? That is precisely what occurs when the *DSM* lists sadism and masochism. Think back to Krafft-Ebing, who postulated that sadomasochism is present in all sexual unions to some extent. What sexual behaviors do you engage in that could be considered a mental illness?

Table 2.1. Sexual Disorders Contained in the *DSM-III-R* (1987) and the *DSM-IV* (1994)

Diagnostic Category	Classification	Description	Present in DSM-III-R, DSM-IV, or Both
Sexual disorders—paraphilias	Exhibitionism	Sexual urges or fantasies, acted on or not, regarding exposing the genitals to strangers.	Both
Note: A new category in the DSM-IV is sexual and gender identity disorders	Fetishism	Sexual urges or fantasies, acted on or not, regarding objects such as bras, women's underpants, stockings, shoes, boots, or other women's apparel. Masturbation to the object is common.	Both
	Frotteurism	Sexual urges or fantasies, acted on or not, regarding touching or rubbing against a nonconsenting person.	Both
	Pedophilia	Sexual urges or fantasies, acted on or not, regarding sexual activity with a person under thirteen years of age. Includes incest. The offender must be at least sixteen years of age and at least five years older than the victim.	Both
	Masochism	Sexual urges or fantasies, acted on or not, involving being humiliated, beaten, or bound or other forms of "suffering" for sexual excitement.	Both
	Sadism	Sexual urges or fantasies, acted on or not, to inflict psychological or physical pain for sexual excitement.	Both
	Transvestic fetishism	Sexual urges or fantasies, acted on or not, to cross-dress.	Both
	Voyeurism	Sexual urges or fantasies, acted on or not, to observe unsuspecting people nude or disrobing or engaged in sexual activity.	Both
	Other paraphilias	Telephone scatologia (lewdness). Necrophilia (corpses). Partialis (exclusive focus on part of the body). Zoophilia (animals). Coprophilia (feces).	DSM-III-R

Klismaphilia (enemas).
Urophilia (urine).

Category	Disorder	Description	DSM
Sexual and gender identity disorder			
Gender identity disorders	Gender identity disorder	Evidence of strong and persistent identification with the opposite sex, accompanied by a desire to be the opposite sex.	DSM-IV
	Gender identity disorder not otherwise specified	Intersex, accompanied by gender dysphoria. Transient, stress-related cross-dressing. Persistent preoccupation with castration or penectomy without a desire to be the opposite sex.	DSM-IV
	Sexual disorder not otherwise specified	Feelings of inadequacy regarding performance that are related to self-imposed notions of masculinity or femininity. Distress about having multiple sexual relationships in which the partners are viewed as objects. Distress about sexual orientation.	DSM-IV
Disorders usually first evident in infancy, childhood, or adolescence—gender identity disorders	Transsexualism	Persistent discomfort with one's assigned sex, with the desire to alter one's assigned sex.	DSM-III-R
	Gender identity disorder, nontranssexual	Persistent discomfort with one's assigned sex, accompanied by cross-dressing.	DSM-III-R
Impulse-control disorders not elsewhere classified	Impulse-control disorders not elsewhere classified	Paraphilia involving impulse control.	DSM-IV
Other conditions that may be a focus of clinical attention	Problems related to abuse or neglect	Sexual abuse of a child. Sexual abuse of an adult.	DSM-IV

OTHER TESTS FOR SEXUAL "PREDATORS"

There are numerous tests that exist to measure the potential risk of recidivism among sexual offenders. Actuarial tests are statistically based,
whereas clinical measures are focused predominantly on subjective impressions of the therapist toward the offender and his behavior. Legally,
clinical tests are generally inadmissible, as there is no standardized
methodology and such tests are based too much on the reliance of the subjective judgment of a clinician. Courts have ruled that clinicians can be biased according to their theoretical training, religion, gender, and political
affiliations. Consequently, actuarial tests have become the main criteria
used by courts in sentencing to assess an individual's likelihood of reoffense and are based on characterizations of "similar" types of offenders.

Actuarial tests can be either static or dynamic. Static factors are those
things that cannot be changed, such as age and offense history. Dynamic
or situational factors are constantly changing and are much more useful
in predicting when an individual will reoffend. These factors include res-
idential stability, family support, employment status, involvement in
drugs or alcohol, and the presence or absence of treatment. Moreover, dynamic factors can be either stable or acute. Stable refers to the persistent
characteristics of the offender, such as cognitive distortions and sexual
arousal; conversely, acute refers to rapidly changing elements that may increase risk, such as substance misuse or isolation (Craig et al. 2005). Situational factors can serve to dramatically increase the stress on an individual, thereby increasing that individual's likelihood of reoffending, or
decrease the stress on an individual, thereby decreasing the individual's
likelihood of reoffending. The vast majority of actuarial tests are static,
meaning that the test relies on historical factors, such as past history of offending and whether the person was capable of maintaining a long-term
intimate relationship. This is extremely important because an individual
designated at low risk on static variables, if overwhelmed with negative
situational influences, may become a fairly high risk offender, and this
will be overlooked by most current types of assessment instruments.
There is one actuarial test currently under development that incorporates
dynamic factors, such as current family and employment situation, community supports, and other variables. Unfortunately, this test is not currently available for use by clinicians or researchers. Table 2.2 outlines the
various actuarial tests used by clinicians and researchers to gather data on
recidivism rates for convicted offenders and to assess the likelihood that
an individual will reoffend.

All the measures listed in the table apply only to adult male offenders,
and the effectiveness of these instruments for female and adolescent offenders has not been established. Although many variables included in

Table 2.2. Actuarial Risk Assessment Instruments[1]

Test	Description	Usage
Psychopathy Checklist—Revised (PCL-R)	Semistructured interviews, supplemented by a review of file information. Assigned rating of absent, some indication, or present on each of the twenty items in the measure.	Measures psychopathy via the characteristics of impulsivity, irresponsibility, and callousness.
Violence Risk Appraisal Guide (VRAG)	Measures twelve items: living with both biological parents until sixteen years of age, elementary school maladjustment, history of alcohol problems, marital status, nonviolent offense history, failure on prior conditional releases, age at index offense, index victim injury, sex of index victim, meeting *DSM-III* criteria for any personality disorder, meeting *DSM-III* criteria for any schizophrenia, and PCL-R score. Assigned ratings of risk from lowest to highest on nine-point scale of risk.	Measures relationship between predictor and violent recidivism (not necessarily sexual recidivism).
Sex Offender Risk Appraisal Guide (SORAG)	Modification of the VRAG, with ten common items. Total of fourteen items measured, including the following four additions to the VRAG: phallometrically measured deviant sexual interests, violent history offense, sexual offense history, and sex and age of index victim. Scores can range from −27 to +51, with individuals assigned rating of risk from lowest to highest on nine-point scale.	Measures relationship between predictor and sexual recidivism.

(continued)

Table 2.2. (Continued)

Test	Description	Usage
Rapid Risk Assessment for Sex Offense Recidivism (RRASOR)	Measures four items: number of prior charges or convictions for sexual offenses, age on release from prior or anticipated opportunity to reoffend in the community, any male victims (yes or no), and any unrelated victims (yes or no). Scores range from 0 to 6, with each item weighted differently according to its relationship to sexual recidivism.	Cursory measure for likelihood of sexual recidivism.
Static-99	Addition to RRASOR and includes ten new items: prior sentencing dates, convictions for noncontact sexual offenses, index offense of non–sexually violent nature, prior non–sexually violent offense, stranger victims, cohabitation status, age, unrelated victims, and prior sex offenses. Scores range from 0 to 12, and individuals are assigned one of seven risk categories from lowest to highest risk of reoffending.	Measures relationship between static, or historical, factors and the likelihood of reoffending sexually.
Minnesota Sex Offender Screening Tool—Revised (MnSOST-R)	Contains sixteen items, including twelve relating to historical information and four to institutional information. Historical items include number of sex/sex-related convictions, length of sexual offending history, offender under supervision at time of any sexual offense, any sexual offenses committed in public, force or threat of force used in any sexual offense, any sexual offense within a single incident involving multiple acts on a single victim, number of different age-groups victimized across all sexual offenses, victims aged thirteen to fifteen years and offender five years older, stranger victim,	Used with persons previously imprisoned for sexual assault to measure risk of reoffending six years plus postrelease. Not validated to assess risk and recidivism.

Measure	Description	Notes
	adolescent antisocial behavior, substantial drug/alcohol abuse in year prior to arrest, and employment history. Institutional items include discipline history while incarcerated, substance use while incarcerated, participation in sex offender treatment, and age at time of release. Items weighted according to statistical relationship between it and sexual reoffending. Assigned one of six risk categories from lowest to highest.	
Multifunctional Assessment of Sex Offender Risk for Recidivism (MASORR)	Assigned ratings from low to high on five-point scale for static items. This score is then combined with subjective analysis of treatment provider regarding motivation, degree of change achieved in treatment, and clinical impression of posttreatment risk.	Higher motivation for treatment and greater change achieved in treatment assumed to be indicators of lower risks to reoffend.
Sexual Violence Risk-20 (SVR-20)	Twenty-item checklist, including elements related to prosocial adjustment, sexual offenses, and future plans. Rating based on review of clinical files and documents, followed by an interview. Items scored on three-point scale. Items measured include sexual deviation, victim of child abuse, psychopathy, major mental illness, substance use problems, suicidal/homicidal ideation, relationship problems, employment problems, past non–sexually violent offenses, past supervision failure, high-density sex offenses, multiple sex offense types, physical harm to victims in sex offenses, use of weapons or threat of death during sex offenses, past violent offenses, escalation in frequency or severity of sex offenses, extreme minimization or denial of sex offenses, attitudes that support/condone sex offenses, lack of realistic plans, and negative attitude toward intervention.	Measures sexual violence via affective and interpersonal personality characteristics and behavioral patterns.

(continued)

Table 2.2. *(Continued)*

Test	Description	Usage
Personal Concerns Inventory—Offender Adaptation (PCI-OA)	Measures fourteen items in a semistructured interview format concerning life goals. Items include home and household matters, employment and finances, partner/family/relatives, friends/acquaintances, love/intimacy/sexual matters, self changes, education/training, health/medical matters, substance use, spiritual matters, hobbies/recreation, offending behavior, current relationship, and other.	Used to measure substance abuse and as a tool to motivate offenders into treatment.
Sex Offense Attitude Questionnaire	Assesses variables related to the level of denial and minimization expressed by the sex offender.	Measures levels of cognitive distortions.
Relapse Prevention Interview	An eighteen-item interview that focuses on the offender's ability to recognize relapse cues, develop coping strategies, and accept future risk. Assigned a rating on a three-point scale from no skills or recognition to good skills and recognition.	Used to assist release decisions.

[1] *Sources:* Barbaree et al. (2001) for all but the SVR-20. Source for the SVR-20: Sjostedt and Langstrom (2002). Additional source for MnSOST: Campbell (2000). Source for PCI-OA: Theodosi and McMurran (2006). Source for Sex Offense Attitude Questionnaire and Relapse Prevention Interview: Wakeling, Webster, and Mann (2005).

the scales (such as empathy, denial, and treatment involvement) have been empirically proven to be unrelated to recidivism risk, they remain included in risk assessment measures. It is significant to note that the scales were designed and are coded based on the behaviors of only convicted sex offenders. As such, the effectiveness of the scales remains untested for individuals who have not been charged with an offense but who may present to a counselor with sexually offensive behavior. For example, many of the scales are not accurate in predicting risk for incest offenders (many of whom may present to a counselor but not be legally charged with an offense), as many incest offenders do not have previous histories of sexual abuse toward other victims. In essence, these instruments are superior at predicting recidivism for static (unchanging) factors only. In addition, because of a myriad of variables, predicting risk is generally very difficult, and the result is that the scales overestimate risk (Craig et al. 2005). As such, the real risk lies in the creation of false positives.

The most consistent factors in the risk assessment instruments are in reference to age, previous convictions, procriminal attitudes, and association and measures of antisocial personality (Barbaree et al. 2001). None of the tests are clinical, meaning that it would be inappropriate to base treatment decisions on the scales, and others, such as the Rapid Risk Assessment for Sex Offense Recidivism and the Minnesota Sex Offender Screening Tool—Revised, are incapable of measuring the effect of treatment on recidivism (Barbaree et al. 2001). All the risk assessment instruments are correlated with each other, meaning that much of the data set that was used to develop the baseline for statistical analysis is the same. However, using the tests in combination with each other does not provide a statistically significant advantage despite the fact that many clinicians and forensic psychologists and psychiatrists do so as part of their testimony for court (Seto 2005).

The U.S. federal government has developed a four-pronged test to ascertain the evidentiary reliability of a scientific theory or technique. The test is as follows: 1) whether it was tested, 2) whether it was subject to peer review and publication, 3) the known or potential error rate, and 4) its widespread acceptance in the field (Campbell 2000). Currently, there are no professional standards available for assessing violent risk despite the fact that risk assessment instruments have been developed (Campbell 2000). In addition, some of the data sets from which the baseline data are derived are lacking information on follow-up periods. Studies have shown this to decrease predictive accuracy and ultimately reduce the sample sizes that can legitimately be included in meta-analyses of sexual offenders (Seto 2005). Perhaps most important, all the commonly used tools for assessing risk fail to fully comply with ethical and testing standards for psychology (Campbell 2000). Consequently, it is questionable for psychologists to use the instruments in legal proceedings, such as civil commitments, to support their clinical judgments of persons charged with sexually based crimes.

There is no one best method for determining the level of risk associated with a particular offender and no comprehensive way to estimate recidivism. Ascertaining these factors requires more than briefly examining limited items from a person's history, diagnosing them as mentally disordered, or labeling someone a sexual deviant as a result of an illegal act. Leading researchers and sexologists have illustrated that most people partake in sexual acts that are illegal—they simply do not get caught. It would be more advantageous to compare the behavior and attitudes of those convicted of sexual offenses to those of "normal" citizens who commit sexual offenses but do not get arrested and to those individuals who do not commit any sexual offenses. This is the only method to determine with any validity why a person offends sexually. Moreover, researchers and clinicians will have to set aside their preconceived notions of "normal" versus "abnormal" behavior or the legal versus illegal dichotomy and instead focus on behaviors involving lack of consent. Without a more holistic approach to measuring the risk to society of violent sexual offenders, society is doomed to exist in a cycle of violence.

3

Is There Any Explanation?

The most important and frequently asked question is why people offend sexually. What drives a person to rape a child, beat a woman into submitting to sexual intercourse, engage in sex with an underage pupil, or become aroused by watching child pornography? The easiest explanations, such as those provided by politicians and the media, refer to "sick" or mentally unstable people and are often completely devoid of fact. Many disciplines have attempted to develop theoretical frameworks to explain why an individual offends sexually and how society responds to such acts. Women are virtually absent in theoretical discussions, thus leaving a huge gap in the literature and drawing into question the validity of theoretical models. Thus, it is important when reading this chapter to be cognizant that the theories developed are based entirely on male sex offenders and, most frequently, female victims. This chapter examines the sexological and sociological/criminological disciplines to examine the varied explanations to sexual offending. Although the idea of theory may seem unimportant in stopping sexual crimes from occurring, it does have several significant benefits. First, theory helps society understand the complexity of an issue. Second, theory helps elucidate the socially constructed nature of sexual offending and how society is organized to respond to the issue. Finally, theory often forms the basis of treatment modalities and public policy related to sexual offenders.

SEXOLOGICAL THEORY

Sexology is an area of study that examines people's sexual attitudes and behaviors. It is subdivided into three areas of concentration: education, research, and clinical applications. There is great debate in the field as to whether a unifying theory of sexology exists, as the field has borrowed heavily from other disciplines in terms of educational theories and clinical applications. Despite theoretical disagreements, sexology may be described as sex positive with a clear desire to avoid labeling people as deviant, perverts, or miscreants because of the behaviors in which they engage. The general consensus within the field is that what people publicly (and sometimes privately) state as their sexual attitudes differ widely from their actual sexual behaviors. Originally, this was empirically proven in Kinsey's series of groundbreaking sex history studies on men (Kinsey et al. 1948) and women (Kinsey et al. 1953). Generally, people are conservative in their sexual attitudes and liberal in their sexual behavior. Kinsey found that many people were regularly engaging in illegal sexual activities, such as homosexual sex, oral sex, anal sex, and sexual activity with minors. These behaviors spanned all social classes and educational levels and demonstrated the extreme variance between culturally sanctioned sexual behaviors and reality. Laws may change and redefine what is and is not socially and legally acceptable, but the behavior of people does not necessarily follow suit. Two theoretical frameworks within sexology through which to understand sexual offending are the sociosexual response cycle and sexual anthropology.

Sociosexual Response Cycle

Although widely used as a clinical model in sexological practice, very little has been formally published about the sociosexual response cycle (SSRC). The theory is taught as part of graduate education in sexology in the United States. The SSRC explores the social responses of individuals to sexual stimuli and how people manage their sexuality. Basically, it analyzes how sexual decisions are made and sees each sexual encounter as a series of choices with various available options. This includes how a person negotiates one's sexual choices, both internally and with potential partners, and how the postsexual experience is handled. For persons who offend sexually, their crimes are seen holistically from the first thought of a sexual encounter to the denial or admittance of the crime afterward. The SSRC is composed of two distinct parts: desire and consideration of options. The sex crime occurs during the second part at the consideration-of-options phase (McIlvenna 2007).

Society condemns many activities that average citizens routinely engage in, and thus sexology supports expanded definitions of sexual options so that inappropriate sexual outlets become unnecessary (McIlvenna 2007). Clinically, the SSRC is used to give offenders permission to be sexual in appropriate ways and provides them with additional sexual options they may have been previously unaware of by exploring sexual fantasies and thoughts that involve consensual activities (McIlvenna 2007). The SSRC is one theory that is actually put into practice by sexologists who use the cycle to teach offenders how to transform their thoughts and fantasies into reality in socially acceptable ways. This is done through taking detailed sexual histories of offenders to learn what the person has read, watched, and been exposed to and the thought processes that influence the person the most profoundly (McIlvenna 2007). The use of this technique has proven to be more accurate than plethysmography, or measuring the engorgement of the penis when exposed to sexual stimuli, in treating sexual offenders and can form part of a treatment program (for a discussion of the various treatment techniques, see chapter 9).

The SSRC in Practice

A man is feeling lonely and rejected by his friends and family. The stress of his job seems overwhelming to him, so he decides to take a walk in the park to clear his head. While on his walk, he becomes increasingly sexually aroused by the women he sees around him. He finds a lone woman walking her dog in a somewhat secluded location and approaches her. As he walks by he makes eye contact with the woman and exposes his genitals. He believes the woman will see this display, interpret it as manly, and become sexually attracted to him. He is looking to feel accepted and wanted. What are the conscious choices this man has made? He knows that he is an exhibitionist and exposes himself when feeling rejected by those close to him. His first conscious choice was to go for a walk alone in an area conducive to offending when he was feeling rejected. His second choice was to view the females in the park as potential sexual partners, persons to which he could expose himself. Next, he arranged himself in a location to have access to a lone female. Finally, he exposed his genitals to the woman and felt a sense of euphoria immediately afterward.

The SSRC contends that people have to ask for what they want sexually and then negotiate for specifics. For sex offenders, the "asking" part can be nonexistent, or the offender may believe that a positive response from the victim, such as a smile or brief conversation, is equivalent to an agreement to engage in sexual activity. At each stage of a sexual encounter, the person checks in with their partner, verbally or nonverbally, to ascertain if what is occurring coincides with previously agreed-on desires. The underlying belief of this theory is that sexual acts are planned and conscious and that choices are made at every stage throughout an encounter. Thus, offenders must be taught to identify the choices they make, become cognizant of their fantasies, develop skills to recognize sexual cues of potential partners, and be able to communicate about a sexual encounter throughout its engagement.

Case Study: Analyzing Intergenerational Sex from Varying Perspectives

Various actors study the issue of child–adult sexual interaction, also termed intergenerational sex. Terminology and use of language is critical when discussing sex offenses, as it sets the tone for how offenders are ultimately treated by the legal system, treatment providers, and the public. This case study examines the use of language for various actors.

The focus of sex researchers studying intergenerational sex is on synthesizing legal, moral, and scientific values and definitions. In terms of practice, the focus is on the impact to the individual and whether sexual and interpersonal adjustment has been affected by the sexual activity. Most of the research conducted on child–adult sexual interaction (CASI) uses statistics generated from the criminal justice community and therefore incorporates terminology and legal definitions of sexual abuse (Cowburn 2005). Legal actors utilize terminology that focuses on the apparent innate harm caused by CASI, and terms such as "pedophile" and "child molester" are common (Holmes and Holmes 2009). For district attorneys, a child molester is an adult who has any form of sexual interaction with a person who is legally defined as a child, whereas a pedophile is defined as an adult who has sexual fantasies and erotic images that focus on children as sexual partners. Importantly, the term "child molester" has no medical or scientific value, and, as such, defining child molesters as socially inept and unassertive is used as a legal ploy to promote conviction rates and engender public outrage. On the other side of the courtroom, the defense attorney seeks to distinguish between "abuse" as harm to the child (e.g., physical injuries or psychic trauma) as opposed to "abuse" as a violation of social norms. There is a separation between wrongfulness and harmfulness. A defense attorney may cite as evidence a study that found that 37 percent of adult male college students who reported engaging in CASI viewed it as positive at the time of the event and that 42 percent viewed it as positive when they reflected back on the incident (Rind, Tromovitch, and Bauserman 1998). The focus of a defense attorney would be on the immorality of the activity as opposed to the harm caused.

When studying CASI, sex researchers often employ the term "sexual coercion" to distinguish it from situations that involve violence; such situations have significantly different social connotations (Cowburn 2005). In scholarly research, use of the term "sexual coercion" allows for a wide array of sexual behaviors to be captured under a very broad category. A major drawback to using the concept of "sexual coercion" is its vagueness, which may lead to exaggeration of research findings and misconceptions regarding the extent and nature of truly abusive sexual behavior between adults and children.

Clinical professionals are also involved in the study of CASI, and the American Psychiatric Association uses terms such as "sexual and gender identity disorders," "pedophilia," "sexual disorder not otherwise specified," and "antisocial personality disorder" to identify persons who engage in sexual behaviors deemed inappropriate. Pedophilia is defined as sexual activity between a prepubescent child (generally under thirteen years of age), with the offender being at least sixteen years of age or five years older than the child. Pedophilia is further subdivided into those sexually attracted to males, females, or both; those who limit their interests to incest; those who are exclusive; and those who are nonexclusive. "Sexual disorder not otherwise specified" refers to a person who engages in a repeated pattern of sexual relations involving a succession of partners who are regarded by the individual as objects to be used. Finally, the American Psychiatric Association uses the term "antisocial personality disorder" to identify persons with a pattern of disregard for and violation of the rights of others. Importantly, these are all clinical terms that often have different meanings than those used within the legal system (Hall and Hall 2007). For instance, "child molestation," a term favored by the criminal justice system, is not synonymous with "pedophilia." For clinicians, a child molester is a person who touches a child in order to obtain sexual gratification and is only four to five years older than the victim (Hall and Hall 2007). Moreover, clinicians will distinguish between hebephilia and infantophilia when diagnosing and treating clients.

Another school of thought emerging from sex therapy is that not all children who participate in intergenerational sex have a negative reaction, as is generally assumed albeit not empirically proven by the mental health profession. This perspective demands that there be a delinking between the types of acts (e.g., coitus, oral sex, or fondling) and the level of closeness shared between the child and adult (Rind, Tromovitch, and Bauserman 1998). The central illustration is to remove the assumptions of "severity" and "seriousness" from therapy and instead focus on the impact to the individual and whether sexual and interpersonal adjustment has been affected by intergenerational sexual activity.

Sexual Anthropology

Sexual anthropology aims to provide a framework with which to understand why people engage in sexual behaviors. The theory contends that it is necessary to learn about society's peripheral behaviors in order to understand average sexual behaviors. Two key elements of sexual anthropology are cultural relativism and symbolizing. Cultural relativism is the belief that one can understand a culture only on its own terms. In other words, American researchers cannot study the sexual behaviors of peoples of other countries simply because they are not privy to the social and sexual nuances of those other countries. Symbolizing is a dynamic process in which researchers participate in the behavior they are studying in order to understand how that behavior accumulated its cultural meaning. What sexual anthropology has discovered is that there is one universal for all cultures: the control of sexual behavior. Moreover, it has been demonstrated that once a culture compartmentalizes a behavior, it becomes normalized, meaning that once society believes that people who commit sex crimes are "deviant," "mentally challenged," "poor and uneducated," or "perverts," it serves to give offenders the status of "other" and normalize the behavior of those not deemed to be sex offenders (e.g., "It's alright what I do because I'm not a pervert like that child offender").

In the late 1800s, a sexologist named Havelock Ellis employed the concept of cultural relativism to the notion of modesty. For Ellis, modesty was used to describe behaviors considered acceptable by the majority of society. As such, North Americans and Europeans considered modesty to be the covering of genitals and breasts in public, whereas in other nations, such as African countries, nudity was the norm because it was believed that what everyone could not see was highly erotic and desired (Brecher 2000). This demonstrates that modesty varies widely between cultures but also over time—it is rare to find African countries where citizens walk around naked, but female toplessness is permitted in some social situations in the United States. Ellis also found that the concept of modesty, however defined, exists in all cultures and is unrelated to sexual behavior (Ellis 1942). In the 1800s, Tahitians would not eat in front of each other because of the sexual connotations eating possessed, and the Victorian-era English thought that it was improper for husbands and wives to bathe together (Brecher 2000; Ellis 1942). Another sexologist, Mary Jane Sherfey, regarded sexuality through the prism of evolution. Sherfey found that if people were freed from their cultural restrictions on sex and fully understood human anatomy, it would become evident that women and men respond similarly to sexual stimuli (Brecher 2000). Thus, it was Sherfey's goal to demonstrate that the supposed difference between men and women, such as the myth that men have more sexual desire than women, is culturally created and not biological.

Sexual anthropology also recognizes that there are differences in sexual behaviors within cultures. In Kinsey's groundbreaking research on sexual attitudes and behaviors, he empirically demonstrated that there are significant differences between the behaviors of the lower and upper classes as well as differences based on gender and religion (Kinsey et al. 1948, 1953). Sexual anthropology analyzes the interconnections of class, gender, and race as structures of dominance and subordination in sexuality. The upper classes tend to self-define appropriate behavior for themselves, which is often very different from what they consider acceptable for those from the lower classes (Weeks 1986). Women's sexuality is recast and reformulated by men to meet male needs and desires, and people of color may be regarded as more animalistic in their sexual activity (Weeks 1986).

The study of sexuality necessitates an understanding of how society believes people should live as well as knowledge of past sexual practices (Weeks 1986). Sexuality exists only through its social forms and social organization, and it is organized through a variety of channels, including kinship and family systems, economic and social organization, social regulation, political intervention, and cultural resistance (Weeks 1986). The family serves as the primary source of sexual socialization, whereby it shapes, structures, and constrains the development and expression of sexuality through a combination of training and a system of rewards and punishments (Davenport 1977). The work conditions faced by people influence their sexual lives, as does the predominant religions of the country and other formal and customary activities (Weeks 1986). The social climate determines the significance that sexual issues have with politicians, the types of laws that are formed to respond, and society's moral regulation, ultimately giving rise to resistance among various factions that in turn may lead to social changes.

It is not possible to study only the rules and regulations a culture has surrounding sex and sexuality, as sexuality has linkages with regulations that may seem unrelated with sex (Davenport 1977). For instance, in some tribal communities sexual violence is perpetrated to test as well as demonstrate the power and social position of a man. In other cultures, such as the Gusii of Kenya, sexual arousal and mating must be connected with hostility and antagonism to be regarded as successful. Gusii women are taught to encourage and then reject men, while men are taught to demand and forcefully take sex (Davenport 1977). In a study of homosexuality in Mexico, a sex crime punishable in the 1970s by fines, spiritual penances, public humiliation, floggings, exiles, galleys, and death, Taylor (1975, 1978) illustrated the discrepancy between overt social mores, public sentiment, and what people actually did sexually. This sex crime was considered so heinous that various agents of social control were trained to uncover gays and "treat" them for what was regarded as a mental disorder.

What is uncovered when we look at sexuality cross-culturally is that when people deviate from what is considered normal sexuality in specific ways, the state and culture work together to take away all control over the lives and bodies of those individuals then stigmatized as "sex offenders." This is evident today in the form of civil commitment laws and lifelong registration for persons who have offended sexually. However, in the United States, one's sexual rights are vested not in the family or the individual but in society as a whole. This is evidenced by the sex crimes laws whereby offenders give redress to society in the form of prison or probation and not to the individual victim or their family. In American culture there is a broad range of sexual behaviors labeled deviant. These behaviors are categorized within a hierarchy (e.g., the worst being offenses against children, the least being exhibitionism or voyeurism) that is based on assumptions about the offender's motivation, the degree of reprehensibility of the act, if specific laws exist to punish the type of crime, and the severity of the sanction (Bryant 1982). Therefore, deviant becomes relative in society and must be analyzed within a framework of social norms and prescriptions.

FEMINIST THEORY

Although there does not exist one unifying feminist theory, there are common threads to all variations of the feminist perspective. One major unifying thread is the structural, as opposed to individual, nature of the problem of sexual violence: "Although there can be individual explanations, individual resolution, and though there is always individual pain, individual wounding, scarring, the issue is not an individual issue but a societal one. We live in a society where men are encouraged to do violence to women and children, subtly and overtly" (Bass 1995: 115). A patriarchal society is one in which men are structurally and ideologically in a superior position to women. Structurally, men continue to hold a majority of positions of power and influence in society, with their labor often more highly valued than the labor of women. Ideologically, feminist theorists believe that a system of patriarchy teaches men that women are inferior and submissive and this permits some men to feel a sense of entitlement over a woman's sexuality. A patriarchal society also teaches women that men hold entitlement over their sexuality. This perspective is revealed by one convicted rapist's view toward women: "Rape is a man's right. If a woman doesn't want to give it, a man should take it. Women have no right to say no. Women are made to have sex. It's all they are good for. Some women would rather take a beating, but they always give in; it's what they are for" (Scully 1994: 166). These messages come across in day-to-day male treatment of women as well as in music videos, billboards, popular music, television and film productions, and magazines. Feminists suggest that a society in which sexual violence is even somewhat condoned (as illustrated by weak punishments for sexual offenses in comparison to crimes such as drug offenses as well as weak punishments for male physical violence against women) serves to preserve male dominance en masse.

Adherence to these beliefs is linked to a greater likelihood of committing offenses against women. For example, men who condone the disrespect of women and surround themselves with like-minded individuals are more likely to engage in some type of abuse (sexual, physical, or emotional) of women (DeKeseredy and Schwartz 1998). In addition, Scully (1994) has found that men who have negative attitudes toward women and who believe in rape myths (e.g., "She asked for it because she was out alone late at night wearing a tight skirt") are most likely to perpetrate a sexual offense against a female. These beliefs are harmful to both men and women in society. One twenty-three-year-old remarks,

> The whole dating game between men and women also makes me feel degraded. I hate being put in the position of having to initiate a relationship. I've been taught that if you're not aggressive with a woman, then you've blown it. She's not going to jump on *you*, so *you've* got to jump on *her*. I've heard all kinds of stories where the woman says "No! No! No!" and they end up making great love. . . . Probably a lot of men think that women don't feel like real women unless a man tries to force himself on her, unless she brings out the "real man," so to speak, and probably too much of it goes on. It goes on in my head that you're complimenting a woman by actually staring at her or by trying to get into her pants. Lately, I'm realizing that when I stare at women lustfully, they often feel more threatened than flattered. (Beneke 1995b: 57; emphasis in original)

Many feminists suggest a close relationship between common modes of expressing sexuality and sexual assault. An analysis of sexual scripts reveals a complex learning process that is tied to cultural norms. "It is gender identity which provides the framework within which sexuality is learnt and through which erotic self-identity is created. Thus men and women learn to be sexual in different ways, to enact different roles in the sexual drama, to utilize different vocabularies of motive. The attributes of masculinity and femininity, learnt from the beginning of childhood and incorporated into expectations of sexual behaviour, provide the motivational and interactional basis of rape" (Jackson 1995: 18–19). Taken one step further, "it may not be that rape is forced seduction but that seduction is a subtler form of rape" (Jackson 1995: 20). In a provocative study of thirty men who admitted to sexually abusing children, Douglas Pryor (1996: 172–73) revealed similar structural explanations:

> The men became interested in sex with children for the same reasons they do with any other adult—they were curious. . . . They experienced sex in the same ways men generally experience sex. . . . They approached and engaged the other party in ways men routinely initiate sex. . . . They reacted afterwards often with feelings of shame, or sometimes no guilt at all, just like the range of reactions others elicit if they are involved in behavior of any type that society frowns heavily on. And they adjusted and coped with these feelings in ways that are commonplace as well—by apologizing to the injured party, by burying themselves in work or alcohol, by denying that what they did was really all that bad or harmful. . . . Ultimately the men appeared to treat the children they victimized as sexual objects. . . . There does not seem to be much that differentiates these men from men who are not offenders except that they crossed what appears to be a thin boundary between ordinary sexual relations and what is defined culturally as extreme sexual deviation.

Assumptions of male and female behavior that form cultural norms also have historically been present even within the criminal justice system, as a woman's sexual history, behavior, and attire were frequently the subject of intense scrutiny during a trial against a sexual offender.

For feminists, the various forms of violence against women are intimately interconnected. As elucidated by Bass and Thornton (1983: 53), "I was not sexually abused. Yet I was sexually abused. We were all sexually abused. The images and attitudes, the reality we breathe in like air, it reaches us all. It shapes and distorts us, prunes some of our most tender, trusting, lovely and loving branches. We learn that this is who a woman is. This is what men think of women. This is what we are taught to think about ourselves. . . . We are all wounded. We all need healing." We are reminded by feminist theorists that sexual relationships and encounters exist side by side and are built on the sexual inequalities that are prevalent in a society:

> Understanding that otherwise normal men can and do rape is critical to the development of strategies for prevention. We are left with the fact that all men do not rape. In view of the apparent rewards and cultural supports for rape, it is important to ask why some men do not rape . . . we may be seeking an answer to the wrong question about sexual assault of women. Instead of asking men who rape "Why?," perhaps we should be asking men who don't "Why not?" (Scully and Marolla 1995: 71–72)

Feminists believe that male violence against women has been institutionalized and in many respects accepted by mainstream society and that we must work to change attitudes and behavior that support and condone violence against women.

SOCIOLOGICAL AND CRIMINOLOGICAL THEORIES

Criminological theories have not been widely applied to the understanding of sexual offenses and sexual offenders. Most criminological texts that cover the area of sex crimes use psychological and/or feminist theories as explanation. And while criminological and sociological theories have not been extensively used to explain such offenses, there are a number that would be of relevance. Sociological and criminological theories approach sexual offending as a phenomenon embedded in the structural elements of society. Sociologists assert that social and cultural factors influence our attitudes toward sexual offenses, what is considered a sexual offense, how we view sexual offenders, and the significance of sexual offenses as a problem in American society. Generally, sociological theories focus less on individual factors than psychological theories and draw attention instead to the social environment of the offender. Of the sociological theories applicable to sexual offending, many focus on social interaction patterns in specific situations as opposed to adopting a structural critique (as in the case of feminist theory). Table 3.1 provides an overview of the sociological approaches to sexual offending.

Social Reaction Theory

Social reaction theory, commonly known as labeling theory, asserts that some behaviors and, therefore, the individuals who engage in such behaviors are labeled negatively by society in general and often by the criminal justice system. Labeling results in an individual being stigmatized by conventional society, resulting in a negative societal response, which frequently fuels the individual's return to the behavior in question. Social reaction theory has its roots in the writings of George Herbert Mead and Herbert Blumer, who suggested that the meanings we assign to events are shaped by our social and cultural experiences.

With regard to sexual offending, labeling theory would explore the ramifications of an individual being labeled publicly as a sexual offender. What happens if a person's sexual offenses are made public? What if family and friends now know? What if coworkers or neighbors know? What if our picture is posted on a sexual offender website for others to find? What if our picture is on a poster in local supermarkets and other venues? How do these actions (labeling) affect the ability of an individual to reintegrate successfully into a community? According to social reaction theorists, once an offense has been widely revealed and is labeled by others as deviant or criminal, the individual may continue the behavior because one has internalized the personality characteristics that other people expect.

Table 3.1.   Overview of Main Points of Sociological/Criminological Theories

Sociological Theory	Main Premise
Social reaction theory	Suggests that some people are labeled negatively by the larger society or those in the criminal justice system. This process of negative labeling results in the individual being shunned and treated differently by conventional society, which may serve to increase the likelihood of recidivism.
Social learning theory	Asserts that behavior is learned through human interaction. As such, individuals learn attitudes that predispose them to sexual offending from personal experience or from those in their close circle of friends.
Social control theory	Suggests that various forms of violence are culturally approved; therefore, individuals do not have to learn this behavior. Instead, theorists seek to examine how human behavior is controlled through close association with institutions and individuals. Examines how self-control and a commitment to conformity deter sexual offending.
Rational choice theory	Asserts that offenders make a rational choice/calculation to commit an offense based on factors such as prior experience with the criminal justice system, individual psychological processes, and situational context.
Life course theory	Emphasizes how involvement in crime relates to life course events, with a focus on continuity and change. Theorists are interested in the factors that influence initiation into crime, factors that influence continued involvement or escalation of involvement, and factors that influence desistance.

The labeling process traditionally goes as follows:

- An individual commits a sexual offense (social reaction theory does not attempt to explain the initial motivation for an offense, so the reasons could be varied).
- This person's behavior is brought to the attention of others or to the attention of the criminal justice system.
- If the victim was a stranger, the likelihood of arrest is higher.

- Some of the individuals who commit a sexual offense are officially labeled as criminals through arrest and/or widespread media exposure, while others are officially labeled through registration and notification procedures; other individuals, primarily offenders who are acquainted with their victim or are a family member of the victim, are not officially labeled or brought to the attention of the criminal justice system.
- The labeled individuals are then viewed negatively by conventional society, which has an extreme negative reaction to such offenders.
- These individuals come to accept and internalize the negative label.
- Acceptance of the stigma leads to an association with others who have been similarly labeled.
- Acceptance of the stigma also may decrease the ability to reintegrate successfully into a community and increase the likelihood of recidivism.

Following this logic, then, the likelihood of subsequent sexual offenses could be decreased if society and the criminal justice system did not publicly label individuals. This theoretical approach would therefore advocate against policies such as community notification because of the potentially stigmatizing effect. A man convicted of attempted sexual abuse of a minor illustrates the impact of a stigma:

> There is so much stigma I hardly know where to begin. People look at child sex offenders as a hideous monster kind of thing. They don't want to be near you. People act like they [sex offenders] are like on the verge of just, like they are lust-crazed animals and I don't think that is the case. . . . It can be anybody. I mean, it can be your priest, it can be your gardener, it can be anybody, you know . . . it could be you. I never pictured myself as a monster. . . . I do see myself as a child molester. I don't see myself as the monster at all, but I see that people will view me that way. (Meloy 2006: 82)

In a study that interviewed sexual offenders, one perpetrator sentenced to community supervision for aggravated criminal sexual abuse said,

> I can honestly tell you I was shocked at the level of stigma I have because of this. I mean, I knew it was bad to have sex with a teenager . . . it is obviously unacceptable and I knew I was going to jail, but ah' I had no idea I would be viewed as some kind of a child molester, predator-type thing. I got hammered by the court for this. All 'cause of the stigma of being a sex offender. . . . The stigma and how you are looked at, it's real bad by the court and everybody. It's like you're a deviant scumbag and we're gonna hammer' ya. I mean how much do they want from me? I have done my counseling, my probation, everything, fine. My therapist says I am not dangerous. They are say'n that I'm okay so why do I have to suffer and my family be stigmatized

for the rest of my life? When is it over? When is enough, enough? (Meloy
2006: 80)

Another perpetrator convicted of a sexual offense against a minor female
said,

> My biggest concern about this whole thing is that I did not want to be labeled
> as a sex offender. I mean, I recognize I am a sex offender. I committed a sex
> offense against a minor. But, I did not want to be *publicly* labeled as a sex of-
> fender. . . . Why don't they label other offenders? Drunk drivers kill people
> everyday but they are not labeled like sex offenders are. (Meloy 2006: 81–82;
> emphasis in original)

Social reaction theory shifts the focus away from the question of why an
individual commits a sexual offense to society's reaction to sexual offenders. This is not to suggest that sexual offenders should not be punished
but that overt notification policies may do more harm than good in rehabilitating a sexual offender. Labeling theorists attempt to address questions such as the following: Why are certain sexual offenses not pursued
as vigorously by the criminal justice system as other sexual offenses? Why
do some sexual offenders become publicly stigmatized and labeled while
others engaging in the very same behavior avoid the societal stigma?
How does the fact that we label individuals affect their lives and their
choices for the future? As such, labeling theory raises some extremely interesting and important questions surrounding sexual offenses.

Social Learning Theory

Social learning theorists believe that behavior is learned from those closest to us. As we grow from children into adults, we learn skills and behaviors through imitating others, trial and error, and positively reinforced
behaviors. Just like we learn to hit a baseball from a parent or from watching our favorite baseball player or learn to ride a bicycle from our older
sibling, we also learn attitudes that are favorable or unfavorable to inappropriate sexual interaction. Sexual beings are not born; they are created.
Most frequently, these types of behaviors are "learned" as a result of being sexually abused as a child or viewing sexual abuse in the home or
elsewhere. Edwin Sutherland (1950) used the term "differential association" to indicate that the key factor in whether an individual would engage in deviant behavior was the group of people with whom he or she
associates. According to this theory, a person engages in deviant behavior
when there are more favorable than unfavorable consequences to such behavior. It suggests that deviance, including sexual offending, is a learning
process that can affect anyone in any culture and that the skills and mo-

tives behind deviance are learned as a result of contact with values, attitudes, and definitions favorable to such behavior. As such, sexual offending behaviors would develop and continue if these "prodeviant" values and behaviors are not matched or exceeded by conventional values and behaviors.

Rewards and punishments also play an important role in social learning theory. Based on whether specific behaviors are rewarded or punished in the group of people we are close to influences the type of behavior we continue in the future. The key for social learning theorists are the groups of people with whom you are closest, and much social learning during formative years takes place within the family. This type of learning provides the foundation for the "intergenerational cycle of violence theory," which suggests that violence and proviolent attitudes are passed from generation to generation in a repetitive cycle.

While the larger society can contribute to learning attitudes that are prodeviant regarding sex, through television, films, video games, music lyrics and videos, sports, and so on, the closer an individual's lifestyle and history matches such a view, the more likely one is to engage in inappropriate sexual behavior. In practice this means that sexual offenders need not personally experience sexual abuse as a child or prodeviant sexual attitudes in the home in order to later offend sexually. Instead, it means that sexual offenders, either in their home life or in society more generally, have internalized such attitudes and have become desensitized to such acts, likely no longer perceiving such behavior as morally suspect. When you consider family as the most significant force in social learning theory, it becomes evident that a more dynamic perspective is required, as many individuals who sexually offend as adults have not been sexually victimized as children, and there are many children who were sexually victimized who did not mature into sexual perpetrators. Learning theory ties intimately the control of women to the way manhood has been perceived and constructed in society. So, while not all men who internalize society's prodeviant position on sex may commit a sexual offense, men in general risk standing up and objecting to such behavior for fear of being labeled negatively by society as less of a man. This becomes an additional quandary in overcoming sexual abuses in society. This learning occurs in cultures globally and is not unique to the United States.

Social Control Theory

Because deviance and crime often result in rewards, social control theorists want to know why some people obey society's rules and others do not. They believe that self-control and a commitment to conformity deter deviant behavior. In other words, people's behavior is controlled by their attachment and association to conventional society. Applied to sexual offending, social control theorists would suggest that society has constructed a continuum of sexual behaviors that are considered appropriate or inappropriate and that the vast majority of individuals choose not to violate social norms. As such, the question for social control theorists becomes, Why do some people follow the rules and others do not?

The dominant social control theorist is Travis Hirschi (1969), who believes that everyone is a potential deviant but that most people maintain control because they fear damaging their relationships with those close to them. As such, Hirschi suggests that deviance and involvement in activities that are against social norms increase as individual bonds to society decrease. That is, the stronger our attachment to conventional society, the more likely it is that we will follow the rules. Hirschi outlined four main elements that serve to bond an individual to society:

- *Attachment* to family, friends, and the community builds respect for others and society's norms.
- If individuals have worked hard to *commit* to society, they are less likely to risk their position by engaging in deviance.
- Strong *beliefs* in honesty, morality, fairness, and responsibility keep individuals tied to conventional values and less likely to violate norms.
- *Involvement* in conventional activities such as sports, community organizations, and social clubs leave little time for deviance.

Building on social control theory, Gottfredson and Hirschi (1990) argue that low self-control or the lack thereof, combined with the opportunity to engage in crime, is the primary influence on criminality. Those with low self-control are believed to be impulsive, risk taking, and shortsighted and will engage in crime if provided the opportunity. It is suggested that individuals lacking in self-control will offend when the opportunity presents itself and will engage in a variety of offenses rather than "specialize" in one type of offense, such as sex crimes. Interview data have confirmed this suggestion and the importance of opportunity for sexual offenders, with those incarcerated for sexual offenses admitting to a history of both sexual and nonsexual offenses (Cleary 2004; Zimring, Piquero, and Jennings 2007), though pedophiles as a group seem to be less "generalist" (Simon 1997).

The tighter these social bonds are to conventional society, the less likely an individual is to risk engaging in deviance or criminal behavior. As such, social control theorists would suggest that in order to reduce sexual offenses against women and children, society must widely condemn these behaviors and be committed to investigating and prosecuting these claims in a manner that provides swift, certain, and proportional punishment by the criminal justice system. This systematic response would create a situation in which an offender would be deterred from committing an offense because of the loss of bonds and humiliation to family, friends, and the community that would result. This may also involve the application of situational crime prevention techniques to nonstranger sexual offenses to prevent a category of offenses (Simon and Zgoba 2006).

Rational Choice Theory

The notion of deterrence in the criminal justice system assumes that individuals make rational decisions and that they can be deterred by the "threat" of punishment for prohibited acts. Specific deterrence seeks to deter an individual who has already committed a crime from committing another offense. An example is an individual who has committed a sexual offense and served his time in prison and is then given community supervision for life in order to deter him from committing a subsequent offense through state monitoring. General deterrence seeks to deter society at large from committing crimes by making "examples" of offenders, thereby instilling the fear of punishment. For example, potential offenders can be deterred from committing a sexual offense (according to the general deterrence model) because they have seen the punishment of individuals convicted of such offenses.

Why, however, are some individuals deterred (by either specific or general measures) and other individuals not deterred? A variety of factors go into an individual's rational evaluation of whether to commit a criminal offense. In sum, an individual conducts a cost–benefit analysis wherein he weighs the potential benefits of committing a sexual offense against what he perceives to be the costs or risks of this act. A potential offender will decide to offend if, in his mind, the benefits of the offense outweigh the potential risks. In order to deter an offender from committing a crime, then, punishment in the criminal justice system must be *perceived* as swift, certain, and severe enough to offset the benefits of a crime. In addition, with sex crimes, extralegal factors, such as a moral inhibition, individual self-control, empathy, and the physical and/or psychological pleasure that may be associated with offending, can play a role in one's decision whether to offend. In addition, the situational context is important. Situational factors include a victim deemed appropriate by the offender as well as the opportunity to offend against this victim. On the basis of factors such as prior experience with the criminal justice system or knowing other offenders involved in the criminal justice system, along with individual psychological processes and situational context, rational choice theorists suggest that the offender makes a rational choice or calculation to commit an offense.

Some studies have been conducted to suggest that sexual offenders are both rational and calculating in the commission of their offenses (Haas and Haas 1990; Meloy 2006; Pithers 1990; Quinsey and Earls 1990; Warren, Reboussin, and Hazelwood 1998). One man imprisoned for rape said, "At the time I didn't think of it as rape, just [sex] . . . but I knew I was doing wrong. But I also knew most women don't report rape and I didn't think she would either" (Scully 1994: 159). Another man convicted for rape expressed a similar sentiment: "I knew what I was doing. I just said, the hell with the consequences. I told myself what I was going to do was rape . . . but I didn't think I would go to prison" (Scully 1994: 159). Both of these men's comments point to a rational calculation prior to committing their offense: each knew the act was wrong, but neither felt that the potential costs or the likelihood of getting caught were significant. Research on rapists has found that the offense and the victim may be planned (Haas and Haas 1990), and indeed some rapists have even planned the script that they follow during the attack (Warren, Reboussin, and Hazelwood 1998). Research on decision making among men who sexually abuse their female children suggests that offenders evaluate opportunities and consider victim characteristics and risk factors (Wakeling et al. 2007). One offender elucidated his "rational" view on reoffending and the impact (or lack thereof) of community notification policies on the likelihood of his reoffense:

> If you're going to reoffend, it doesn't matter if you're on TV, in the newspaper, whatever, you're going to reoffend. And there's nothing to stop you. It's a choice you make. . . . The only person that can stop it is the sex offender himself. And that's one of the choices he makes. If he chooses not to offend anymore and he chooses to take part in treatment and deal with the situation like a real human being and to have empathy in his life, then he won't reoffend. (Zevitz and Farkas 2000b: 387)

Rational choice theory is very subjective in that what one offender may consider a "benefit" of offending another may consider a "risk." As such, this theory is very individual in scope and may not prove useful in creating broad policy solutions to sexual offending.

Life Course Theory

Life course theory emphasizes how involvement in crime relates to life course events, with a focus on continuity and change. Theorists are interested in the factors that influence initiation into crime, factors that influence continued involvement or escalation of involvement, and factors that influence desistance. Life course criminologists examine trajectories or long-term patterns of behavior and study the influence of transitions or turning points in one's life pathway that may change a pattern of behavior. It is believed that there are events in the life course that can change a person's trajectory, leading one to crime or moving one away from crime (Sampson and Laub 1993). This perspective was popularized and applied to "traditional" types of crime in *Crime in the Making: Pathways and Turning Points through Life* (Sampson and Laub 1993), which proposed an age-graded theory of social control. Life course theory builds on social control theory and suggests that the nature and types of social controls and bonds change over a person's life course. This theory involves three main premises:

- Environmental factors are mediated by family and school during childhood and adolescence, and this can be used to explain crime during this period.
- There is frequently continuity in involvement in crime and/or antisocial behavior from childhood through adulthood across a range of life domains.
- During adulthood, bonds to family and employment can alter earlier propensities toward criminal activity (Sampson and Laub 1993).

Life course theory links social environment and informal social control as a mediating process in an attempt to explain persistence and desistance in criminal involvement and deviance.

Theorists of this perspective believe that antisocial or delinquent childhood behavior is linked to adult deviance and criminality in a variety of settings and that only by changing an individual's social bonds with society can we alter involvement in a criminal lifestyle. Using this perspective to examine sexual offenses would involve an examination of how "the age of the offender may influence the type, severity, and frequency of violence . . . [and] victimization might have very different repercussions depending on the victim's stage in the life course" (Payne and Gainey 2005, 121). Most important, a life course approach encourages the conceptual linkage of various forms of violence and therefore could be extremely useful for examining sexual violence should researchers choose to apply it to this area of study.

THE USEFULNESS OF THEORY

The observation that sexual offenses have been a part of human history is often overstated, but it holds true. People throughout history have been perpetrating these behaviors for a variety of reasons, not all of which are fully understood. Many scholars and laypeople alike are interested in learning why people deviate from social convention, and theory seeks a systematic way to explain and predict variation in sexually abusive behaviors. Why do some people commit sexual offenses and most do not? What are the motivations for such crimes? Is there a "type" of offender whom society should avoid? Are the answers found in the individual's biological or psychological makeup or in society at large? Is there hope for rehabilitating offenders, and how can we predict who will reoffend? While each theory approaches sexual offending behaviors from a different perspective, no particular theory can claim to completely understand them. That is, no one theory can explain all sexual offending behaviors, and no theoretical explanation can provide an all-encompassing picture of why different types of people engage in different types of sexually abusive behavior. Theoretical approaches are used to explain varied dimensions of the issue; each provides a lens through which the issues can be better understood. It provides a starting point to answer the question of "why." Theory is perhaps most useful in that these explanations inform policy and point the way toward answers in minimizing sexual violence, healing survivors and communities, and reintegrating offenders into society.

4

Historical Sexual
Offending Laws

The social responses to sexual violence have varied throughout history, oscillating between a focus on mental health and punishment, pity, and revenge. The focus, however, has always been transitional. The United States has experimented with the clinical model, which considers sex offenses a mental health issue requiring medical intervention; the justice model, which regards sex offenders as deviants who should be punished; and the community safety model, which classifies sex offenders as evil predators who should be indefinitely confined. More recently, the hybrid model has gained popularity. This model, a combination of previous models, acknowledges that sex offenses are rooted in issues of mental health that require treatment but also views incarceration as a legitimate means of punishment and deterrence (Zilney and Zilney 2008). This chapter elaborates on these models and then traces the history of sexual offending laws beginning in the 1930s.

SOCIETAL RESPONSES TO SEXUAL OFFENDING

The clinical model focused on diagnoses, prognoses, and treatment in which indeterminate confinement was considered mandatory if recidivism risk was moderate to high and *possibly* accompanied by a mental disorder. However, assessing risk is not an exact science and relies on historical factors as opposed to current variables, thereby producing many moderate- and high-risk rankings. In addition, the clinical model placed the concept of dangerousness solely on the individual, regarding the person rather than the behavior as pathological. This model resulted in offenders serving longer sentences than if they were processed only through the criminal justice system. Offenders were incarcerated in a psychiatric facility and on treatment completion were brought for trial on criminal charges and often then received lengthy prison sentences (Hacker and Frym 1955). The clinical model was based on the behaviors outlined in the *Diagnostic and Statistical Manual of Mental Disorders* (*DSM*) and was entirely sex negative in orientation. The foundation of this model is that sexuality is so powerful and overwhelming that it can destroy a person's life.

The justice model emphasized providing a "just" and fair punishment. Proponents of this model advocated for fixed sentencing rules to reflect the seriousness with which society views sexually based crimes. Further, this model based sentencing on the current actions of an individual as opposed to an assessment of potential future risk (Petrunik 1994). This model is much more punitive than the clinical model and focuses on the need to provide retribution to both society and the victim for sexual harms.

Conversely, the community safety model gained increasing popularity in the 1980s and 1990s, as the public believed that victims' rights were taking a backseat to the due process rights of criminals. This model was designed to provide maximum safeguards for the public and consequently severely restricted the rights of those suspected or convicted of sexually based crimes (Petrunik 1994). The foundation of this model is that the greater social good takes precedence over the rights of individuals. It aligns closely with the missions of the women's and victims' rights movements, which believe that treatment and rehabilitation must not be at the expense of community safety (Petrunik 1994). This model is tempered by the belief that persons convicted of sex crimes will eventually reenter society, so there is a need to slow the rate of reintegration through restrictions on movement, employment, and social networks. One difficulty with this model is the tendency to presume guilt prior to a finding of guilt at trial. The fact that a person is accused of a sex crime must mean that there was enough evidence to support the charge, and therefore guilt is presumed. This model assumes a clear demarcation between right and wrong and appropriate versus inappropriate sexual behavior. However, there are often shades of gray. For example, if a woman has sex with her partner even though she is uninterested and agreed to sexual relations simply to ward off a fight, is this consensual? Is this rape?

Currently, a hybrid model is most often used by the criminal justice system in dealing with sexual offenders. This model attempts to combine some of the common themes present in the other models by focusing on the mental disorders of offenders as well as the need for punishment. The assumption is that sex offenders are mentally unstable, as evidenced by the fact that most illegal behavior is found within the *DSM* but that the social good must be served through instituting penalties for sexually offensive behavior. If treatment is available and if it is cost effective, it may be offered to incarcerated sex offenders, but their ability to attain parole is not necessarily enhanced by their participation in treatment.

CASE STUDY: THE CHANGING AGE OF PUBERTY

In order to illustrate how changing social conditions and mores impact society's notions of appropriate and inappropriate sexual behavior, the changing age of puberty is examined. Although puberty is considered primarily a biological event, it occurs within a social context, and its reality is experienced differently depending on one's culture, religion, ethnicity, class, and family of origin. Therefore, age is not necessarily a reliable indicator of puberty, as physical and emotional development can occur over extended periods when pubertal processes are under way. The difference in the experience of puberty is the result of several sources of maturational heterogeneity in both physical and psychosocial development that are not necessarily reflected by age (Dorn et al. 2006). Development in puberty is influenced by physiology, behavior, drug metabolism, motivation, emotion, and some aspects of cognitive development.

It was G. Stanley Hall in 1904 who first defined adolescence and developed key themes that encompassed the phases of puberty. Hall contended that adolescence must be analyzed from an interdisciplinary perspective, as it included numerous elements, such as formative role context and the malleability of adolescents as individuals and adolescence as a phase in life (Shanahan, Erickson, and Bauer 2005). Hall's work included the physiological patterns of growth (e.g., height, weight, and proportion of parts), criminality and sexuality, treatment of adolescence as a phase in literary sources, perceptions and the senses, cognition, religion, and pedagogy (Shanahan, Erickson, and Bauer 2005). The focus was on the prevalence/frequency of phenomena within the phase of life labeled adolescence in order to extrapolate common themes or experiences. Thus, in the early 1900s, adolescence was considered the stage between childhood and adulthood where individuals assumed increasingly adult roles and responsibilities, including those related to physicality, mental and emotional development, cognitive changes, and changes in social roles. Adolescence was regarded as both social and physiological, while puberty remained purely physical.

During Victorian times, pubescence was believed to occur between thirteen and fifteen years of age, at which point changes in the body were especially evident (Haroian 1994). During this historical period, sexual exploitation of children was common, yet there began a slow shift in societal mores regarding the treatment of children. Although childhood was deemed a phase free of sexualization, adults were constantly surveying youth and punishing them for their sexual curiosity and activity (Haroian 1994). Puberty was a time in which the sexual experiences of females caused devaluation by family and peers, yet girls were also taught that they could withhold or use their sexuality as a commodity. Conversely, boys were taught that sex is their natural right, as is the pursuit of sexual gratification. It was also during this period that Freud postulated his theory of adolescence as a particular stage in psychosexual development. Slowly, academics moved away from the belief that puberty was a biologically determined event, but the concept of puberty as a stage in the life cycle remained popular (Connell 2005).

In 1948, Kinsey defined adolescence as a stage representing steady progress of development where maximum growth was achieved. Kinsey contended that adolescence usually occurred between the middle teenage years and early twenties and provided an introduction into adulthood through sexual experience (Kinsey et al. 1948). Between the 1950s and 1970s, age consciousness, categorizing, and the ubiquity of age-based norms became predominant in the United States (Raby 2002). These concepts were intimately linked to capitalist initiatives and the increasing consumer culture of the postwar years. American culture was focused on making life easier through the use of technology and celebrating the spoils of war and prosperity. Despite the rapid social change occurring, adolescence continued to be regarded as a predictable stage of life, homogeneous to all groups. It was during this period that adolescence came to be associated with dangerous and reckless behavior and images of ungovernable teens in need of control (Raby 2002).

Media attention began to focus on the risk-taking behaviors of teens, such as drug and alcohol use, depression, and sexual promiscuity. Society began to form a very clear understanding of what adolescence and puberty entailed and emphasized a longer transition period to adulthood. Puberty and adolescence continued to be merged concepts and were defined as occurring roughly between ten and nineteen years of age. The reasons for this change in age were predominantly economic. Society could no longer support unskilled labor in the numbers it had previously, so emphasis was placed on increased schooling or training for teenagers. Increasingly, structural factors (e.g., unemployment), internal factors (e.g., anomie), peer-related factors (e.g., sex, drugs, and alcohol), and adults (e.g., drug dealers, pimps, and child molesters) came to shape the experience of adolescence from the 1950s through the 1970s (Raby 2002). Adolescence was now denoted by the cessation of physical and physiological changes.

Adolescence and puberty were socially as opposed to academically defined through American culture. The growth of the educational system played a key role in the emergence of adolescence as a social category and in the emergence of a youth culture (Connell 2005). It is during the school years that sexual decision making and the exploration of emerging sexualities take on prime importance (Halpern 2006; Michels et al. 2005). This held special significance in the 1970s at the height of the sexual revolution. Many youth became initiated into partnered sexual activity and partook in activities that would form the pattern of their subsequent behavior. Youth in high school viewed traditional heterosexual sex as their movement into adulthood, a definable moment in their lives that signified their maturity and ability to become adults. Moreover, the teen years became an important time in establishing personal boundaries and applying those boundaries to a variety of situations. Adolescence became a time of learning to communicate and negotiate sex while simultaneously acquiring basic sexual techniques that could be transferred to adulthood (Haroain 1994; Sarrel and Sarrel 1979).

Despite the fact that menstrual and fertility growth becomes stable at approximately fourteen years of age, the age range for adolescence has now been extended into the twenties. Puberty is currently linked to the capacity to perform sexually but has minimal if any connection to actual sexual behavior. In other words, sex is allowed in adolescence/puberty but not for reproduction, as youth are not deemed to be socially or morally responsible enough for such a commitment (Graber and Sontag 2006). The transition continues from the completion of high school to the decision-making challenges of whether to pursue higher education, enter the labor market, move out of the family home, and possibly marry and parent. Demographic, sociocultural, and labor market shifts have made the years between eighteen and twenty-five more transitional than in previous generations. The paths that previously existed for youth and that helped define puberty, such as termination of high school or marriage, now no longer exist for most social groups.

The sexual behavior of youth has also changed throughout the years. The Internet is now providing a source of information and entertainment that relieves sexual anxiety previously dealt with through peer-to-peer interaction. A large majority of teens (98.9 percent of males and 73.5 percent of females) have viewed Internet pornography by fifteen years of age (Wallmyr and Welin 2006). Moreover, as adolescents age, their likelihood of viewing pornographic materials increases. This is in stark contrast to research that highlights the increasing sexual inexperience of adolescents. Currently, only 61 percent of high school graduates have ever reported having coitus (Sieving et al. 2006). Puberty is a time of greater focus on the perceived behaviors and values of peers; consequently, initiation into sexual activity is directly related to the cohort in which the youth associates (Sieving et al. 2006).

Several themes emerge when reviewing the history of puberty. Beliefs about adolescence tend to mirror the economic cycle. In times of economic downturn, such as in the early 1900s, adolescence was defined as being mostly biologically determined and progressing through predefined stages. This belief enabled society to terminate puberty early to ensure that there was an adequate workforce to staff factories and provide manual labor. This also coincided with a relative lack of concern about the sexual behaviors and possible abuse of teens. Conversely, in the economic prosperity of the postwar years, adolescence and puberty were extended to include the later teen years. The reason for this extension was based on an enhanced educational system and society's increasing reliance on skilled labor. This was the time in history when concern over the sexual abuse of teens and children started to take center stage in society and legislation emerged defining prohibited behaviors. In recent years, adolescence and puberty have been pushed into the twenties, and youth are now expected to focus on educational attainment and sociosexual development prior to leaving their family of origin. This helps to explain the increasing social movement to extend the legal age of consent in many states. Moreover, the age of puberty is correlated with sociocultural factors, such as race, class, ethnicity, religion, and family of origin. Puberty is not a homogeneous stage in life despite the fact that each person experiences similar physical and physiological changes. Puberty is experienced differently and at different times, depending on one's environment. Despite the fact that society and the academic community cannot agree on the distinction between puberty and adolescence, it remains clear that puberty is more than a collection of biological processes. Puberty and adolescence are in large measure socially defined concepts that are vulnerable to change and redefinition. It remains to be seen if the age ranges encompassing puberty will continue to expand and incorporate more and more criminal sanctions to sexual behavior with and between adolescents.

A WAR ON SEXUAL OFFENDERS BEGINS IN THE 1930s

The historical roots of U.S. sex offender laws are found in the 1900s in the United Kingdom with the introduction of dangerous offender legislation that initially applied predominantly to property offenses and allowed for indeterminate imprisonment for repeat offenders. At this time the notion of a "sexual psychopath" was equated with immorality, and thus the focus was primarily placed on gay men and other "indecent" offenses. By the 1930s, the definition narrowed, and the focus shifted to "perverts" whose sexual urges caused increasingly violent behavior. It was at this point that the legal and medical fields began to merge; the result was the medicalization of sexual crimes. It was believed that indefinite confinement in a psychiatric facility was the only way to deal with sexual offenders, as their mental or personality disorders predisposed them to sexual crimes and violence. Although legal regulation of sexual behavior can be traced to the earliest of civilizations, it is important to recognize that as the social, moral, and political landscape of society changes, so too does the definition of a sexual offense, a sexual offender, and the socially appropriate response to such offenders.

In early America, morality statutes prohibited offenses such as homosexuality, sodomy, fornication, adultery, and bestiality. Sodomy was a catchall term in the law, with definitions varying widely by state and describing consensual behaviors usually between homosexuals. For example, consensual sodomy in New York State carried a maximum term of imprisonment of one year in the 1940s but a potential sentence of life imprisonment in Georgia. This was the environment in which sexual psychopath legislation was created in the 1930s.

Official statistics indicate a rise in documented sex crimes starting in the 1930s; however, caution must be taken in interpreting these figures, as most arrests during this time frame were for consensual homosexual encounters between adults. As such, much of the record reflects the homophobia present during this period and therefore the "morality" of the time as opposed to the level of serious sex "crime" that was occurring. There were, however, a series of violent sexual offenses that occurred in a relatively short period of time across the United States, beginning with the case of Albert Fish, that gave rise to a new set of laws in response to public outrage.

In the early to mid-1930s, the media seemed focused on sexual violence, with many news articles geared toward an examination of the murder and sexual assault of children (Lucken and Latina 2002). The true panic surrounding sexual offenders came when the story broke of Albert Fish in New York State. Fish was alleged to have sexually assaulted, killed, and cannibalized a twelve-year-old boy, although it was believed that he violated hundreds of other children and killed as many as fifteen children prior to his apprehension in 1934. His case was followed by the public with much fascination until he was executed in 1936. This incident overlapped with a serial rapist named Gerald Thompson, who in 1935 was on trial in Illinois for rape and murder. It was alleged that he had a diary listing the names of eighty-three women he sought to seduce, rape, and kill. He was found guilty at trial and sentenced to die in the electric chair. A couple of years later, in 1941, a thirty-six-year-old black taxi driver named Jarvis Theodore Roosevelt Catoe admitted to raping and choking ten women of various ages and racial groups. This was widely reported in the media, and he was electrocuted for his crime in 1943 in Washington, D.C.

In addition to these widely publicized sexual offenses and murders, there were other high-profile cases during this time period, and while all of them were not sexually related, they struck further fear in the public. One of these was the kidnapping and murder of the Lindbergh baby, which resulted in the execution of Bruno Haumptmann in 1936. In addition, a serial killer in Cleveland dubbed the Torso Killer was active between 1935 and 1938, and while there were suspects in this case, no one was ever charged. There was another serial killer of approximately twenty women in Texas who was dubbed the Alligator Man, active in the 1930s, who committed suicide before he could be arrested and brought to trial. Finally, between 1938 and 1942, six people were murdered on the border of Pennsylvania and New Jersey in what were called the Lover's Lane murders. In this case a man named Cleveland Hill served less than twenty years before he was paroled.

Primarily because of intense media representation of these select cases, the public came to believe there was an epidemic of sexual offending and came to associate sexual offenses with serious violence and murder. Mothers came to fear that there were predators lurking the streets like Albert Fish, and the "sex offender" became synonymous in the eyes of many with the "child sex killer," fueling a conservative approach to crime control. Although at the time this was occurring the concept of a "moral panic" had not yet been developed, in hindsight we can understand these events sociologically using this concept. Noted sociologist Stanley Cohen (1972: 9) formulated the notion of a moral panic to refer to when

> a condition, episode, person or group of persons emerges to become defined as a threat to societal values and interests; its nature is presented in a stylized and stereotypical fashion by the mass media; the moral barricades are manned by editors, bishops, politicians, and other right-thinking people; socially accredited experts pronounce their diagnosis and solutions; ways of coping are evolved or . . . resorted to; the condition then disappears, submerges or deteriorates and becomes [less] visible. Sometimes the subject of the panic is quite novel and at other times it is something which has been in existence long enough but suddenly appears in the limelight. Sometimes the panic passes over and is forgotten, except in folklore and collective memory; at other times it has more serious and long-lasting repercussions and might produce such changes as those in legal and social policy.

Using the language of "moral panic" to discuss societal responses to sexual offenses is not meant to minimize the consequences to those victimized by such offenses. It is instead meant to denote the exaggerated and misdirected nature of societal fear and as a response the misdirected policies that have been created that do not serve to effectively prevent sexual violence.

The case of Albert Fish, although not common, in a time of moral panic is perceived as the "typical sexual offense," and individuals committing minor sexual transgressions are believed to be on a path of escalation to serious sexual perversion and violence. In addition, police crack down on offenses that in the past would not have resulted in arrest or prosecution (petty offenses such as homosexuality, prostitution, or exhibitionism). This leads to the perception that the rate of sex crimes is increasing as the police focus their attention on all types of sexual offenses, thus driving up arrest rates. In addition, further fueling the moral panic cycle, the local media are more likely to report these events and to place local crimes (no matter how minor) into the context of sexual offenses occurring nationwide, leading once again to the perception that the rate of such crimes is increasing not only on a local but also on a national level. As such, the result is that the public believes sex crimes are increasing as a result of increased media coverage and increased police response rather than as a result of an *actual* increase in sex crime rates.

When the public believes something as serious as sex crimes is increasing, there is a natural reaction of concern for personal safety and the safety of one's children. In response, the public demands that lawmakers respond with appropriate legislation. In the 1930s, J. Edgar Hoover, who headed the Federal Bureau of Investigation, responded with a declaration of a "war on sex crimes" that mirrored the fear of the citizens (Lucken and Latina 2002). In this state of fear, lawmakers and the public alike lost sight of the reality that sexual homicides are very rare incidents and it is against this backdrop that sexual psychopath laws were created. By the late 1930s, "public indignation ha[d] reached almost a mass hysteria which ha[d] affected not only the public but also official authorities. . . . A sheriff in New York recommended shooting every child attacker on the spot" (Wertham 1938: 847).

As the Lover's Lane murders ended in 1942, the panic of the 1930s drew to a close, although peaks in media coverage and hysteria over sexual offenders are noted again from 1947 through 1950 and 1953 through 1954 (Jenkins 1998). A 1946 article suggested that "the shadow of the sex criminal lies across the doorstep of every home" (Harris 1946: 4). A 1947 *Time* magazine article reported that in Massachusetts there were at least 1,040 known sex offenders who had been released from prison because their sentences had been served ("Mother Knew Best" 1947). And the media started reporting cases in earnest again in the late 1940s, beginning in 1947 with a twenty-two-year-old woman nicknamed "Black Dahlia" who was found brutally murdered and mutilated in California. Her case sparked massive media attention, and the crime went unsolved. (Indeed, this case continues to draw media attention, and in 1987 a book was written based on this case and a film created in 2006 starring Scarlett Johansson and Hilary Swank.) Near the end of 1949, there were three young girls murdered in unrelated incidents within a very short time span, further fueling the public's fear.

In an attempt to debunk the stereotypes surrounding sexual offenders perpetuated by the media, an article was published in 1950 by *Time* magazine, although the title of the article, "The Unknown Sex Fiend," belies its purpose. The short article in its entirety read as follows:

> Sex crimes, flamboyantly headlined in the press, are currently troubling both public and police. After seven months of poring over statistics and case histories, New Jersey's Commission on the Habitual Sex Offender last week issued a report. One of its main conclusions: the average citizen knows little about the scope and nature of sex crimes, but he is oversupplied with misinformation on the subject. Some of the popular convictions which the commissioners would like to correct: (1) That the sex offender progresses to more serious sex crimes. Statistics clearly show that "progression from minor to major sex crimes is exceptional." (2) That dangerous sex criminals are usually repeaters. Actually, of all serious crime categories, only homicide shows a lower record of repeaters. (3) That sex offenders are oversexed. Most of those treated have turned out to be physically undersexed. (4) That there are "tens of thousands" of homicidal sex fiends abroad in the land. Only an estimated 5% of convicted sex offenders have committed crimes of violence. The commission's cool, if not too reassuring, report: "Danger of murder by relative or other intimate associate is very much greater than the danger of murder by an unknown sex fiend." ("The Unknown Sex Fiend" 1950)

While it was noteworthy that this article appeared at all in the mainstream media, the New Jersey Commission on the Habitual Sex Offender issued an enormous report on sexual offending, and *Time* magazine featured an extremely short segment of the report, indicating near the end that it is "not too reassuring."

Although the media have an important impact on informing public perception, especially with regard to issues of crime—and indeed the media make up one factor that drives legislative and social change—this is not a one-way, causal relationship. That is, there were states wherein sex crimes occurred and were widely publicized by the media, where this publicity was translated to increased public fear; however, sexual psychopath legislation was not passed (Galliher and Tyree 1985). The government normally has some response to the fear of the public; however, in many cases the result was the establishment of a commission (in at least fifteen states) to study the "growing" problem of sexual violence.

Despite the reaction of the public to the media portrayals of high-profile rape/murder cases and the establishment of commissions to research the sexual violence, the criminal justice system generally did not take such offenses very seriously during this historical period. Charges of rape, often resulted in plea bargains or convictions for assault, if charges were even filed. Statutory rape charges were overwhelmingly dismissed or reduced to a misdemeanor offense. The likelihood of dismissal or acquittal for the accused in the case of a less serious sexually related offense, such as indecent exposure or impairing the morals of a minor, was even greater. This was a different historical time, a time in which women and children held a much different role in society, a time in which men were legally permitted to rape their wives, a time in which physical corroboration of a sexual assault was necessary in a court of law, and a time in which child sexual abuse was not considered a social problem. The major outcomes of this time period were research from the commissions and intellectual communities and the legislative establishment of sexual psychopath laws.

Sexual Psychopath Legislation

The prevailing ideology of the 1930s was that sexual offenders were mentally sick individuals who should be afforded treatment and preventive detention in a mental health facility as opposed to confinement in a traditional prison setting. This was an era that advocated rehabilitation, although some critics argued that the adoption of a rehabilitation model also increased the power afforded to the state and decreased the due process protections of the individual. Sexual psychopath laws provided for the *involuntary* and *indefinite* commitment of an individual who was deemed a "sexual psychopath" in a psychiatric facility. The language of this legislation varied by state, was very vague, and may have more accurately reflected the moral views of the time than the predatory or violent tendencies of the offender, as suggested by Jenkins (1998: 13): "the ever-flexible concept of the molester, the abuser, or the predator provides an invaluable gauge for the state of current social ideologies."

These laws were based on the belief that sex offenders are driven by uncontrollable impulses and could be stopped only by eliminating the impulse and placing the offender in jail until "cured." While there were constitutional challenges to these laws that addressed issues of double jeopardy and the lack of protections afforded in a criminal trial, those are elaborated on in greater depth in chapter 7, which discusses the modern-day version of sexual psychopath laws, termed "sexually violent predator laws." In 1937, Michigan passed the first sexual psychopath law, which was later declared unconstitutional for violating the principle of double jeopardy and lacking the protections afforded by a jury trial. It was, however, revised and approved in 1939. In 1938, Illinois enacted a law that passed measures of constitutionality when tested in 1940 because it leaned more on the procedural elements of an insanity hearing as opposed to a criminal trial and because it permitted committal without a criminal conviction. Several states followed shortly afterward (1939 in California and Minnesota; 1943 in Vermont; 1945 in Ohio; 1947 in Massachusetts, Washington, and Wisconsin; 1948 in the District of Columbia; and 1949 in Indiana, New Hampshire, and New Jersey). By the end of the 1950s, the District of Columbia and twenty-six other states had adopted sexual psychopath laws. One interesting provision of these laws was that in order to be declared a sexual psychopath in many states, one need not have been found guilty of a sexual offense—they just had to be deemed at risk of sexual compulsivity.

Although there was variation by state, most of the sexual psychopath laws shared similar language that involved several key elements. The elements usually involved in the statutes (but not all had to be present in a single offender) included the following:

- The commission of a crime of a sexual nature
- A focus on the compulsive nature of the individual's pathology
- The assumption that the offense or a similar offense will be repeated
- An assumption of escalation of offenses
- Potential risk to community safety
- The belief that treatment is possible (Group for the Advancement of Psychiatry 1977)

By way of example, following is the 1955 California Sexually Psychopath Act:

[S]exual psychopath means any person who is affected, in a form predisposing to the commission of sexual offenses, and in a degree constituting him a menace to the health or safety of others, with any of the following conditions:
(a) Mental disease or disorder.
(b) Psychopathic personality.
(c) Marked departures from normal mentality.
When a person is convicted of any criminal offense, whether or not a sex offense, the trial judge, on his own motion, or on motion of the prosecuting attorney, or on application by affidavit by or on behalf of the defendant, if it appears to the satisfaction of the court that there is probable cause for believing such person is a sexual psychopath . . . , may adjourn the proceeding or suspend the sentence, as the case may be, and may certify the person for hearing and examination by the superior court of the county to determine whether the person is a sexual psychopath. . . . When a person is convicted of a sex offense involving a child under 14 years of age and it is a misdemeanor, and the person has been previously convicted of a sex offense in this

or any other state, the court shall adjourn the proceeding or suspend the sentence, as the case may be, and shall certify the person for hearing and examination by the superior court of the county to determine whether the person is a sexual psychopath. . . . When a person is convicted of a sex offense involving a child under 14 years of age and it is a felony, the court shall adjourn the proceeding or suspend the sentence, as the case may be, and shall certify the person for hearing and examination by the superior court of the county to determine whether the person is a sexual psychopath. (California Welfare and Institutions Code § 5501, 1955)

A second case in point, although Illinois uses the language of a "sexually dangerous person" instead of "sexual psychopath," the statute requires "demonstrated propensities toward acts of sexual assault or acts of sexual molestation of children" (Ill. Rev. Stat. ch. 38 §§ 105-1.01-12, 1965). In Illinois this mental condition could have resulted in indefinite confinement in a psychiatric hospital until the point at which the individual's recovery from this condition could be demonstrated.

These statutes were presumably exacted to protect the community from sexually violent offenders yet were used to examine individuals for acts that would be considered minor or even consensual. Not all those examined by mental health professionals as "sexual psychopaths" or "sexually dangerous persons" were obviously committed, but even those who were committed were usually not involved in violent acts. More than 50 percent of those committed in Illinois were for morally offensive but passive acts, such as exhibitionism (Burick 1968). This was also the case in New Jersey, where "psychiatric hospitalization . . . was reserved for petty sex offenders who seemed likely to escalate their crimes. . . . Serious sex offenders were almost invariably returned to the criminal justice system for punishment" (Cole 2000: 299). As illustrated by Ploscowe (1960: 223):

> These [sexual psychopath] laws were passed to provide a means for dealing with dangerous, repetitive, mentally abnormal sex offenders. Unfortunately, the vagueness of the definition contained in these statutes has obscured this basic underlying purpose. There are large numbers of sex offenders who engage in compulsive repetitive sexual acts, which may be crimes, who may be mentally abnormal but who are not dangerous. The transvestite, the exhibitionist, the frotteur, the homosexual who masturbates another in the privacy of his bedroom or in a public toilet, the "peeping tom"—are typical of large numbers of sex offenders who are threatened with long-term incarceration by present [laws].

Although sexual psychopath laws were on the books, they were not used nearly to the extent as sexually violent predator laws are today with most states during this period committing fewer than twenty individuals per year on average (Jenkins 1998).

Just having passed the law, however, was portrayed to the fearing public as a very positive outcome, as exemplified in the *Indianapolis Star* in 1948:

> Indiana today is one step nearer an enlightened approach to the growing menace of sex crimes. A proposed new law to institutionalize sexual psychopaths until pronounced permanently recovered has been drafted by a special state citizens' committee which helped the attorney general's office to study the problem. . . . Such a law should become a realistic, practical answer to the sex crime problem. This type of legislation has succeeded elsewhere and is long overdue in Indiana. (quoted in Sutherland 1950: 146)

Even academics got on the bandwagon:

> The manner in which the people of the United State have tried to deal with sex offenders is perhaps the outstanding enigma in the whole history of attempts in this country to protect innocent individuals and to guard the social interest. Fixed penalties—running up to twenty years imprisonment—are established for crimes of rape, with no provision for adjudication on the basis of circumstances and without reference to the possible psychopathy of the offender. Moreover, we continue to rely upon fines, jail sentences and reformatory commitment as a means of controlling inveterate sex offenders whose conduct not only defies such treatment, but generally grows worse with it. As we well know, some of the most heinous sex offenses on record have been committed by "fiends" whose backgrounds were marked by repeated fines and jail sentences. (Reinhardt and Fisher 1949: 734)

Sexual psychopath legislation was passed on the basis of some faulty assumptions. Passage of this legislation assumed that the rate of sex crime was increasing so rapidly that it required proactive measures and was based on the belief that the criminal justice system was not effectively dealing with sex crime recidivism. One of the reasons used for the introduction of sex offender legislation was the need for continuous treatment. It was believed that sex offenders required lengthy prison terms in order to participate in uninterrupted counseling, and for those who were not amenable to treatment (such as the functionally illiterate), prison was the only means to protect society. It was also based on the assumption that offenders "persist in their sexual crimes throughout life; that they always give warning that they are dangerous by first committing minor offenses; that any psychiatrist can diagnose them with a high degree of precision at an early age, before they have committed serious sex crimes; and that sexual psychopaths who are diagnosed and identified should be confined as irresponsible persons until they are pronounced by psychiatrists to be completely and permanently cured of their malady" (Sutherland 1950: 142).

The legislation is set on the foundation of the medical model—on the model of rehabilitation and the ideal that sexual offenders can be identified and treated by the psychiatric profession. As illustrated by the Criminal Justice Mental Health Standards, however, this legislation rests

> on six assumptions: (1) there is a specific mental disability called sexual psychopathy . . . ; (2) persons suffering from such a disability are more likely to commit serious crimes, especially dangerous sex offenses, than normal criminals; (3) such persons are easily identifiable by mental health professionals; (4) the dangerousness of these offenders can be predicted by mental health professionals; (5) treatment is available for the condition; and (6) large number of persons afflicted with the designated disabilities can be cured. (La Fond 2000: 157)

What if these assumptions were incorrect? What if sexual offending was not a mental disorder that could be identified by mental health professionals? What if psychiatrists could not predict which sexual offenders would be likely to commit violent sexual offenses and which ones would simply commit offenses we found morally objectionable? What if the treatment methods designed did not work? And how would a mental health professional be able to tell when a sexual offender was "cured" of the disorder and unlikely to reoffend? There were so many questions circling around the sexual psychopath legislation, but this medicalization model was the one that had taken hold during this period, with the asylum population peaking during the mid-1950s. Atascadero State Hospital in California in the 1950s experienced success with the treatment of those confined under sexual psychopath legislation. Over a three-year period in the mid-1950s, approximately two-thirds of offenders were discharged because hospital officials believed they were no longer a threat to the public and most of those released did not recidivate (Jenkins 1998).

The nationwide lean toward treatment did not last long, however, as the public soon began to realize that many of the individuals who were supposed to be getting treatment were not. Instead, individuals were being indefinitely confined under sexual psychopath legislation in psychiatric facilities without the benefit of treatment. This provided the grounds to challenge sexual psychopath laws and the U.S. Court of Appeals ruled that an individual deemed a sexual psychopath could not be held in confinement without treatment. In response, some states made legitimate efforts at treatment and rehabilitation. In 1963, Oregon passed the last sexual psychopath statute and actually constructed the first treatment facility specifically for sexually dangerous offenders in the United States. By this time, twenty-six states had similar legislation despite claims of poor treatment, treatment bordering on torture (such as electroconvulsive therapy), or no treatment. It was believed that less than 25 percent of offenders were ever "cured" by such treatment (La Fond 2000).

Concerns Regarding Sexual Psychopath Laws

As the 1960s ended and the 1970s began, concerns began to arise with sexual psychopath legislation, many of which are the same as with modern-day sexually violent predator legislation. A major concern was the subjective nature of determining who was a sexual psychopath for the purposes of admittance to a psychiatric facility as well as for the purposes of release. For many critics, "the concept of the 'sexual psychopath' is so vague that it cannot be used for judicial and administrative purposes without the danger that the law may injure the society more than do the sex crimes which it is designed to correct" (Sutherland 1950: 142). So there are serious civil liberty concerns surrounding individuals involuntarily committed for an indefinite period of time, especially when they are committed for an offense that is merely "morally offensive" and not sexually violent. There were also more specific justice-related concerns:

> Legal and political conservatives saw the laws as a violation of traditional principles of justice and as an ominous intrusion of psychiatric or psychological justifications into accepted standards of guilt and responsibility. The statutes could also provide a way for dangerous criminals to evade proper penal sanctions. Law-and-order concerns might explain why legislation was less popular in the South and West: only five of the eleven states of the former Confederacy had passed statutes by the 1960s. This is an important commentary on the political constituencies favoring the reform of sex crime laws, which were often initiated by the more socially progressive jurisdictions of the Midwest and by the more industrial and urban states. Although later attacked as repressive, the laws were seen at the time as a desirable advance in employing humane principles of therapy and medicine in the treatment of offenders. (Jenkins 1998: 90)

Although the laws may have started out with the rehabilitative model in mind, eventually psychiatrists became uncomfortable with their close alliance with law enforcement and the quick turnaround time line in which they were expected to provide a diagnosis of sexual psychopathy. The mental health profession eventually grew leery of the "sexual psychopath" terminology and the ambiguity surrounding the concept and came to question the assumption that the "minor" sexual offenders who were being confined to facilities would escalate to violent offenses. Legal decisions passed in the early 1970s made involuntary commitment of sexual offenders extremely difficult unless they posed imminent risk of harm to themselves or others, and eventually the sexual psychopath laws were repealed and those individuals confined under this legislation were moved to prisons.

REFORM OF THE 1960s AND 1970s

The 1960s and 1970s was a period of vast societal change, and social movements for civil rights, women's rights, victims' rights, and offenders' rights started to change the legal landscape. One organization on the forefront of these changes was the American Humane Association, which advocated for the protection of all vulnerable family members from violence. Other social movements questioned the existing goals of the criminal justice system. There was a concern for the possibility of overcriminalization, and thus there began a move toward decriminalization, including in 1970 an assertion by the Presidential Commission on Obscenity that pornographic materials do not result in significant harm. Part of this push behind legal reforms was the growing criticism of psychiatry as a discipline of control and the decline of the notion of the prison as a place where rehabilitation is possible. Laws from the late 1950s through the mid-1970s reflected this change and relaxed restrictions on morality and consensual sexual behaviors. Notable in the 1960s and 1970s was the influence of women's groups and victims' rights groups.

In the 1970s, women's groups brought significant attention to the issue of violence against women, both within and outside of the home, and grassroots groups worked to bring this knowledge to the general public. In terms of sexual violence, women's groups worked to challenge stereotypes about rapists as "strangers lurking in the bushes or in a dimly lit parking garage" and advocated that sexual violence against women needed to be viewed as a structural problem in society and linked it to the oppression of women in society more generally. This perspective was advanced in 1975 by Susan Brownmiller, who published her now-classic book on rape titled *Against Our Will*, which argued that "rape is nothing more or less than a conscious process of intimidation by which *all* men keep *all* women in a state of fear" (Brownmiller 1975: 15, emphasis in original).

Women's groups were also instrumental in reforming rape laws, an integral part of the feminist movement of the 1970s and beyond that is elaborated on in chapter 8. Through reforms in the law, feminists sought to "get tough" on sexual offenders and transfer concern of the criminal justice system and society to victims. One of the major goals of rape law reform was to overcome the stereotype of the "black stranger" offender. Feminists wanted the criminal justice system and society generally to understand that rape could occur in a variety of situations, involve a diverse array of individuals, and did not necessarily conform to the rape myths that had historically pervaded societal views. Law plays an important role in shaping cultural perceptions, and therefore reformers sought to expand the list of potential sex crimes to include incest offenders, acquaintance rape, marital rape, rape that did not involve serious physical harm, and assailants who did not fit the "stereotype" of a rapist (Corrigan 2006).

In the late 1970s and early 1980s, women's groups and other social welfare groups turned their attention to the issues surrounding child abuse, which during this time period first became identified as a serious social problem. The federal Child Abuse Prevention and Treatment Act was passed in 1974; this mandates by law the reporting and investigation of all abuse allegations, provides federal funds to states in support of this mission, establishes the Office on Child Abuse and Neglect, begins the collection of data on this issue, and sets forth minimum definitions of what constitutes child abuse. (This has been amended several times and was reauthorized in 2003 in the Keeping Children and Families Safe Act.) In addition, the Department of Health and Human Services in 1974 created the National Center on Child Abuse and Neglect, and several private groups developed, including the National Committee for the Prevention of Child Abuse and the Children's Defense Fund. Women's groups were integral to the development of all these endeavors during the 1970s and 1980s.

Victims' groups also played an important role, as they encouraged victims to report offenses to the authorities, worked to make law enforcement personnel and others within the criminal justice system knowledgeable about the dynamics of sexual violence, worked to protect the privacy of victims, and worked with women's group to create rape crisis centers. One of the most notable writings in this genre is Diana E. H. Russell's *The Politics of Rape: The Victim's Perspective* (1974), which focuses on the individual suffering that results from a sexual assault as well as the importance of victims mobilizing together to create change. This was—and remains—an extremely important contribution to the victims' rights literature. The reforms advocated by these two groups changed the push toward decriminalization and the moral laissez-faire attitude prevalent in the 1960s to one of moral conservatism in the late 1970s and early 1980s.

Reminiscent of the scarlet letter of historical times, a man twice convicted of child molestation has been ordered upon release from prison to relocate to a new residence and place a sign with text at least three inches high in front of his home and in the window of any car he drives reading the following "DANGEROUS SEX OFFENDER NO CHILDREN ALLOWED." This condition would extend for the length of his five-year term of probation ("Unusual Sentence Stirs Legal Dispute" 1987).

THE 1980s

Moral conservatism of the 1980s resulted in earnest investigations into child-oriented pornography, a whole new area of research being published referred to as "recovery literature," and American society was inundated with books on the subject of rape, incest, and child sexual abuse. The message in the media was that sexual violence was an epidemic in our society for women and children and that we should be afraid.

Beginning in the very early 1980s, child pornography was viewed as a widespread social threat that the public and legislators believed should be harshly punished. But could this have been one of those "moral panics"? According to one researcher,

> In reality, child porn was never manufactured domestically on any large scale after the 1970s, and continuing arrests and seizures could be sustained only by steadily expanding the definitions of what was illegal and by emphasizing the role of pornography consumers rather than only the makers or distributors. This expansion assimilated anyone connected with the use of child pornography, however tenuously, with the predatory activity of actual pedophiles and child sex rings. . . . The assumption was that photographs and videos would be shared or sold through widespread vice networks. The phenomenon of pornography rings became linked in the public mind with the idea of the pedophile as an organized career criminal, a violent predator who was potentially capable of abduction and serial homicide and who usually hunted in packs. The scandals of the early 1980s led law-enforcement agencies and the media to suggest that child pornography was often the work of organized pedophiles and that pedophiles, individually and in rings, molested large numbers of children, sometimes abducting their victims. Although a new departure in the stereotype of the molester, the sex ring idea developed immense force and retained a grasp on the public imagination long after the most extreme charges concerning these operations were discredited. (Jenkins 1998: 146)

So the 1980s brings to the forefront the media-linked connection between child pornography and child sex rings. Is this the fetish of the evolved pedophile or a gross overestimation of the child pornography problem? Keep in mind that once the public sees something in the media, "it becomes part of the public's image of the problem and may help justify new public policies" (Best 1990: 46). The association of child pornography with violence soon expanded to an association, advocated by victims' rights groups and women's groups, between adult pornography and more generalized violence, resulting in moral conservatives and feminists aligning forces in the 1980s to pass ordinances outlawing pornography in many jurisdictions. In the case of sexually explicit material depicting adults, however, the courts disagreed, and therefore printed matter that many moralists and feminists consider offensive and obscene is protected by the Constitution. By way of an update, while there may have been merely a suspicion of widespread child pornography in the 1980s, it has become a reality in the twenty-first century. Nonelectronic child pornography has been difficult to get for at least twenty years, but this not the case with electronic child pornography, and unfortunately "the role of law enforcement in regulating supply [of child pornography] is approximately zero" (Jenkins 2001: 4). Child pornography is a social issue that is widely condemned and stigmatized because "by definition, the subjects of child pornography cannot give any form of informed or legal consent to their involvement in this trade, and it is a reasonable suspicion that, even when children are just depicted nude, they are subject to actual molestation" (Jenkins 2001: 4). So while the link between child pornography and child abuse sex rings of the 1980s was indeed a moral panic and continues to remain questionable, the seriousness of the child pornography problem today should not be underestimated.

In the 1980s, laws began to change as child sexual abuse cases started to get prosecuted that permitted modifications for child testimony in court that included closed-circuit testimony, and a field of therapy emerged whose specialty it was to detect and treat child sexual abuse. Part of this field was to prepare child witnesses for court, and one way this was done was through the use of play therapy. This was new ground in the 1980s. As stories of child pornography and child sex rings were told in the media, so were stories of ritualistic abuse. There were several high-profile cases in the 1980s of alleged satanic and ritualized abuse of children involving many perpetrators committing serious physical and sexual abuse. The most sensationalized case was the McMartin preschool scandal in California in 1983, a full discussion of which is beyond the scope of this book. Implicitly tied to the McMartin trial was the debate over "recovered memories" with therapists asserting that many victims repress memories of sexual abuse and may need assistance in recovering these events because of trauma and critics arguing that the memories are not "recovered" but instead false and planted by the therapist (as was determined in the trial of the McMartin case). In the 1980s, this debate caused such a media stir that it had many in the public (falsely) wondering if sexual abuse of women and children was really a serious problem or if many women and children were "falsifying" these memories either on their own or at the "suggestion" of their therapist. This scandal set the women's movement and the child protection movement back considerably. As the 1980s ended and the 1990s began, cases emerged that were extreme and high profile, children were brutalized by previously convicted sexual offenders, and a new panic of stranger danger emerged that set off a new and even tougher set of laws targeting sexual offenders.

II

THE CRIME
AND THE CRIMINALS

5

Laws, Laws, and More Laws

In the United States renewed interest in harsh sex offender legislation was encouraged by high-profile sexual assaults and murders of children during the 1990s. This has put the United States on the forefront of the passage of innovative sex offender legislation designed to prevent future crimes. These laws, however, have been targeted at offenders who are strangers, and the offenders in the case studies in this chapter were strangers despite the fact that women and children are most at risk from individuals they are married to, are dating, or are related to or know as family friends. These laws were passed quickly and were not based on empirical evidence of sexual offenders and sexual offenses. Perhaps not surprisingly, then, these laws have failed to serve the protective functions for which they were intended:

> The reality is that sex offenders are a great political target, but that doesn't mean any law under the sun is appropriate. "Illinois Measure Would Move Some from Sex Offender List" 2006)

THE CREATION OF A MORAL PANIC IN THE 1990s

The public is fearful of those portrayed in the media as "beasts," "devils," "perverts," "fiends," or "evil" (Kitzinger 2004). "Citizens cannot understand a sex attack on a child, and this incomprehensibility fuels reactions of fear. . . . The attack and investigation become front-page news . . . describing the failure of the justice system to protect vulnerable persons, which fuels a strong public reaction. . . . Government officials then feel compelled to act" (Lieb, Quinsey, and Berliner 1998: 11). The themes that are most prevalent in the media, despite this not being the most common perpetrator of abuse, are those of stranger danger, where the perpetrator is someone unknown to the victim:

> Stranger-danger stories have great appeal to journalists. The random and public nature of such attacks makes every reader or viewer potentially at risk from the "pervert on the loose." Such cases often combine sex and murder. They also have ongoing narrative momentum (the appeal by parents for the missing child, the eventual tragic discovery) and they come with their own available images (the little girl in her school uniform, the security video footage of her last journey, the police searching wasteland). (Kitzinger 2004: 128)

This becomes problematic when an overwhelming majority of individuals get their "reality" about crime from the television. The "reality" most citizens get about sexual offenders and sexual offenses becomes significantly skewed, and the policies and laws they support are based on this skewed perception. The media create fear, reinforce stereotypes and rape myths, and perpetuate misinformation about sexual offenders and sexual offenses (Benedict 1992; Carringella-MacDonald 1998; Dowler 2006). In response, the public has overwhelmingly supported laws that do not work to protect women and children from the types of sexual offenses by which they are most likely to be victimized.

WASHINGTON STATE AND SEXUAL PREDATOR LAWS

Earl Shriner was a man with a history of contact with the criminal justice system. In the 1960s he served a term in a mental facility after allegedly murdering a male classmate. On release, he was repeatedly charged with molestation in 1977, 1987, and again in 1988. While in prison, there were attempts to commit Shriner to a mental health facility involuntarily; however, those efforts failed despite his expressed desire to rape and torture children. He was released from prison after serving the full length of a fixed sentence for sexual assault. In 1989 in Washington State, Shriner abducted a seven-year-old boy. The boy was brutally sexually assaulted, had his penis severed, and was left to die. A massive media and public outcry occurred, and within six months Washington's legislature passed sweeping legislation that would impact sexual offenders.

Laws passed in response to the Shriner case are termed special commitment laws or sexually violent predator laws. These laws, passed in many states using almost verbatim language as in Washington, take effect only when an offender is about to be released from serving an assigned prison term and have at their foundation the assumption that "experts" can identify which offenders have the potential to cause future harm and treat these offenders so that they will be safe for release. These laws permit the state to confine offenders deemed "mentally abnormal and dangerous sex offenders" to a secure mental facility until they are deemed safe for release (Zonana, Bonnie, and Hoge 2003). Individuals eligible for indeterminate commitment under Washington State's sexual violent predator legislation include convicted sexually violent offenders (even juveniles) whose sentence is about to expire as well as those charged with a sexually violent offense and found incompetent to stand trial or not guilty by reason of insanity. Some of the controversies surrounding sexual predator laws are elaborated on in chapter 7, though the foundation of these laws should resound with the familiarity of the sexual psychopath laws of the past.

Sexual predator laws, however, have important differences from the sexual psychopath laws of the 1930s, 1940s, and 1950s. First, current statutes do not necessarily require an offender to suffer from a "serious mental disorder." Second, the sexual behavior of the offender need not be in the "recent" past in order for the state to seek civil commitment. Third, in many states no legitimate treatment program is required to be in place in order for an offender to be confined under a civil commitment statute. Finally, current legislation requires that an offender serve the term of imprisonment in its entirety *prior* to the state seeking civil commitment. Thus, many critics argue that "the primary goal of predator statutes is to provide a mechanism for continued confinement of sex offenders considered at risk of reoffending who can no longer be confined under the criminal justice system" (La Fond 2000: 159). As such, there are many civil liberty arguments surrounding this legislation.

THE CASE OF JACOB WETTERLING AND THE WETTERLING ACT

In 1989 an eleven-year-old boy named Jacob Wetterling, his ten-year-old brother, and an eleven-year-old friend were riding bikes in St. Joseph, Minnesota, when confronted by a masked man with a gun. The man told two of the boys to run away into the woods, and he abducted Jacob, who has never been found. There was a halfway house located fairly close to the incident, so there was suspicion that perhaps a previously convicted sexual offender had something to do with Jacob's disappearance, but a perpetrator was never located. Several years later a federal law, formally called the Jacob Wetterling Crimes Against Children and Sexually Violent Offender Registration Act, was named in his honor.

The Wetterling Act requires all states to have registration protocols for sex offenders or risk the loss of federal funds for crime-fighting measures. Each state has a mandatory registration law that requires sex offenders to register their home address with authorities. Who this information gets passed to varies by state and by the tier at which the offender is assessed (elaborated on in chapter 7), though in most states this information is accessible to the general public via a website or CD-ROM. This law was amended in 1996 and evolved into a community notification law.

Many states include language in this law that effectively excludes family members and close family friends from designation as a sexual predator. For example, the Wetterling Act provides that a "predator" must register and defines predatory behavior as "an act directed at a stranger, or a person with whom a relationship has been established or promoted for the primary purpose of victimization" (Jacob Wetterling Crimes Against Children and Sexually Violent Offender Registration Program, 42 U.S.C. § 14071[a][3][E] [2001]). The rationale behind this definition of predatory, as established by two court rulings, is that an offender who targets family members or acquaintances poses less risk to the general community than an offender who targets strangers (*In re G.B* 1996 and *In re R.F.* 1998). However, how can this be measured? Does the court contend that incest, spousal rape, and acquaintance rape are less harmful than stranger attacks? Without evidence to support this position, the court is continuing to protect the societal structures that cause sexual violence in the first place: lack of education about sex and sexuality, secrecy surrounding sex and sexuality, misogyny, and a general devaluation of women and children in American culture.

THE CASE OF MEGAN KANKA AND MEGAN'S LAW

It was 1994 in Hamilton, New Jersey, when a young, middle-class white girl named Megan Kanka was raped and asphyxiated. The convicted perpetrator was a neighbor, a paroled sex offender name Jesse Timmendequas, who resided with two other paroled sexual offenders. Timmendequas had been imprisoned for a second offense against a child and had plea-bargained to a term of ten years (Pallone 2003). It is believed that Megan went to the neighbor's house under the pretense of meeting his puppy. After sexually assaulting and murdering Megan, the perpetrator disposed of her body in a nearby park. This case sparked outrage and intense media attention, as the public felt helpless to prevent sexual victimization of children. Megan's mother was reported as saying, "We knew nothing about him. If we had been aware of his record, my daughter would be alive today" (Human Rights Watch 2007: 47). The solution (within a month of Megan's murder) was registration and community notification legislation, referred to commonly as "Megan's Law," for sexual offenders, which became the guideline for all other states (sixteen states followed New Jersey's lead within the same year as Megan Kanka's murder). Even the federal government eventually followed.

Although the first community notification law was enacted in 1990 in Washington State after the offense by Earl Shriner, Megan's Law created statutes that were replicated nationwide. Megan's Law requires sex offenders to register with the police at various time intervals, depending on their tier level, and in many states requires law enforcement officials to notify communities when a sex offender moves into the neighborhood. The notification of community members and the notion of who has the right to be notified is the most controversial aspect of this law, which is elaborated on in chapter 7. There are no national standards, so depending on the state and on the offender's tier status, varying degrees of information about the offender are available to the public. Based on a psychological assessment of the offender, he is assigned a tier, ranging from 1 to 3. Tier 3 offenders are deemed at high risk to the public, tier 2 offenders are deemed at moderate risk to the public, and tier 1 offenders are deemed to be the lowest risk to the public. In order to notify the community, letters may be delivered by police to various community organizations or to neighbors, website notification may be involved, or billboard notification is possible. Broad dissemination of information about offenders who are subject to community notification occurs in states such as New Jersey, Oregon, and Washington, including to local organizations, residents, and the media. In states such as Connecticut, Georgia, and New York, discretion is given to probation and parole officers who can notify anyone they deem appropriate. And in states such as Arkansas, Michigan, South Carolina, Vermont, and Virginia, disclosure of information is only to individuals submitting a written request. In addition, some states have special labeling procedures, such as a designation on one's driver's license, like in Delaware.

An example of community notification: "Readers of the . . . *Bucks County Courier-Times* in Pennsylvania were greeted, on May 25, 2001, with a front page headline 'Sex Offender Living Here,' introducing a story concerning a 25-year-old man whom we shall call John Doe. He, and his auto, were pictured in front of a particular building in the apartment complex in which he had taken up residence: both a street address and an apartment number were provided. The story explained that Mr. Doe had pled 'nolo contendere' [no contest] . . . to unlawful sexual contact in the second degree in a neighboring state in 1999, apparently involving an offer to engage in sexual congress with an underaged prostitute (and therefore prosecutable as attempted statutory rape); thereafter, he paid a fine and was placed on probation. The offense did not rise to the level of severity that, in the state in which it was committed, required placement on the Megan's List registry. Because of a job change, he moved to Pennsylvania in March 2001—thereby encountering Catch-22. A senior officer of the local police department told the *Courier-Times* that anyone convicted of a sex offense in another state is automatically placed on 'community notification' status, even though the offense of which he/she had been convicted would not warrant such placement had the offense been committed within Pennsylvania." (Pallone 2003: 87–88)

Although these types of laws may empower community members, they may also produce a perpetual sense of fear in the public. As for the offender, such laws decrease the possibility of community reintegration; label offenders, making it difficult to secure housing, employment, and other opportunities; and undermine their rehabilitative efforts. President Bill Clinton summed up the purpose of Megan's Law in his presidential radio address on August 24, 1996: "Nothing is more threatening to our families and communities and more destructive of our basic values than sex offenders who victimize children and families. Study after study tells us that they often repeat the same crimes. That's why we have to stop sex offenders before they commit their next crime, to make our children safe and give their parents piece of mind" (cited in Human Rights Watch 2007: 47). Megan's Law amended the Jacob Wetterling Act to make parents feel safe and protected from the recidivating sexual offender. It did not matter if this information was not based in fact, and it did not matter if this law failed to apply to the individuals most likely to take parents' peace of mind.

THE CASE OF POLLY KLAAS AND THREE-STRIKES LAWS

In 1993 a slumber party was taking place in a middle-class California neighborhood. During this party, a twelve-year-old white girl named Polly Klaas was abducted from her bedroom window. The public was shocked and outraged and assisted in the search for Polly for several weeks. The police eventually arrested a previously convicted child molester named Richard Allen Davis, who led them to the body of the young girl. He was convicted and sentenced to the death penalty for kidnapping, rape, and murder. Prior to the conviction for the kidnapping, rape, and murder of Polly Klaas, Davis had served fifteen years in prison for a variety of sexual offenses. However, because of plea bargaining, he was able to plead guilty to offenses that would not trigger mandatory registration, meaning that no one was aware that a former sexual offender was living in the neighborhood. Polly's murder by a repeat offender enraged the public, and the media publicized this case incessantly, resulting in overwhelming public support in California for Proposition 184. This proposition was to increase penalties for repeat felony offenders. This meant that an individual committing a second felony after a first felony of a violent or serious nature was to be subject to sentencing standards twice as long as typical for a second felony. A third felony conviction would result in a sentence of twenty-five years to life imprisonment. This proposition is commonly referred to as "three-strikes" legislation and was passed in March 1994. While supporters of such legislation argue that it serves as a general deterrent to potential three-time offenders, there is little evidence to suggest that reduction in serious crime has resulted due to the implementation of three-strikes laws.

Pam Lyncher was the victim of a sexual assault at the hands of a stranger who was able to plea-bargain to a sentence of twenty years. In response, she became a victims' rights advocate. In 1996 the Pam Lyncher Sex Offender Tracking and Identification Act was named after her. This is a national database that permits the Federal Bureau of Investigation (FBI) to track the location of a specific tier of offenders.

THE CASE OF AMBER HAGERMAN AND THE AMBER ALERT

In 1996 neighbors witnessed a young girl being pulled off her bike and forced into a truck. The kidnapped girl was nine-year-old Amber Hagerman of Arlington, Texas. Authorities searched extensively, and Amber's body was found several days later in a drainage ditch close to her home with her throat slashed. Despite following all valuable leads, Amber's killer was never found. What did develop in response was the AMBER Alert system, which stands for America's Missing: Broadcast Emergency Response. This system provides repeated broadcasts about details of an abducted child and the perpetrator, including physical description, vehicle description, and any other useful details. This information is broadcast via television, radio, highway notification signs, and text message in order to garner tips from the public. A federal version of the AMBER Alert was adopted in 2003, and as of 2005 all states have this program. The system seems to be most effective when there is an existing relationship between the victim and the offender, as information about the offender is readily available to issue the alert. The U.S. Department of Justice reports that 80 percent of abductions that included an AMBER Alert have resulted in recovery of the child (U.S. Department of Justice 2005).

THE CASE OF JESSICA LUNSFORD
AND THE JESSICA LUNSFORD ACT

In 2005 a nine-year-old white girl was abducted from her Homosassa, Florida, home. Media coverage was widespread, and three weeks after her abduction, a neighbor and registered sexual offender admitted to sexually assaulting and killing Jessica Lunsford and disposing of her body in a shallow grave in his backyard. The suspect was a previously convicted sexual offender with a borderline-retarded IQ who had been able to relocate his residence without notifying authorities. In addition, he had failed to attend mandated counseling sessions. Recently, transcripts have surfaced that he admitted to law enforcement that he sexually abused a female family member in the early 1990s, an offense for which he was never arrested or charged. In 2007 John E. Couey went to trial; however, his confession had been suppressed by the court because police had ignored his requests for an attorney. The prosecution charged him with first-degree murder, kidnapping, sexual battery, and burglary. He was found guilty and, despite his borderline intelligence and the ban on execution of the mentally retarded, sentenced by a jury vote of ten to two to the death penalty.

A few short weeks later elsewhere in Florida, a thirteen-year-old white girl was abducted from her Ruskin, Florida, home. Given that this was the second child abduction in such a short time frame, the media were in a state of frenzy, the public was outraged, and even Jessica Lunsford's father went to Ruskin to join in the search for Sarah Lunde. A week after her disappearance, Sarah Lunde was found dead in a nearby lake. The man who ultimately confessed to choking Sarah to death was a convicted rapist who had earlier dated Sarah's mother. David Onstott admitted to detectives that he murdered Sarah; however, the confession was never heard at trial because the court ruled that Onstott was denied proper access to an attorney prior to giving the statement. There were a few statements he made to others that linked him to Sarah's murder. After a two-week trial in August 2008, David Onstott was found guilty of second-degree murder and sentenced to life in prison.

A short time after Jessica Lunsford was found sexually assaulted and murdered, the Jessica Lunsford Act was passed unanimously in the Florida legislature, providing for a twenty-five-year mandatory minimum sentence for an individual convicted of sexual assault of a child under the age of twelve. This law also requires lifetime electronic surveillance once the perpetrator was released. Using many of the provisions of the 2005 Jessica Lunsford Act, as of 2007 more than thirty states had followed Florida's lead and created legislation with a mandatory minimum sentence of twenty-five years to life for certain sexual offenses against children. Although this law can be applied to incestuous offenders, as is the case with other types of legislation, it is rarely used for such offenses. In addition, twenty-two states authorize electronic monitoring for some offenders following their release from prison. By way of example, California's Proposition 83 provides for lifetime electronic monitoring for felony registered sexual offenders as of 2006.

Dru Sjodin was a college student who was kidnapped, raped, and murdered in 2003 by a tier 3 sexual offender who had recently been released from serving twenty-three years in prison. The perpetrator was Alfonso Rodriguez Jr., and he was found guilty in 2006 in federal court because he had transported Sjodin across state lines. He was sentenced to the death penalty. The Dru Sjodin National Sex Offender Public Registry (NSOPR) was launched in 2006 and allows for real-time access to nationwide data regarding sex offenders. A potential problem with the registry is that it always lists the age of the victim at the time the offense occurred; however, it updates the age of the offender each year, and this can be extremely misleading, especially in cases involving statutory rape charges. For example, you look on the website and find out that your male neighbor (now age thirty-seven) was convicted of sexually assaulting a fourteen-year-old female. What the website does not reveal is the context: the neighbor may have been eighteen years old and dating the female at the time, and the offense may have been statutory in nature. Instead, you get the idea that he is a child molester. The press release regarding the NSOPR states that "there are over 500,000 registered sex offenders nationwide and statistics have shown the recidivism rate for these offenders is high. Access to public registry information nationwide is essential for citizens to help identify sex offenders beyond their own streets or neighborhoods" (Department of Justice 2005). Actual statistics regarding recidivism of sexual offenders are elaborated on in chapter 6.

THE ADAM WALSH ACT

The Adam Walsh Act was signed into law on the twenty-fifth anniversary of a young boy named Adam Walsh being abducted in Florida from a shopping mall. Adam was found murdered sixteen days later, and the perpetrator was never found. This act is backed by $47 million to fund the programs it entails and includes the Sex Offender Registration and Notification Act (SORNA), which seeks to establish a comprehensive and national system for the registration of sexual offenders. The idea is to streamline the system so that all states will have identical information posted about sex offenders online (name, address, birth date, employment, photo, and so on). This legislation organizes sex offenders into three tiers and mandates that tier 3 offenders (the most serious offenders) update their whereabouts in person with law enforcement every three months for life, tier 2 offenders update their whereabouts every six months for twenty-five years, and tier 1 offenders update their whereabouts every year for fifteen years. The law also provides that failure to register and update information is a felony and mandates the registration of sexual offenders as young as fourteen years of age. Under SORNA, failure to follow the registration guidelines can result in a fine of up to $250,000 for an offender and/or imprisonment of up to ten years. Critics have challenged the constitutionality of the registration requirement; however, it was upheld by the court in July 2008.

Although laws vary by state, incest offenders are usually omitted from website registration, and in New Jersey this was a provision sought by the New Jersey Coalition Against Sexual Assault. Here a father describes his daughter's friends finding a notification at school: "My daughters went to school and had a situation where there was a newspaper that was on the table and some of the kids came back up to my oldest daughter and basically started teasing her, saying, 'You know, I heard that your daddy played sex with you.' The impact of that goes beyond measure" (Zevitz and Farkas 2000b: 384). Because the posting of offender information online, including a photo and address, would be harmful to the victim as well, victims' rights groups have lobbied in many states to have incest offenders exempt from this type of legislation. It is worthy to note that victim information is not listed on the registration website, only the general crime in which the individual was convicted. To exclude incest offenders ultimately renders the registration useless, as familial and acquaintance offenders make up the majority of sexual offenses and sexual offenders. It is shortsighted for victims' rights groups to suggest that stranger danger is the most important and devastating form of sexual offending. Estimates are that as of 2004, only 18 percent of tier 2 and 3 offenders in New Jersey who were eligible for inclusion in the online database were actually included because of appeals and exemptions (Corrigan 2006).

This act also has some other provisions, including the elimination of the statute of limitations for prosecuting child abduction and felony child sexual offense cases. It has established a federal DNA database and funds Global Positioning System monitoring of sexual offenders. It also permits victims of child abuse to sue their offender in civil court for damages. In addition, it imposes some mandatory minimum sentencing:

- Thirty years minimum for the rape of a child
- Ten years minimum for sexual trafficking offenses involving children
- Ten years minimum for offenses involving coerced child prostitution
- Increasing the minimum terms of imprisonment for offenders who travel between states with minors

Finally, the act has created some loopholes that create some obvious due process concerns, including giving federal hearing officers the authority to civilly commit an individual in federal custody and permitting the U.S. attorney general to apply this law retroactively. All states in the United States must comply with the Adam Walsh Act and the provisions of SORNA by July 27, 2009, or their federal grant funding may be reduced. The Adam Walsh Act is yet another example of how government is responding to fearmongering instead of objective fact. It is hoped that civil libertarians will challenge this law and that political wrangling and poor science will not sway the U.S. Supreme Court.

CASTRATION LAWS

Perhaps the most invasive strategy has been the attempt to prevent future sexual offenses through castration. Involuntary sterilization of sex offenders and other habitual criminals was permitted by law in the early 1900s by many states until it was struck down by the Supreme Court in 1942 in *Skinner v. Oklahoma*. Although it was historically used as a method of treatment, laws have once again been passed to mandate it under some circumstances beginning in the 1990s. In 1996, California implemented the first chemical castration (testosterone-reducing injections) or surgical castration laws in a very long time, and several other states followed with almost verbatim legislation. These laws typically apply to sex offenders seeking early release from prison and require individuals to take drugs to reduce their sex drive, though no provision exists that professionals are available and knowledgeable to administer and monitor this process. Indeed, in Colorado, the court *must* order a certain tier of child molester to take antiandrogen treatment as a parole condition without determining the medical appropriateness of the treatment for each offender. In Florida, qualified repeat offenders *must* be ordered by the court to submit to weekly chemical castration injections, and even first-time offenders can be given this sentence. Some of the risks and benefits of castration as a treatment method are elaborated on in chapter 9.

INTERNET RESTRICTIONS

In recent years, governments at both the state and the federal level have begun to devote financial resources to the prevention of crimes against children committed on the Internet, specifically crimes of sexual exploitation. In 2008, the two major social networking sites, MySpace and Facebook, added significant safeguards to protect minor users from potential sexual offenders. Some of these changes included a ban on use by those convicted of a sexual offense, limited searching ability by adults for users who are under the age of eighteen, and a task force that seeks to improve methods of verifying user identity information. On occasion, these social networking sites search the profiles of their users. For example, in August 2008, MySpace deleted 146 profiles belonging to sexual offenders after comparing the profiles with the state's sex offender registry. This procedure resulted in the removal of almost 250 profiles by MySpace in 2007 ("MySpace Deletes 146 Profiles of NE Sex Offenders" 2008). In addition, in 2007, the Department of Justice announced that there were fifty-nine state and local agencies involved in Internet Crimes Against Children (ICAC) task forces nationwide. These task forces have been in existence since 1998 and have made more than 10,000 arrests (Department of Justice 2007) to aid in preventing sexual criminal activity targeted at children. These task forces are part of the Project Safe Childhood initiative of the Department of Justice, whose

> goal is to investigate and prosecute crimes against children facilitated though the Internet or other electronic media and communication devices. Project Safe Childhood is implemented through a partnership of U.S. Attorneys; ICAC Task Forces; federal partners, including the FBI, U.S. Postal Inspection Service, Immigration and Customs Enforcement and the U.S. Marshals Service; advocacy organizations such as the National Center for Missing and Exploited Children; and other state and local law enforcement officials in each U.S. Attorney's district. Other aspects of the program include increased federal involvement in child pornography and enticement cases; training of federal, state, and local law enforcement on investigating and prosecuting computer-facilitated crimes against children; and community awareness and educational programs. (Department of Justice 2007)

Given the ease of distribution of child pornography electronically and access to minors online, such initiatives will become increasingly important.

On the Internet, sexual deviants are able to "justify" their desires in children as elaborated in a *New York Times* article in 2006: "Acts of molestation are often celebrated as demonstrations of love." The article quotes a man who writes about a "consensual sexual relationship" he has been having with his ten-year-old daughter for the past two months. "Whatever guilt Sonali [the man's screen name] felt for the relationship was eased by the postings of other pedophiles . . . the most dangerous element of the pedophile Internet community [is] its justification of illegal acts. Experts described the pedophiles' online worldview as reflective of 'neutralization,' a psychological rationalization used by groups that deviate from societal norms. In essence, the groups deem potentially injurious acts and beliefs harmless. That is accomplished in part by denying that a victim is injured, condemning critics and appealing to higher loyalties—in this case, an ostensible struggle for the sexual freedom of children" ("On the Web, Pedophiles Extend Their Reach" 2006).

Other laws target offenders who have a history of using the Internet to access or target their victims. A law passed in New Jersey in 2007 bans sexual offenders who utilized the Internet in the commission of their crime from using the Internet for personal purposes, with an exemption for work required as a part of employment or in the search for employment. Monitoring takes place through the use of installed computer equipment, periodic computer scans, and polygraph examinations. Failure to comply could result in eighteen months of imprisonment and a $10,000 fine. This type of law is a relatively recent phenomenon, with similar legislation seen only in Florida and Nevada ("No Internet for Some Sex Offenders in New Jersey" 2007). Because this is a relatively new area, the future is likely to see further restrictions for offenders.

THE DEATH PENALTY

Recently, constitutional challenges to the death penalty as a form of cruel and unusual punishment resulted in a stay of execution for many offenders on death row. One case that prompted a consideration of the cruel and unusual nature of the death penalty occurred in Florida in 2006 wherein a lethal injection took thirty-four minutes to execute a condemned man, which is more than twice the "normal" or anticipated length of the procedure. The first execution in Florida since the Supreme Court ruled in November 2007 that the lethal injection protocol is acceptable was in July 2008. The condemned man was Mark Dean Schwab, who was convicted of kidnapping, raping, and murdering an eleven-year-old boy named Junny Rios-Martinez in 1991. The murder of Martinez took place a mere month after Schwab was granted early release on a charge of raping a thirteen-year-old boy. Because of this case, Florida passed the Junny Rios-Martinez Act of 1992, which prohibits the early release of sexual offenders from prison and prohibits credit for good behavior for sexual offenders ("Florida Executes Child Killer" 2008).

This case involved the sexual assault and murder of a child, but can an offender be sentenced to die for a sexual offense that does not result in murder? Supreme Court rulings in 1976 and 1977 barred the death penalty for rape cases as unconstitutional; however, several states (Florida, Louisiana, Montana, Oklahoma, South Carolina, and Texas) passed laws permitting the death penalty for child rape under the guise that the Supreme Court decisions referred to the sexual assault of only adult women, not children. Nevertheless, a man has not been executed in the United States for a sexual offense in which the victim was not murdered since 1964. Did the Supreme Court justices bar execution for the rape of women? Or did they mean children too? This was the question before the Court in 2008.

Patrick Kennedy was on death row at Angola Prison in Louisiana, convicted of rape in 2003 of his eight-year-old step-daughter. A prosecutor argued, "In my opinion the rape of a child is more heinous and more hideous than a homicide. . . . It takes away their innocence, it takes away their childhood, it mutilates their spirit. It kills their soul. They're never the same after these things happen" ("Rape a Child, Pay with Your Life, Louisiana Argues" 2008). Conversely, an appellate attorney reminded that "when we look at what it means to be cruel and unusual, this is exactly the kind of thing that raises these serious concerns of the constitutionality of Mr. Kennedy's death sentence" ("Rape a Child, Pay with Your Life, Louisiana Argues" 2008). This case also brings up historical issues of race, as Patrick Kennedy is black and resides in a southern state where racial discrimination is always a factor of consideration (even when the victim is also black, as in this case). "All 14 rapists executed by Louisiana in the past 75 years were African American . . . [and] nationwide from 1930 to 1964, nearly 90 percent of executed rapists were black" ("Rape a Child, Pay with Your Life, Louisiana Argues" 2008).

The Court has decided. In June 2008 in a five-to-four ruling, the Supreme Court asserted that execution of child sexual offenders is unconstitutional and violates the Eighth Amendment's prohibition against cruel and unusual punishment. The justices stated that "we cannot sanction this result when the harm to the victim, though grave, cannot be quantified in the same way as the death of the victim" (*Kennedy v. Louisiana*). The Court further stated that "by in effect making the punishment for child rape and murder equivalent, a State that punishes child rape by death may remove a strong incentive for the rapist not to kill the victim. Assuming the offender behaves in a rational way, as one must to justify the penalty on ground of deterrence, the penalty in some respects gives less protections, not more, to the victim, who is often the sole witness to the crime" (*Kennedy v. Louisiana*). The Supreme Court thus concluded that the death penalty was not a proportional punishment for the crime of child rape.

Some in Louisiana were outraged, including Governor Bobby Jindal, who immediately signed into law the Sex Offender Chemical Castration Bill. In a press release, the governor said,

> The Sex Offender Chemical Castration Bill is a good bill, and I am especially glad to sign it into Louisiana law today, on the same day the Supreme Court has made an atrocious ruling against our state's ability to sentence those who sexually assault our children to the fullest extent. Those who prey on our children are among the very worst criminals imaginable. Not only as the Governor of this great state, but as a father of three children, I believe that sexually assaulting a child is one of the very worst crimes and I am glad we have taken such strong measures in Louisiana to put a stop to these monsters' brutal acts. I want to send the message loud and clear—to the Supreme Court of the United States and beyond—make no mistake about it, if anyone wants to molest children and commit sexual assaults on kids they should not do so here in Louisiana. Here, we will do everything in our power to protect our children and we will not rest until justice is won and we have fully punished those who harm them. (State of Louisiana 2008)

In addition, the press release indicated details of other measures during the most recent session of the legislature supported by the governor, including

> the passage of SB 143 to prohibit a sex offender from wearing a mask, hood or disguise during holiday events and from distributing candy or other gifts on Halloween to persons under eighteen years of age; SB 517 which provides for the lifetime registration of sex offenders; SB 510 to double the minimum sentence for computer-aided solicitation of a minor; HB 770 to prohibit the use of text messaging by sex offenders; and SB 514 to increase the minimum sentence for the molestation of a juvenile by five-fold. (State of Louisiana 2008)

Governor Jindal is pandering to his constituency with the excellent political target of sexual offenders, but that does not mean that any of these provisions, like a ban on text messaging, is going to improve the safety of women and children from sexual violence.

Fitting squarely within a crime control model, the United States has passed legislation in an attempt to prevent sex offenders from committing future crimes. In fact, in 2005 alone, lawmakers passed more than one hundred sex offender laws, which is double the number passed in 2004. While many of these laws have effects that could reasonably be argued infringe on the due process rights of sex offenders, in America's quest to reduce crime, lawmakers and the public are unconcerned with the individual liberties of "sexual predators." Quoting the executive director of the Jacob Wetterling Foundation, Nancy Sabin,

> We keep getting sidetracked with issues like castration and pink license plates for sex offenders, as if they can't borrow or drive another car. . . . Don't get me wrong, we need extreme vigilance for some. But these people are coming from us—society—and we have to stop the hemorrhage. We have to stop pretending that these people are coming from other planets. (Janus 2006: 1)

Focusing selectively on the rare but powerful cases that have spawned harsh laws against offenders hurts the struggle against sexual violence generally. Sexual violence and abuses pervade society, and turning our attention to the atypical dangers or the dangers from strangers who are portrayed as recidivating sexual deviants does not make us safer. This diverts our focus from the structural elements in society that contribute to the victimization of women and children (Janus 2006). "The politics of sexual violence forces the majority of the risks of sexual violence underground, making them invisible in the political discourse. Risks that fall outside the predator template simply cannot figure into the public discourse. Because the risks must remain invisible, we are deflected from a sensible and effective fight against sexual violence" (Janus 2006: 144). If we truly want community protection from sexual abuses and violence, these are the roots we need to explore. There is "no inherent contradiction between protecting the rights of children [and women] and protecting the rights of former offenders" (Human Rights Watch 2007: 130). The rights of everyone are protected if policies are established that are based on empirical evidence, case-by-case evaluation, and professional supervision as opposed to political rhetoric, pandering, and the panic that derives from tragedy.

6

Counting the Problem

When I talk to people about statistics, I find that they usually are quite willing to criticize dubious statistics—as long as the numbers come from people with whom they disagree. (Best 2001: xi–xiii)

As the public's fear continues to increase and as we pass stricter legislation targeting sexual offenders, it is important to evaluate what we know statistically about sexual offending. Are we experiencing an epidemic of sexual offenses? Are there significantly more sexual offenders, and are they more aggressive and predatory in their attacks than other violent offenders? The media would have citizens believe that there is an epidemic of sexual predators that we have never before experienced. Is this true? An examination of the studies conducted regarding sexual offending will give us a more accurate picture of the "typical" sexual offender, the type of offenses committed most frequently, and the "typical" victim of sexually related offenses. While sexual offending is a difficult social issue to measure because of the myriad factors that contribute to underreporting, viewing these statistics in combination will give us a fairly good idea of the dynamics of sexual offenses and sexual offenders.

In 2001, Joel Best wrote an illuminating book titled *Damned Lies and Statistics: Untangling Numbers from the Media, Politicians, and Activists*. In this book, Best (2001) notes that much of the general public simply accepts at face value the statistics presented to them in the media because we are led to believe that statistics are objective facts. We see statistics about the epidemic of sexual offending presented in news articles, we hear politicians lament about the increase in these types of crimes, and too often we accept this as truth, believing that numbers are not to be questioned. Best (2001) stresses that statistics are "products of our social arrangements" and are brought to our attention for particular purposes. He outlines the importance of asking ourselves three critical questions when viewing or hearing a statistic about a social issue: Who created the social statistic, and how might their personal beliefs or professional affiliations influence the statistic? Why was the statistic created, or what is the purpose for which the statistic will be used? How was the statistic created, or what was the methodological design of the project? Together, answers to these three questions provide a solid foundation on which to critically evaluate the truthfulness (and usefulness) of statistics (Best 2001). This is not to say that statistics can be used to prove anything and should not be trusted; it is merely a note that consumers of research must be diligent in evaluating statistics on social issues before accepting and passing these numbers on to others as hard-and-fast truth. "People create statistics: they choose what to count, how to go about counting, which of the resulting numbers they share with others, and which words they use to describe and interpret those figures. Numbers do not exist independent of people; understanding numbers requires knowing who counted what, why they bothered counting, and how they went about it" (Best 2004: xi–xiii). When using statistics as a basis for the consideration of policies and legislation, it is paramount that our evaluation be critical.

PREVALENCE AND INCIDENCE OF SEX OFFENDING

The definition of sexual offenses has changed dramatically throughout history, and currently there remains inconsistency between jurisdictions regarding behaviors that are considered sexual offenses. For example, there are many states in the United States in which consensual sodomy is considered an illegal sexual offense, whereas in many other states consensual sodomy is legal. Another example is that age of consent varies by state, from fourteen to eighteen. As such, those states with higher statutory ages of consent will likely have higher rates of violations and therefore the highest concentration of sexual offenders. These inconsistencies in legislation necessarily impact the measurement of sexual offenses from state to state and the comparison of statistics across regions. That being said, most jurisdictions agree that a sexual offense involves lack of consent. For lack of consent to exist, it is generally agreed that there is 1) force or threats, 2) a statement implying the desire not to participate in said activity, or 3) an individual who is unable to consent, because of age, mental capacity, or physical capacity or because the individual is under the care of the state.

There are two primary ways in which sexual offenses are counted. The first source of knowledge regarding sexual offenses and offenders is derived from arrest and conviction data obtained by law enforcement. The Uniform Crime Report (UCR) in the United States counts crimes that are reported to law enforcement by participating agencies. This was updated in 1982 with the National Incident Based Reporting System (NIBRS). When included in NIBRS, only the most serious offense committed in an incident is recorded. For example, if a woman is murdered and sexually assaulted, the offense will be recorded in the UCR as only a murder and not as a sexual assault. While only a small number of murders also involve the victim being sexually assaulted, the method of counting offenses used in NIBRS will necessarily result in undercounting in some circumstances. In addition, NIBRS does not include statutory sexual offenses. Perhaps the most problematic aspect of NIBRS, however, is that it includes only offenses reported to law enforcement, thus overlooking the dark figure of sexual offenses. The "dark figure" is the number of crimes not reported to the police, and in the case of sexual offenses, there are myriad reasons that a victim would not report a sexual crime to the authorities.

To overcome the methodological flaws of NIBRS, the second significant way in which sexual offenses are counted is the use of the National Crime Victimization Survey (NCVS). This is a national survey conducted annually of a randomly selected population to help assess the dark figure of sexual offenses and other types of crimes. Victimization studies involve participants self-reporting crimes that have impacted their lives over the previous twelve-month period. One potential disadvantage to this type of study is the possibility that participants may forget some incidents or may experience a problem with recollection of when an incident occurred, resulting in overreporting of a crime. Those completing a victimization survey are asked about the types of victimizations they have experienced as well as demographic characteristics about themselves and the alleged perpetrator involved in the offense. Victimization surveys indicate that most types of crime, including sexual offenses, are significantly underreported to the police, thus decreasing our understanding of the true prevalence of such offenses in society.

The third source of information regarding sexual offenses and offenders, though not nearly as common, are studies conducted by researchers. The UCR and victimization surveys are government studies that make up much of what we know about sexual offenses. There are, however, several other studies that have focused, for example, on the dynamics of sexual offending through in-depth interviews with sexual offenders or the experience of victimization through detailed analysis of sexual experiences. These studies typically involve detailed analysis of either the victim or the offender population.

CHILD SEXUAL ABUSE

By way of definition, noncontact sexual abuse may include sexual comments, voyeurism (watching), exhibition (showing) of one's genitals to a child, sexual harassment, and sexually related contact via the telephone or Internet. Contact sexual abuse may include touching or penetration (completed or attempted) or involvement of a minor in prostitution or pornography. Incest involves contact or noncontact sexual abuse of a child with whom the adult is related by blood or marriage. Statistically, the most frequently occurring incestuous relationship is between a father and daughter, with mother–child incest rarely reported.

"Pedophile" is a word used frequently in the media and has become synonymous with "child molester" of any type. Technically, however, this is incorrect. Pedophilia involves a sexual interest or desire in children who have not yet reached puberty and is extremely rare despite media reports to the contrary. "Hebephile" is the term used for those offenders sexually interested in individuals who have reached puberty and would commonly apply to most heterosexual men in America. While society views pedophiles as mentally deranged monsters, a reasonably high percentage of men in one study reported attraction to children. In a study of male undergraduates, 21 percent admitted a sexual attraction to children, 9 percent admitted to sexual fantasies involving children, 5 percent admitted to masturbating to sexual fantasies involving children, and 7 percent indicated they may engage in sexual activity with a child if they would not be apprehended and punished (Briere 1989). Statistically, pedophiles are typically male (Murray 2000), though recently in the media there have been some cases reported of females (specifically teachers) having sexual relations with minor boys (though these women are, more accurately, hebephiles because the boys have usually reached puberty). As a group, pedophiles usually are age specific (with about a four-year age span) and gender specific with their choice of victim.

Data regarding the prevalence of child sexual abuse comes from a variety of different sources, one of which is the National Child Abuse and Neglect Data System. The Department of Health and Human Services collects data from state child protective agencies and reports annually on child abuse, with separate data collected for child sexual abuse. In 2005, child protection workers investigated 83,810 cases involving sexual abuse, which is 9.3 percent of all cases investigated by child welfare workers (Administration on Children, Youth, and Families [ACYF] 2007). According to the report by the ACYF, almost all these cases were confirmed (ACYF 2007). Despite almost 83,600 cases of confirmed child sexual abuse in 2005 (ACYF 2007), this is a significant decline from the previous year. Between 1992 (estimated 150,000 cases) and 2000 (estimated 89,500 cases), the number of substantiated child sexual abuse cases decreased by 40 percent (Office of Juvenile Justice and Delinquency Prevention [OJJDP] 2004). This was after a period of increased sexual abuse substantiations from 1977 to 1992 (OJJDP 2001). This pattern of decline in child sexual abuse appears to be "real" and not a statistical fluke, as it was present in twenty-six states and is also replicated in victimization surveys (OJJDP 2001).

Analysis of NIBRS data from 1991 through 1996 revealed that 33 percent of sexual assaults reported to law enforcement involved a victim ages twelve through seventeen, and 34 percent of sexual assaults reported to law enforcement involved a victim under the age of twelve (Bureau of Justice Statistics [BJS] 2000). Of all sexual assault cases reported, juveniles accounted for 84 percent of forcible fondling reports, 79 percent of forcible sodomy reports, and 75 percent of reports of sexual assault involving an object. Of all sexual assault cases reported to law enforcement, 69 percent of victims under the age of six were female, 73 percent of victims under the age of twelve were female, and 82 percent of victims under the age of eighteen were female (BJS 2000). Of those sexually victimized under the age of six, 97 percent are victimized by a family member (Snyder 2000). Males made up 15 percent of those under the age of eighteen who were sexually assaulted with an object, 20 percent of those under the age of eighteen who were victims of forcible fondling, and 59 percent of those under the age of eighteen who were the victim of forcible sodomy. The NIBRS data revealed that a male's risk of victimization is greatest at age four and that a female's risk of victimization is greatest at age fourteen. In addition, rape of an individual prior to the age of eighteen is a significant variable in increasing one's likelihood of being sexually assaulted as an adult (BJS 2000). Although research has not fully elaborated why this is the case, factors such as low self-esteem or negative associates may play a role in further victimization.

Female Sexual Offenders

Overwhelmingly, sexual offenders are male, so little is known about the female sexual offender. Perhaps the most widely known study regarding female sex offenders was conducted in the 1980s using the National Incidence Study on child abuse and integrating it with two other surveys. Statistical estimates revealed that 5 percent of females and 20 percent of males were victimized by a female perpetrator (Finkelhor 1984). This remains, however, an extremely understudied area of research. Female-perpetrated sexual abuse could be underreported because these events disproportionately involve a familial victim, which is the least reported type of sexual violence (Travin, Cullen, and Protter 1990). In addition, women are involved in caretaking roles, which involve legitimate touching; therefore, there may be confusion over whether an abusive act occurred. Indeed, some sexually abusive acts may be "dismissed" as part of a routine of child care. Part of this explanation is tied to a larger cultural denial of a maternal figure as abusive. Investigations of women's perpetration of sexual abuse are three times as likely to be classified as "unfounded" as allegations of sexual abuse made against a male (Denov 2004):

> Socially, we, as a culture, find it particularly difficult to think that women would sexually abuse children. Our Judeo-Christian heritage places enormous emphasis on women as warm, nurturing mothers. Furthermore, we are, at best, culturally ambivalent about female sexuality. We struggle with the notion of women—particularly mothers—being sexual at all. (Larson and Maison 1987: 30)

The stereotype exists of the woman as a caregiver who would not intentionally harm a child. Add to this that teen male victims may be reluctant to define the incident as abusive but instead may define it as "sexual experimentation." Such incidents are portrayed in films such as *American Pie* (1999), where there were sexual encounters between adolescent boys and adult women (e.g., see Cavanagh 2005):

> Society romanticises and minimizes the impact female molesters have on their young male victims. If a boy discloses abuse, he may not be believed. If he physically enjoyed the molestation, he does not perceive himself as a victim, despite the fact that he may be suffering from the effects of abuse. Many will suggest that he should have enjoyed the experience. If he did not enjoy aspects of the abuse, he may fear that he is homosexual. Either way the young male victim of the older female is placed in an untenable position. (Mayer 1992: 49–50)

As a result of the lack of research in this area, care needs to taken in making any sort of generalizations based on these data, which often involve very small samples.

Mary Kay Letourneau has been dubbed in the press "America's Most Famous Pedophile," likely for being one of the first high-profile female sexual offenders. As a thirty-five-year-old schoolteacher, she had sexual relations with a sixth-grade student. When arrested, Letourneau was pregnant with the victim's child, and she pled guilty in 1997 to two counts of child rape in the second degree. She served 7.5 years in prison and, once released, married the boy she was convicted of sexually assaulting. In recent years, there have been a handful of similar female-teacher/male-student cases that have made prime-time news.

Female sexual offenders make up a small percentage of offenders: approximately 3 percent according to one study by the Correctional Service of Canada (1996) and 5 percent in another study (Grayston and DeLuca 1999). In Washington State, between 1985 and 1992, women made up a mere 1.6 percent of convicted sexual offenders (Song, Lieb, and Donnelly 1993). Over a ten-year period from 1987 to 1997, of all offenders referred to a psychiatric facility in South Carolina, only fifteen (1.57 percent) were women. In this study, twelve of the women reported a history of sexual abuse, ten of the women admitted to sexually abusing their own children, and the other five women admitted to molesting acquaintances. The victims in these cases ranged in age from two to seventeen, and a male codefendant was present in seven of the fifteen cases. The study found that offenders had low levels of education and were typically employed at a low-wage job (Lewis and Stanley 2000). Of note, however, this study was conducted on women referred to a psychiatric facility and should therefore not be generalized.

A common thread running through the research that has been conducted on female sexual offenders is that they have experienced a history of sexual abuse (Fehrenbach and Monastersky 1988; Lewis and Stanley 2000; Travin, Cullen, and Protter 1990). Another common thread is the presence of a co-offender who is typically male and is present in more than half of cases involving a female sexual offender (Grayston and DeLuca 1999), though recent research challenges this claim (Ferguson and Meehan 2005). In addition, many studies find that most victims are known to the offender (Vandiver and Walker 2002). Although a handful of researchers have attempted to classify female offenders into typologies, these typologies are not discussed here because the research is so sparse and so lacking in generalizability as to make the typologies next to meaningless.

We talk generally of female sexual offenders in terms of child sexual abuse because the notion of a female raping a male seems incomprehensible to many, though, to be clear, all states as of the year 2000 have gender-neutral language with regard to statutory rape laws, meaning that an adult female can be prosecuted for having sexual relations with a minor male. Conversely, if the male is eighteen years of age or older, several states have laws that do not even allow for the crime of rape to occur, including Idaho, Indiana, Maryland, Mississippi, and North Carolina. By way of example, Idaho provides that rape can be perpetrated only by a male against a female: "Rape is defined as the penetration, however slight, of the oral, anal or vaginal opening with the perpetrator's penis accomplished with a female under either of the following conditions" (Idaho Statutes 2003 11 § 18-6101). There is a separate statute for men who are raped; however, once again the perpetrator must be male: "Male rape is defined as the penetration, however slight, of the oral or anal opening of another male, with the perpetrator's penis, for the purpose of sexual arousal, gratification or abuse, under any of the following circumstances" (Idaho Statutes 2003 11 § 18-6108).

The complexity that accompanies disclosure of sexual assault seems to be magnified when the perpetrator is a woman, whom society still perceives to be relatively harmless and innocent sexually despite the high-profile media attention of a handful of female teachers in recent years. Even professionals are often ambivalent and dismissive as they must learn to deal with this underreported aspect of sexual offending.

INTERNET SEXUAL OFFENSES

Internet sexual offenses are a relatively new and burgeoning area of offending, and as such it is extremely difficult to estimate the number of individuals who fall victim to predators on the Internet. In addition, this is a widely underreported crime and difficult for law enforcement (and even parents) to detect. The Internet is used for a variety of sexual purposes including pornography (both adult and child), facilitating prostitution, and sites that cater to a variety of paraphilias with the expressed purpose of linking those with similar sexual preferences. The Internet also provides venues, such as chat rooms, where potential sexual offenders can meet potential victims. The Texas Office of the Attorney General (2001) suggests that sexual solicitation has happened to one in five young people online, though this is only an estimate.

Research suggests that individuals using the Internet for sexually predatory purposes are disturbed emotionally or psychologically and use this venue to avoid confrontation (Deirmenjian 1999; Quayle, Vaughn, and Taylor 2006). Increasingly we have become a detached, online society, and the anonymity of cyberspace provides an ideal atmosphere for sexual exploration and experimentation that could lead to manipulation or coercion. This may involve behavior such as that depicted in *Dateline*'s *To Catch a Predator* series wherein agents from Perverted Justice acted as young boys or girls in response to the expressed sexual interests of adults in chat rooms. Internet sexual offenses are a relatively new area for which law enforcement is just starting to garner the resources to deter predators in this arena. New laws are being enacted (as elaborated on in chapter 5) to prevent offenders from using the Internet for this purpose, and future studies will likely have better estimates of the amount of sexual abuse that begins online.

ADULT SEXUAL OFFENSES

Myths surrounding the sexual assault of women, called "rape myths," abound, fueling the underreporting of this crime. Myths are believed by both women and men and influence both reporting of these offenses as well as criminal justice responses. Such myths include the following: that "a woman who says no really means yes and eventually will give in," that "on some level women want to be raped," that "if a woman really wanted to defend herself against a rapist, she could," and that "many women lie about being raped because they regret having sex." Each of these myths serves to bring shame to the victim and therefore discourages a woman from reporting.

There are other reasons a woman may not report a sexual offense as well. She may feel embarrassed and not want others to know, or she may not understand that she was legally sexually assaulted, which may be especially true in the case of statutory rape (where an older man has sexual intercourse with a minor female). A victim may not want to allege abuse against someone she knows, or a victim may fear there is no "proof" of rape and therefore be less willing to report it to the authorities. The victim may fear the response of police or the ordeal of an investigation by the criminal justice system or might fear retribution by the offender. Or an individual may not want the stigma associated with being labeled a rape victim. For these reasons or a variety of other personal reasons, this remains an underreported crime.

Adult sexual offenses include sexual assault or rape by a stranger, acquaintance, date, spouse, or rape that occurs in jail or prison. This may include completed or attempted rape, completed or attempted sexual coercion, or completed or attempted sexual contact. The UCR (2007) measures discussed here define forcible rape as "the carnal knowledge of a female forcibly and against her will . . . assaults and attempts to commit rape by force or threat of force are also included; however, statutory rape (without force) and other sex offenses are excluded." Table 6.1 provides the number of forcible rapes and the forcible rape rate per 100,000 female inhabitants over a period extending from 1987 to 2006. From this representation, a decline beginning in 1992 and extending to 2006 is apparent. There is some regional variation, with 38.6 percent of all forcible rapes occurring in the South, 25.4 percent in the Midwest, 23.9 percent in the West, and 12.2 percent in the Northeast (UCR 2007).

Another very useful source of data is the victimization survey. The most recent victimization survey revealed that there were 209,880 rapes or sexual assaults in 2004 (BJS 2006). Of these, 30 percent of sexual assaults and

Chapter 6

Table 6.1.   Forcible Rapes in the United States, 1987–2006

Year	Number of Forcible Rapes	Forcible Rape Rate per 100,000 Female Inhabitants
1987	91,111	37.6
1988	92,486	37.8
1989	94,504	38.3
1990	102,555	41.1
1991	106,593	42.3
1992	109,062	42.8
1993	106,014	41.1
1994	102,216	39.3
1995	97,470	37.1
1996	96,252	36.3
1997	96,153	35.9
1998	93,144	34.5
1999	89,411	32.8
2000	90,178	32.0
2001	90,863	31.8
2002	95,235	33.1
2003	93,883	32.3
2004	95,089	32.4
2005	94,347	31.8
2006	92,455	30.9

Source: Uniform Crime Report (2007).

42 percent of rapes/attempted rapes were reported to the police for a total of 70,700 incidents reported to the law enforcement. The data indicated that 44 percent of whites assaulted reported the crime to the authorities, in comparison to only 17 percent of blacks. Reporting also varied by age, with those ages thirty-five to forty-nine most likely to report an assault (BJS 2006). The survey inquired as to why a woman would not report a rape or sexual assault, with 22 percent indicating the reason was because it was a private matter and an additional 18 percent suggesting that they reported the incident to another official. Of those who did report the crime to the police, 17 percent chose to do so in order to prevent the offender from committing a future offense (BJS 2006).

In most of the cases (65 percent), the offender was known to the victim. In all reported rape/sexual assault cases of a black victim, the offender was also black. When the victim was white, 45 percent of offenders were white, 34 percent were black, and 20 percent were of another race. Regardless of the race of the victim, 33 percent of offenders were white, 49 percent were black, and 15 percent were of another race. Overwhelmingly (83 percent of the time), there was a single offender. In approximately one-quarter of the incidents (26 percent), the offender was believed to be under twenty-one, about one-quarter of the time the offender was perceived to be between twenty-one and twenty-nine, and about half the time the offender was believed to be over the age of thirty (BJS 2006). In cases with more than one offender, 72 percent of the time, the offenders were believed to be under the age of twenty-one. In 98 percent of the cases, the offender was male. In only 36 percent of cases did the victim perceive the offender to be under the influence of alcohol and/or drugs, and in 85 percent of cases, there was no weapon used (BJS 2006).

Because so few rapes are reported, statistics reveal a very skewed picture of the typical victim. Table 6.2 provides victim demographic information from victimization surveys. Studies reveal that though sexual assault can cross all race and class lines, the most typical victimization is of someone from an economically depressed household (with an income of less than $7,500 per year), an individual who is separated or divorced, or an individual who lives in an urban area in the Southeast region of the United States (BJS 2005). Keep in mind, however, that the offenses most likely to be reported (approximately 75 percent of victims report stranger rapes) are not the offenses most likely to occur (65 percent of offenders know their victim) (BJS 2006; Holmes and Holmes 2009).

OFFENDER PROFILE AND INCARCERATION RATES

Just as the "typical victim" is not the one described by the UCR data reported by law enforcement, we must be cautious in suggesting that the "typical offender" is the one reported to the authorities or the one imprisoned. Studies reveal that the type of offense most likely to be reported is one committed by a stranger and one involving violence; thus, it stands to reason that the offenders in prison should be those who committed offenses against strangers and those who used higher levels of violence than is "typical." As such, we cannot make generalizations from these data about the "average" or "typical" sexual offender who has not been caught, reported, or prosecuted.

Most studies show that the sexual offender who has been brought to the attention of the authorities is male (98.6 percent) and about 65 percent of the time is white (for forcible rape; in the case of other sexual offenses, the offender is white 73 percent of the time). In addition, the offender is usually over the age of twenty-four (UCR 2007). Approximately 40 percent of all rapes reported to the police result in an arrest, and juveniles account for only 15 percent of forcible rape arrests, as indicated in Table 6.3 (UCR 2007).

Of the total 14,380,370 arrests in 2006, 24,535 were for forcible rape, and 87,252 were for other sexual offenses (not including prostitution) (UCR

Table 6.2.   Demographic Characteristics of Rape/Sexual Assault Victims, 2005

Demographic	Victimizations per 1,000 Persons Ages 12 and Older
Gender	
Male	0.1
Female	1.4
Race	
White	0.6
Black	1.8
Other	0.5
Hispanic origin	
Hispanic	1.1
Non-Hispanic	0.7
Age	
12–15	1.2
16–19	3.2
20–24	1.1
25–34	0.7
35–49	0.6
50–64	0.6
65 or older	0.0
Household income	
Less than $7,500	2.2
$7,500–$14,999	0.6
$15,000–$24,999	1.4
$25,000–$34,999	1.7
$35,000–$49,999	0.9
$50,000–$74,999	0.5
$75,000 or more	0.6
Marital status	
Never married	1.4
Married	0.2
Divorced/separated	1.5
Widowed	0.8
Location of residence	
Urban	1.5
Suburban	0.7
Rural	0.1

Source: Bureau of Justice Statistics (2006).

2007). As of 2004, there were 59,700 prisoners sentenced under state juris-diction for rape and 94,100 for other sexual assaults (UCR 2007). Most sexual offenders imprisoned have victimized someone they did not know despite the fact that most victims are assaulted by someone they know (BJS 1997). Of those arrested for child sexual abuse, most admit to previous molestation of children for which they were never arrested (Petrosino and Petrosino 1999).

Table 6.3. Arrest Percentages by Age for Forcible Rape and Other Sexual Offenses, 2006

Age	% of Total Arrested for Forcible Rape	% of Total Arrested for Other Sexual Offenses
Under 18	15	18
18–20	15	11
21–24	15	11
25–29	14	11
30–34	11	9
35–39	11	10
40–44	8	10
45–49	6	7
50–54	3	5
55–59	2	3
60–64	1	2
65 and over	1	2

Source: Uniform Crime Report (2007).

Once brought to the attention of the authorities, approximately half of those charged with rape are released pending trial, with about half of these individuals required to post a monetary bond. About 80 percent of offenders pled guilty, and slightly more than two-thirds received a prison sentence (BJS 1997). In comparison to the total prison population, sexual offenders make up less than 5 percent of the total correctional population in the United States. In addition, despite the link between serious violence and sexual offenses in the media, less than 2 percent of murder cases involve rape or another sexual offense (BJS 1997).

A significant number of offenders receive a community sentence. Approximately 234,000 convicted sexual offenders each day are under the care of correctional authorities, with about 60 percent of these offenders under community supervision (BJS 1997). Of state prisoners incarcerated for sexual assault, two-thirds report having a victim under the age of eighteen, and 58 percent of these offenders report having a victim twelve years of age or younger (BJS 1997). The average sentence is almost fourteen years, with approximately 2 percent of those convicted of rape serving a life sentence (BJS 1997). From 1993 to 2002, the number of sexual offenders incarcerated has increased by 74 percent, while the overall state prison population has experienced only a 49 percent increase (Lucken and Bales 2008).

Some states have what is called Special Sex Offender Sentencing Alternatives (SSOSAs), which are used very selectively. These permit a suspended sentence and require treatment for qualified offenders. In order for an offender to qualify, he must have no prior record of sexual offenses and must not be charged with a sexual offense involving violence. In addition, these types of sentences are usually used in cases in which there is a relationship between the offender and the victim. This type of sentence is designed to benefit both the community and the offender but is sparingly approved by the courts (Sentencing Guidelines Commission 2004).

Washington State reviewed its sentencing laws with regard to sexual offenses in 2004 in response to a legislative mandate. In 2003 there were 27,213 felony sentences imposed, and 1,403 involved sexual offenses, which was consistent with the national average of about 5 percent. In 2003 in Washington State, the average length of sentence for all felonies was 37.3 months, and the average length of sentence for sexual offenses was 90.8 months. Only murder had an average sentence length longer than sexual offenses. Therefore, states are not very willing to impose community sentences, despite their availability. In Washington State in 2003, SSOSAs were used for only 207 of 857 eligible offenders (Sentencing Guidelines Commission 2004).

Juvenile Sexual Offenders

Recall from the UCR (2007) mentioned earlier that 15 percent of those arrested for forcible rape in 2006 were under the age of eighteen and that 18 percent of those arrested for other sexual offenses were under the age of eighteen. Problematic is that it can be difficult to separate normal childhood sexual exploration among peers from sexual offending. Finkelhor (1980) estimated sibling sexual abuse at about 13 percent of the population, yet this type of offense is rarely reported, as it is perceived as youthful experimentation. Just like with knowledge regarding the female sex offender population, knowledge regarding juvenile offenders is limited both because of their relatively small numbers and because of limited research in this area. As such, great care needs to be taken in making generalizations. The theoretical perspectives discussed earlier cannot be adequately applied to juvenile offenders because such offenders vary dramatically from adults in level of maturity, development, and understanding of issues of sexuality.

In one study only 4 percent of youth arrested for a sex crime recidivated. Research also indicates that most adult offenders were not formerly youth offenders: less than 10 percent of adults who commited sex offenses had been juvenile sex offenders. Applying registration, community notification, and residency restriction laws to juvenile offenders does nothing to prevent crimes by the 90 percent of adults who were not convicted of sex offenses as juveniles. It will, however, cause great harm to those who, while they are young, must endure the stigma of being identified as and labeled a sex offender, and who as adults will continue to bear that stigma, sometimes for the rest of their lives. (Human Rights Watch 2007: 9)

Research finds some of the same characteristics in juvenile sex offenders as in adults, such as lowered self-esteem, poorly developed social skills, difficulty forming attachments, family problems, and substance abuse issues (Epps 1999). Not all research supports Epps's findings, but most research finds these characteristics more frequently in juvenile sexual offenders compared to other, nonoffending populations. A significant study of juvenile offenders conducted by the National Adolescent Perpetrator Network (NAPN) and spanning thirty states found that 90 percent of offenders are male—most having committed other, nonsexual offenses, with only 7 percent committing exclusively sexual offenses—and that 96 percent of the time the victim is also a juvenile. In addition, 90 percent of the victims are known to the offender, 39 percent are related by blood, the average number of victims per offender is 7.7, and many juvenile offenders have experienced both physical and sexual abuse during childhood and adolescence (NAPN 1993).

Because research on juvenile sexual offenders is in its infancy, there are many contradictory findings, and therefore much research has yet to be accomplished before determining patterns in juvenile offending, motivations, and the proper treatment methods. Because of the early nature of this research, a debate exists as to whether we are dealing with "children at risk" or "risky children." That is, are juvenile sexual offenders the "risky children" who are going to grow up to be the monstrous predators portrayed by the media, or are they "children at risk" acting out as a result of social problems that are occurring at home and in their neighborhoods, such as domestic violence or substance abuse? Despite not really knowing a lot about the juvenile sex offender population, there are more than 800 treatment programs geared to juvenile offenders across the country, and juveniles are forced into many of the same legislative rules as adult sexual offenders, such as registration and community notification, in more than half the states that have these laws. This means succumbing to the stigma of a "sexual offender" label for an act they may have committed when they were twelve or thirteen years of age.

RECIDIVISM RATES

Studies vary dramatically in findings regarding recidivism of sexual offenders for a variety of reasons, most notably a varied methodological design. Researchers do not use a consistent period of measurement (obviously, the longer the period of study, the higher the rate of recidivism), some studies count only new sexual offenses as recidivism, other studies count any offense, and some studies measure technical violations (e.g., failure to notify a change of address within the specified time limit) as recidivating, while other studies do not. In addition, how do we measure who committed another offense? Do we rely on self-reports, do we use arrest data or conviction data, or do we consider the offender a recidivist only if he is incarcerated? All these questions affect how a researcher "measures" or "counts" recidivism and therefore how high the recidivism rate is in a study. To add to the complexity of the issue is the already mentioned problem that sexual offending is underreported—whether it is a first or a second offense, it is underreported.

What is clear is that the public believes that sex offenders have a much higher recidivism rate than they actually do regardless of which level of measurement we use. A study was conducted in Florida a mere six months after Jessica Lunsford and Sarah Lunde were murdered inquiring about public perceptions regarding sexual offenders. Participants in the study estimated sexual offender recidivism at approximately 75 percent and suggested that this was the group of criminals who were most likely to reoffend (Levenson et al. 2007). This indeed is not the case.

In a 2000 study using a population of sexual offenders on probation and a follow-up period of almost five years, a rearrest rate of 35 percent was found for nonsexual offenses, and a 5.6 percent rearrest rate was found for sexual offenses (Kruttschnitt, Uggen, and Shelton 2000). A study using a three-year follow-up period found a rearrest rate for nonsexual offenses of 43 percent and a rearrest rate for sexual offenses of 5 percent (BJS 2003). Some studies have found slightly higher rates of recidivism, ranging from 9 percent (Zgoba and Simon 2005) to 12 percent (Meloy 2006). In a 2004 meta-analysis of sex offenders found guilty and/or incarcerated, Harris and Hanson found an average recidivism rate of 24 percent over a fifteen-year period (Webster, Gartner, and Doob 2006). Research has revealed that not all types of sexual offenders have similar rates of recidivism and that offenders who have experienced sexual victimization themselves during childhood have higher rates of recidivism (Meloy 2006). Sexual offenders whose victims are adult women typically have the highest rates of recidivism at approximately 40 percent (Snyder 2000), whereas heterosexual offenders with a child victim in the family have the lowest rates of recidivism at approximately 3 percent. Other research has found that rapists reoffend in a shorter time frame after release from prison in comparison to child offenders (Furby, Weinrott, and Blackshaw 1989; Quinsey, Rice, and Harris 1995); however, child offenders have a higher likelihood of eventually reoffending than rapists (Lussier, LeBlanc, and Proulx 2005; Prentky et al. 1997).

When examining the effect of treatment on recidivism, a meta-analysis of forty-three studies in Canada, the United States, and Britain found that recidivism rates over a four-year period were approximately 12 percent for treated and 17 percent for untreated offenders. Further, over a five-year period, recidivism ranged from 10 to 15 percent, depending on the type of treatment provided and whether the participants completed therapy (Hanson et al. 2002). A study of more than 23,000 sexual offenders found that the best factors determining recidivism are sexual "deviancy" and not general criminological factors (Stadtland et al. 2005). How sexual deviancy is defined varies substantially between studies and can include any behavior not presently deemed culturally acceptable. This definition leads to obvious problems when analyzing studies from different countries, as culturally sanctioned or acceptable behavior varies greatly according to culture, religious affiliation, political structure, and the ethnic composition of society.

In Washington State and in many other states with sexually violent predator legislation, the department of corrections can make a referral for sexual predators who meet the requirements for commitment. For individuals who meet the requirements, it is then up to the attorney general's office to decide whether to file a petition to seek to have the offender committed under this legislation. One study involved a six-year follow-up of 135 sexual offenders who met the requirements under legislation regarding sexually violent predators but for whom no petition was filed by the attorney general's office and the individuals were therefore released. Twenty-three percent of the men were convicted of a new felony offense of a sexual nature (29 percent of these recidivists had participated in the treatment program available in the prison facility), 10 percent were convicted of a new felony offense of a nonsexual nature, and 19 percent were convicted for failure to register as a sexual offender. In this study, age had a significant impact on sexual reoffending with the youngest age-group at the highest risk. Interestingly, none of the offenders who were over the age of fifty had committed another sexual offense, and this would be explained nicely by life course theory (Washington State Institute for Public Policy 2007b).

What is clear in the research is that the longer individuals remain in the community offense free, the less likely it is they are going to recidivate (BJS 2003). In addition, there are a variety of factors that can reduce sexual recidivism, such as community-based treatment, intensive supervision programs, broad-based community notification for tier 3 offenders (Duwe and Donnay 2008), participation in Circles of Support and Accountability (Wilson, Picheca, and Prinzo 2005), and the reduction of transience. Simply releasing sexual offenders into the community after serving a sentence without proper reintegration skills is setting them up for reoffending and ensuring that sexual offending remains an element with which society must perpetually contend.

7

Controlling Offenders

In an interview with Human Rights Watch, one law enforcement official reported, "The expansion of state sex offender registries to include more offenses and longer registration periods has really compromised our ability to monitor high-risk sex offenders." (Human Rights Watch 2007: 45)

The level and types of controls placed on an offender revolve around the likelihood of his recidivating. Many types of sexual offenders have very low rates of reoffending; however, the identification of those offenders at a high risk of reoffending is an extremely difficult but important goal of the criminal justice system. Recall from chapter 2 the types of assessment instruments used to predict recidivism. Utilizing these techniques, states that use a tier system to assess risk place offenders into one of three categories. Tier 3 offenders are deemed at high risk to the public, tier 2 offenders are deemed at moderate risk to the public, and tier 1 offenders are deemed to be the lowest risk to the public. Assessment of risk of offenders impacts sentencing options and alternatives, the tier to which they are assigned, community notification and registration procedures, residency restrictions, and the likelihood that treatment will be successful in diminishing their risk of future offenses. Assessment of risk is also used to determine whether an offender will be released or civilly committed. This chapter elaborates on controls on sexual offenders through awareness programs such as community notification and registration programs, through community management policies such as residency restrictions, and through civil commitment legislation. Another method of community management—and one that is often mandated by the criminal justice system—is treatment; however, because of the various types of treatment and history of treatment, this is given separate coverage in chapter 9.

CONTROL OF SEXUAL OFFENDERS THROUGH AWARENESS

Recall from chapter 5 that in 1989, an eleven-year-old boy named Jacob Wetterling was abducted by a stranger near his home in Minnesota. Because a halfway house for recently released sex offenders was located nearby, there was speculation that someone from that facility had something to do with Jacob's disappearance. Jacob's parents became activists for children, and several years later a federal law called the Jacob Wetterling Crimes Against Children and Sexually Violent Offender Registration Act was named in honor of Jacob Wetterling. Jacob's mother, Patty, now has the following response to broad-based community notification policies:

> I based my support of broad-based community notification laws on my assumption that sex offenders have the highest recidivism rates of any criminal. But the high recidivism rates I assumed to be true do not exist. It has made me rethink the value of broad-based community notification laws, which operate on the assumption that most sex offenders are high-risk dangers to the community they are released into. (Human Rights Watch 2007: 4)

Community Notifications and Registration Programs

As a reminder, community notification and registration laws first occurred in 1990 in Washington State but became widespread later in the 1990s after the sexual assault and murder of Megan Kanka in New Jersey. In response, registration and community notification legislation, referred to commonly as "Megan's Law," for sexual offenders was passed, becoming the guideline all other states and the federal government eventually followed (by 1998). This law requires sex offenders (in many states even juvenile sex offenders) to register with the police and in many states requires officials to notify communities when a sex offender perceived to be dangerous moves into the neighborhood. In 2006, on the twenty-fifth anniversary of the abduction of Adam Walsh, the Adam Walsh Act was signed into law, organizing sexual offenders into three tiers. This act also indicated that offenders were committing a felony if they failed to register and update their information with law enforcement, the frequency of which depended on their tier assignment. Tier 1 offenders are required to update their whereabouts every year for fifteen years, tier 2 offenders are required to do so every six months for twenty-five years, and tier 3 offenders are required to update their whereabouts with law enforcement every three months for life. In order to ensure compliance with registration, some states, such as Illinois, Kansas, Oklahoma, and Utah, are involving the department of motor vehicles and mandating a one-year expiration date on a sex offender's driver's license in order to keep track of changes in residence.

Australia, Canada, France, Ireland, Japan, and the United Kingdom each have registration laws for sexual offenders; however, they vary widely from that of the United States. The only country with a similar system of notification laws is South Korea. In Canada, the Corrections and Conditional Release Act requires that the Correctional Service of Canada notify the appropriate law enforcement personnel on the release of a sexual offender. The law then varies at the provincial level regarding distribution of this information to the public; however, disclosure is always at the discretion of the police. The Canadian government also maintains a National Sex Offender Registry to provide law enforcement access to information regarding convicted offenders; however, the public does not have access to this registry (Human Rights Watch 2007).

The registration with law enforcement is not the part of the law that is controversial; rather, it is the public notification aspect. Who has the right to be notified? Why are communities notified when a sexual offender moves into the neighborhood but not a murderer, someone who has been convicted of drunk driving, or someone who has been convicted of selling drugs to children? There is wide discrepancy from state to state regarding who has the right to know, and the ten states that use a tier classification system for offenders have a more "objective" system of notification than the states that do not use a tier classification system. There are varying degrees of information about the offender available to the public, and there are varied methods by which this information is delivered, be it by media release, door-to-door distribution of information by law enforcement, letters mailed to residents, registration lists, websites, or town hall meetings. Some of these methods require citizens to search out information on their own (websites or registration lists) and therefore afford the offender more privacy, whereas others are extremely broad and make privacy and community reintegration for the offender very difficult (media release, door-to-door distribution, or letters to residents). The impact of these policies on community safety and the likelihood of the individual reoffending are discussed later in this section.

By way of example, Minnesota uses a tier classification system and uses law enforcement personnel to release information to the public regarding sexual offenders at the highest tiers (Zevitz and Farkas 2000a). Notification regarding tier 1 offenders (who are the lowest-level offenders) is only to the victims of the crime and any witnesses, law enforcement agencies in the region, and anyone else deemed relevant by the prosecutor's office. By way of example, "In many states, people who urinate in public, teenagers who have consensual sex with each other, adults who sell sex to other adults, and kids who expose themselves as a prank are required to register as sex offenders" (Human Rights Watch 2007: 5). Tier 2 notification includes all individuals listed for tier 1 offenders as well as day care facilities, schools, and any other organizations where there are potential victims of the offender in question. Notification of tier 3 offenders is broad based and public and includes revealing the offender's residence. This usually occurs by way of a town hall meeting as well as distributing information via media release and posting information on the website of the Minnesota Department of Corrections for access by the public at a later date. Some states include additional labeling procedures to identify sexual offenders. For example, Delaware, Alabama, and West Virginia require offenders to have a recognizable designation on their driver's license indicating that they have been convicted of a sexual offense. Other states have been more creative in trying to "identify" sex offenders. Ohio attempted to pass a law requiring convicted sex offenders to have a fluorescent license plate, and though this was supported by much of the public, it seemed to die in the legislative halls, never to be heard from again.

In Alabama, if you are an adult convicted of soliciting an adult prostitute, you will be required to register as a sexual offender for life, with no possible way of petitioning the state to be removed from the sex offender registry (Human Rights Watch 2007).

The registry aspect of these laws also varies by state, though compliance with the Adam Walsh Act should put all states in line with one unified system by the end of July 2009. Most online sex offender registries list the victim's age at the time of the offense (e.g., female victim, age fourteen); however, many update the offender's age each year (e.g., male offender age thirty-six now, but the website does not indicate that he was nineteen when the offense occurred), which can be extremely misleading, especially in the case of statutory offenses. In addition, most states list the statute or cite from the statute, making it very difficult for the average citizen to understand. User-friendly, easy-to-understand registries were found in Alabama, Minnesota, New Jersey, North Dakota, and South

Dakota. Studies have found that the clearer the registry is, the less likely there will be confusion by the person who is searching the statute and therefore the less likely there will be further difficulty for the offender to reintegrate into the community.

Much of the public (including Megan Kanka's mother and former Attorney General Janet Reno) view notification and registration laws as paramount to protecting children from sexual victimization. According to survey research conducted in Washington State, the public is overwhelmingly familiar with notification laws (81 percent). In fact, 63 percent believe that such laws encourage released offenders to abide by the law, and 78 percent feel a greater sense of safety knowing the whereabouts of sexual offenders. In this same study, 84 percent of the participants felt that notification laws may make reintegration into the community more difficult for sexual offenders yet support these laws anyway (Lieb and Nunlist 2008). Another study was conducted in Florida a mere six months after Jessica Lunsford and Sarah Lunde were murdered inquiring about public perceptions regarding sexual offenders and community notification policies. In this study, 95 percent of those surveyed believed that the public should be informed of the name of a sexual offender and be provided with a photo, and 85 percent believed that a home address should also be provided. Approximately 76 percent supported this policy for all sexual offenders, regardless of the seriousness of the individual's offense. Of participants in this study, 83 percent felt that community notification was effective in reducing sexual violence, though 73 percent either partially or completely agreed that they would support such a policy even without scientific evidence demonstrating that it reduced sexual abuse (Levenson et al. 2007). So these are policies that have demonstrated widespread public appeal even if the public recognizes that the policies may impede the reintegration of offenders into the community and even if there is no "proof" that it will make communities safer. Having these policies in place for *all* offenders, regardless of the seriousness of the offense, makes people *feel* safer from stranger danger, yet it has been proven that statistically most sexual offenders are individuals *known* to the victim, not strangers.

Released offenders, however, have challenged the constitutionality of community notification laws in two U.S. Supreme Court cases. In the first, the question dealt with the Fifth Amendment double-jeopardy clause and whether registration and notification laws constitute a second punishment. In *Smith v. Doe* (2003), the Supreme Court ruled that the law is regulatory and is not therefore a second punishment. As well, it does not violate the ex post facto clause of the Constitution, meaning that even offenders who were convicted of a sexual offense *prior* to the establishment of a registration and notification law can still be required to comply with these laws. Therefore, registration and community notification laws are constitutional despite the recognized harm that results for the individual, as indicated by Supreme Court Justice Clarence Thomas:

> Widespread dissemination of offenders' names, photographs, addresses, and criminal history serves not only to inform the public but also to humiliate and ostracize the convicts. It thus bears some resemblance to shaming punishments that were used earlier in our history to disable offenders from living normally in the community. While the [majority of] the State's explanation that the Act simply makes public information available in a new way, the scheme does much more. Its point, after all, is to send a message that probably would not otherwise be heard, by selecting some conviction information out of its corpus of penal records and broadcasting it with a warning. Selection makes a statement, one that affects common reputation and sometimes carries harsher consequences, such as exclusion from jobs or housing, harassment, and physical harm. (*Smith v. Doe* [2003])

Justice Thomas points out some of the negative consequences of community notification laws that will be elaborated on later.

"In Louisiana, in addition to the state's right to notify the community, a child sex offender on probation or parole is required to notify his neighbors personally of his address and criminal record. If he lives in a city, he must, at his own expense, mail a notification to all of his neighbors living within a one-mile radius of his home, and he must take out a classified advertisement in the local newspaper and register with local school superintendents. A judge may also force the offender to wear special clothing or post signs on his home or bumper stickers on his car labeling him as a sex offender" (Earl-Hubbard 1996: 810–11).

The second Supreme Court case addressed the issue of cruel and unusual or excessive punishment. In *Connecticut Department of Public Safety v. John Doe* (2003), the Supreme Court ruled that the posting of photographs of convicted sexual offenders online is constitutional, as these laws were not deemed a barrier to an individual's personal freedom. Since 2003, courts at the state level have upheld these laws, and the Supreme Court has refused to hear any further cases addressing the constitutionality of sexual offender legislation.

Although these types of laws may empower community members, they may also serve to produce a perpetual sense of fear in the public. As for the offender, such laws may decrease the possibility of community reintegration because of the labeling effect, which may make it difficult to secure housing, employment, and other opportunities, and undermine their rehabilitative and treatment efforts. In addition, these laws are extremely expensive for law enforcement. One unforeseen consequence of notification laws is that some offenders are able to plead guilty to other offenses as part of a plea negotiation, which would allow them to avoid registering as a sexual offender. One such offender indicated, "For me, the most important thing, even more important than doing time in jail was avoiding the sex offender label. They are seen as the scum of the earth and I wanted nothing to do with that label. I don't want people seeing me that way" (Meloy 2006: 81). This example is also illustrative of the incomplete nature of sexual offender registration lists. This particular individual committed a sexual offense but, because of the plea agreement, will never be classified with similar offenders. However, the overarching question becomes, do these laws work?

A twelve-year-old neurologically impaired boy who admitted to sexually touching his eight-year-old stepbrother will have to register as a sexual offender for fifteen years according to a New Jersey court. The boy was sentenced to a suspended term at a youth facility and three years of probation and currently resides at home ("New Jersey Court Says 12-Year-Old Must Register as a Sexual Offender" 1996).

Do These Laws Work?

If offenders have difficulty reintegrating and if law enforcement spends more time and money ensuring that offenders comply with registration and notifying the public of an offender's whereabouts, this would all be worthwhile if these laws significantly reduce the recidivism of sexual offenders, right? These laws were designed under the assumption that they were going to increase public knowledge, which was going to increase public safety. Even Megan Kanka's mother said, "We knew nothing about him. If we had been aware . . . my daughter would be alive today" (Human Rights Watch 2007: 47). So has knowledge made society safer?

From the perspective of the offender, the answer is a resounding "no." Seventy-five percent of sexual offenders interviewed in one study (Meloy 2006) suggested that community notification would not be a deterrent to recidivating, and most offenders indicated that they perceived the law as unfair. But what does the research reveal about the relationship between community notification laws and recidivism rates? A study in California in 1988 found that these laws made it easier to find and apprehend an individual suspected of a sexual offense because the police had offender address information on file; however, the research did not find any influence on recidivism rates (Lewis 1988). Several studies in later years in other states also found no significant reduction in sexual recidivism rates against either children or adult women due to community notification laws (Adkins, Huff, and Stageberg 2000; Schram and Milloy 1995; Vasquez, Maddan, and Walker 2008). Another study, however, employing more statistical control and advanced analysis, conducted on data from the states of Washington and Wisconsin, both with tiered systems of risk management for sex offenders, found some reduction in sexual recidivism from community notification (Barnoski 2005; Zevitz and Farkas 2000a). In addition, a recent study in Minnesota found that broad community notification for the most serious sexual offenders (tier 3 offenders) was effective in significantly reducing sexual recidivism over an average eight-year period. The offenders in this study on release were placed on intensive supervision, so it was not entirely clear whether it was the community notification or the intense oversight that impacted the lowered recidivism rate. As the authors indicated,

> For offenders on ISR [intensive supervision], the increased surveillance that results from broad community notification likely creates a more rigorous version of ISR in that both community members and supervision agents can closely monitor the offender . . . level 3 sex offenders may be aware they are subject to constant scrutiny, but they cannot confirm whether they are, in fact, being observed at all times. As such, these offenders may ultimately internalize the perception of constant surveillance by monitoring their own behavior. In deterring—or at least delaying—sexual recidivism, what may be important is not that sex offenders are actually being monitored at all times, only that they think they are. (Duwe and Donnay 2008: 442)

The major limitation to research regarding whether community notification programs are effective in reducing sex crimes is that these studies are unsure what aspect of the notification process actually reduces sexual offending. That is, current studies cannot control for the role of intensive supervision that normally accompanies broad-based notification, and studies cannot control for the community treatment of offenders that also normally accompanies those individuals who are required to register as a tier 3 offender. These are serious limitations that must be examined, as it is entirely possible that community notification has no impact on sexual recidivism at all (as many early studies indicate), and it is either treatment or intensive supervision (or the combination of these two factors) that decreases the likelihood of an offender recidivating.

Effects on Community Reintegration

Research remains unclear about the positive impacts of community notification laws in terms of decreased recidivism. We know that these policies increase feelings of public safety, but what are the effects of these laws on the lives of the offenders? Years of criminological literature reveals that the factors that encourage continued desistance from offending include integration or reintegration into the community, management of individual stress, and establishment of a stable lifestyle. This means that the offender must find a community with supportive friends and/or family, a stable place of employment and residence, and develop appropriate social relationships. Obviously, broad-based community notification policies can hinder all aspects of reintegration for an offender trying to reestablish a life. Recall from chapter 3 the discussion of social reaction theory, which suggests that some people are labeled negatively by the larger society or those in the criminal justice system. Social reaction theory argues that this process of negative labeling results in the individual being shunned and treated differently by conventional society, which may serve to increase his likelihood of recidivism.

Once community members find out that a sex offender has moved into the neighborhood, regardless of his offense, he is at a decreased likelihood to form a significant relationship or friendships; will have more difficulty finding employment, which is often the hallmark of successful community reintegration; will have difficulty locating housing; and will likely experience increased feelings of societal detachment. One male offender who was convicted of criminal sexual abuse and kidnapping of a minor suggested, "Community notification can be a real problem for sex offenders. We learn about 'red flags' in treatment. These are the things that can set a sex offender off and make him offend again" (Meloy 2006: 87).

Offenders may also experience harassment by community members who may not have all the facts of the case. Although the Supreme Court in *Doe v. Poritz* suggested that this would not be a problem and that the public would act responsibly with the information obtained from such laws, a smattering of vigilante cases have occurred across the country. Studies suggest that about one-quarter of offenders report being the victim of some sort of vigilante justice (Bedarf 1995), and approximately 40 percent worry about being the victim of harassment (Meloy 2006). One offender indicated, "One day after I registered I got this note in the mail. It was my name, address, and my charge highlighted and downloaded off the Internet. The note said 'I'm watching you.' It scared the hell out of me" (Meloy 2006: 86). Another offender suggested,

> Registration ain't all bad, know what I'm saying. But, there are a lot of nuts out there so you got to be real careful. That's why a lot of ex-offenders don't

register because they don't want people to know who they are and come kill them or burn down their house or something, know what I'm saying? And now that I got to register I am on the Internet for ten years. My picture is on the Internet for ten years. I don't want nothing bad to happen to me, but I am afraid that registering on the Internet will make something bad happen so that's why a lot of guys don't even register. They're afraid. (Meloy 2006: 87)

Because of harassment and the resulting stigma, offenders may decide to move to a different location and decide not to register with law enforcement. This will negatively impact the accuracy of registration lists and put extra work on law enforcement personnel. A study in Tennessee revealed movement without follow-up registration by 28 percent of convicted sexual offenders (Finn 1997), and nationwide estimates of compliance with registration guidelines range from 25 to 54 percent (Avrahamian 1998).

In interviews conducted with 239 sexual offenders residing in Connecticut and Indiana, researchers found both positive and negative results of notification laws. Almost 75 percent of participants admitted that they were more motivated to stay offense free to "prove something" to others, approximately one-third believed that neighborhoods were more safe, and about the same number felt that being watched by neighbors helped them decrease their risk of reoffending. Conversely, there were many negative results as well. A significant percentage of the offenders felt stressed, avoided various activities as a result of notification, felt isolated from the community, felt decreased hope regarding the future, or feared for their safety. In fact, 10 percent of those interviewed in the study had experienced a physical assault or injury that they attributed to the notification. In addition, approximately 20 percent of offenders indicated loss of employment due to notification (Levenson, D'Amora, and Hern 2007).

These laws are geared toward stranger offenders, as community notification of family offenders would target not only the offender but the victim as well. As such, while the public may *feel* safer, these laws are not protecting society from the most common type of sexual victimization, which is the known offender. A major difficulty with notification laws is that there is no scientific evidence to suggest that these laws significantly reduce recidivism rates for tier 1 or tier 2 sexual offenders, but there is scientific evidence to suggest that these laws make community reintegration of offenders of these tiers more difficult. The safety the public feels from the implementation of these laws is false because it "protects" against a very small percentage of sexual offenses. In addition, adding all sexual offenders to a registration list and notifying the public of all sexual offenders makes it next to impossible for law enforcement officials to keep track of everyone. In 2003, the state of California admitted to "losing" approximately 33,000 convicted sexual offenders (Human Rights Watch 2007), amounting to 44 percent of individuals who should have been registered and monitored by merely one officer. If the goal is to protect the public from the truly dangerous sexual offenders, registries and notifications must focus on the most dangerous of offenders and not overwhelm the public with notification of offenders in the neighborhood who are no real threat. The authors of the most recent study of these laws suggest that

> applying broad community notification to level 1 and level 2 offenders would not likely produce an appreciable reduction in sexual recidivism given that the baseline rate for these offenders is already relatively low (e.g., a 3-year rearrest rate of 5–7 percent) . . . [and] . . . it is unclear whether community notification has an impact on non-sexual recidivism, which comprises roughly three quarters of the reoffenses committed by sex offenders. (Duwe and Donnay 2008: 443)

Therefore, both for the safety of the public and to avoid stigma for offenders, policies should be geared toward the most potentially dangerous offenders. For low-level offenders, registration and notification may become more burdensome on the offender than the value of public knowledge obtained by the process (Levenson and Cotter 2005; Tewksbury 2005).

In that vein, there are a variety of suggestions for improvement of how these laws are implemented, many of which are offered by Human Rights Watch (2007). First, the law should be reasonably narrow in scope and not apply to an overly broad range of offenses so as to be useless in terms of community feelings of safety and security and prevention of sexual abuses. This would include the periodic reevaluation of risk assessment of offenders to determine whether their registration is still necessary or whether their level of dangerousness has declined to a point that their registration is deemed no longer pertinent for public safety. Second, the law should extend for a reasonable length of time and should be determined by the likelihood of continued harm to the community. As of 2007, seventeen states had lifetime registration, yet statistics indicate that the longer an offender remains offense free, the less likely he is to reoffend, making lifetime registration unnecessary for an overwhelming number of offenders. Further, a shift in access from the public to only law enforcement would limit many of the negative public consequences of sex offender registries. When community notification is required, Human Rights Watch suggests that the

> meeting should be designed as an opportunity for education about where the risk for sexual victimization lies and how to prevent sexual abuse before it occurs. Organizations to include in the development and implementation of these community meetings should be victim advocacy groups, sexual violence prevention and response professionals, and sex offender treatment and management agencies. (Human Rights Watch 2007: 18)

This would help the public recognize that the dangers of sexual violence and abuse come not only—and indeed not primarily—from the individuals listed on sex offender registries. Finally, individuals listed on public registries should be given the opportunity at periodic intervals to challenge their inclusion on the registry. An individual should be able to present evidence of rehabilitation through treatment, a significant amount of time without a sexual offense (or a nonsexual offense), or a significant change in one's life situation in order to end the requirements of community notification (Human Rights Watch 2007). This would have individuals working toward a positive goal rather than working against the barriers posed by community shaming often posed by notification legislation.

CONTROL OF SEXUAL OFFENDERS THROUGH COMMUNITY MANAGEMENT

An overwhelming percent of probation and parole departments in the United States have adopted "conditions" for sexual offenders, with many of these departments dedicating officers specifically trained in sexual offenses to the monitoring of sexual offenders. Recall from chapter 6 that approximately 60 percent of sexual offenders are supervised in the community, involving either probation or parole (Bureau of Justice Statistics 1997). Community management involves the cooperation of police, probation and parole officers, treatment providers, agencies providing victim services, social service agencies, child service agencies, housing authorities, employers, and other personnel. Most oversight is through probation and parole officers who are responsible for ensuring that the conditions imposed on the offender are enforced on a routine basis. Because sex offenders are a unique population, different from the "typical" street criminal, it would be advantageous to have specialized probation units to oversee the implementation of conditions. Such specialized units would involve probation officers with reasonably small caseloads who are aware of the triggers that sex offenders may face and who can assist offenders in reintegrating into the community through substance abuse treatment programs, encouraging individuals to join social groups to avoid isolation and depression, encouraging therapy to deal with sexual issues, and being aware of items that may indicate reoffending behavior (such as video games, children's magazines, and so on).

Halloween Community Management

In some states, sex offenders who are on probation or parole are required to report to one location for a period of detention. In other states, offenders are given a curfew, and police patrol the neighborhood to ensure compliance. In Illinois and Tennessee (among other states), an offender cannot dress in a costume. In many states, offenders cannot decorate their residence. Many states require the posting of a "No Candy" sign on the front of an offender's residence. In many of these states, possession of Halloween candy or a costume can result in a violation and a potential prison sentence ("Sex Offenders Locked Down in the Dark for Halloween" 2007).

In a 2000 report, the Center for Sex Offender Management (CSOM 2000) outlined several recommendations to help sexual offenders succeed on probation that would be part of a successful community management plan. These included participation in treatment, even if this means paying out of pocket if not covered by insurance; payment of restitution to the victim; no planned contact with children; finding a residence in a community that is approved; socializing with only adults (non–sex-offending adults); no use of pornographic material; work in an appropriate location to minimize exposure to the offender's preferred type of victim; no alcohol or drugs; willingness to submit to any drug, polygraph, penile plethysmograph, or any other tests on request; and conforming to Internet restrictions as well as a willingness to consent to a computer search when asked. Although these are recommendations by the CSOM (2000) for successful probation, many of these "suggestions" have not been empirically tested, and therefore it is questionable whether they have any impact at all on improving probation or serve merely to minimize any sense of personal freedom or dignity of the individual. The CSOM (2000) also recommends frequent contact between the probationer and the family in order to provide support and to recognize potential triggers before they lead to a reoffense.

Community management frequently involves what is termed a "containment approach," which involves teaching offenders to control their behavior through management of their feelings and situational stressors. This involves working in concert to get the offender to recognize the factors in the environment that cause him stress and may lead him to consider offending again. These may be loss of employment, stress in a relationship, a fight with a friend or family member, loss of social ties, and so on. Just like an alcoholic has "triggers" that may cause him to "fall off the wagon," so too does a sex offender have elements in the environment that may lead him to consider offending. It is important that he recognize when these variables are starting to occur and learn how to deal with them in a way that does not involve offending. The containment approach involves conditions imposed by the criminal justice system that may include required treatment, intensive supervision, or other conditions tailored specifically to the individual offender to decrease his likelihood of reoffense. It may also involve polygraph exams to monitor compliance with the program. In addition, testing for sexually transmitted diseases and HIV may be involved, raising some serious questions with regard to ethics and privacy concerns (CSOM 2002). A paroled offender discusses the difficulty with moving on with his life:

> The rules are humiliating—a constant reminder. It's hard to, in a manner of speaking, to move on and try to put things behind when you're constantly reminded by the rules that you are a sex offender and the rules more or less make you feel like it just happened yesterday. . . . The rules don't allow you to have a normal life and the rules are a constant reminder that you're not a normal person. . . . The only thing is when, *when* does there come a time to move on. (Zevitz and Farkas 2000b: 385; emphasis in original)

The goal of community management is a balanced and multidisciplinary approach that protects community safety while successfully reintegrating the offender into the community. Not all community management, however, is so "balanced." A case in point is residency restriction laws.

Residency Restrictions

States continue to expand and refine laws that restrict where sex offenders may live, work, or visit. Eighteen states passed such laws in 2006. Among them, Kansas now prohibits transitional release facilities for offenders deemed sexually violent from being within 2,000 feet of facilities where children congregate. It includes local restrictions on where sex offenders may reside. Maryland requires the state's parole commission to establish restrictions on where sex offenders may live, work, and visit. In Washington, legislation directs the Association of Washington Cities to develop statewide standards for determining residency restrictions on sex offenders. The least restrictive laws are in Illinois, which has 500-foot distance requirements, whereas California prohibits certain sex offenders who are on parole from residing within a quarter mile of elementary schools and within thirty-five miles of a witness or victim (Levenson and Cotter 2005). These laws were passed in great numbers in many states despite no empirical research to demonstrate that residency restrictions lower recidivism or make communities safer.

From the perspective of the offender, most indicate that the restriction would not impede their reoffending if they wanted to reoffend. One offender remarked that residency restrictions "serve no purpose but to give some people the illusion of safety" (Levenson and Cotter 2005: 174). Another offender noted the lack of logic behind some of the regulations: "I couldn't live in an adult mobile home park because a church was 880 ft away and had a children's class that met once a week. I was forced to move to a motel where right next door to my room was a family with three children—but it qualified under the rule" (Levenson and Cotter 2005: 175).

New York State law requires emergency shelter to be provided to homeless individuals, including homeless sex offenders. So officials in Long Island decided to put homeless sex offenders in movable trailers and relocate them in various places around the county on a regular basis so as not to "offend" any one community for too long ("The Toxic Offender" 2007).

In many jurisdictions, all tiers of sex offenders are subject to residency restrictions, and these laws may have no time limit and therefore theoretically extend past the time an offender is required to register as a sexual offender. As they exist, residency restrictions have the unintended consequence of overwhelming a select group of communities with sexual offenders because there are so few areas in which offenders are permitted to reside. For example, in one trailer park in St. Petersburg, Florida, ninety-five of the 200 residents are convicted sexual offenders, leading some to believe this is a "paradise for sex offenders" ("Trailer Park Becomes Paradise for Sex Offenders" 2007). While the benefits for the offenders are obvious in that it affords them a place to live and begin their process of reintegration without risk of violating a residency restriction, it unintentionally has the consequence of making many of the neighbors uncomfortable and lowering the property values. Moreover, it places convicted sex offenders together for extended periods of time, therefore increasing the risk of having them associate with one another and thereby increasing the likelihood of recidivating.

These laws, combined with the unwillingness of landlords to rent to sex offenders, makes it difficult for many offenders to locate housing on release from prison, leaving many of them homeless and in an enormous catch-22, as they are required by law to register an address with law enforcement or face imprisonment. Not all states are like New York, which requires the state to provide emergency shelter for offenders. Other states leave homeless sex offenders in violation because they are precluded from living in homeless shelters, as described by this Texas individual:

I was homeless—I went to two homeless shelters—told them the truth—I was a registered sex offender—I could not stay. No one helps sex offenders I was told. The 3rd shelter I went to—I did not tell them. I was allowed to stay. November 2002 I was to register again—my birthday. If I told them I lived at a shelter—I would be thrown out—if I stayed on the streets I would not have a [*sic*] address to give—violation. So I registered under my old address—the empty house, which was too close to a school. Someone called the police— told them I did not live at that address anymore—I was locked up, March 2003. I was given a 10-year sentence for failure to register as a sex offender. (Human Rights Watch 2007: 103)

In June 2008, another challenge came to Georgia's sex offender restrictions, initially heralded as the most stringent in the nation. Georgia law prohibits a convicted sexual offender from working, living, or loitering within 1,000 feet of schools, parks, gyms, swimming pools, bus stops (there are approximately 150,000 bus stops in the state of Georgia), or anywhere else children may choose to gather. The law also bans working or volunteering at houses of worship. Violation of the law can result in imprisonment of between ten and thirty years. Five registered sexual offenders filed a lawsuit because the ban on church volunteerism deprives them of the potential "rehabilitative influence" of religion ("Georgia: Sex Offenders Sue over Church Ban" 2008).

Residency restriction laws, however, have recently been challenged in the courts on behalf of sexual offenders and overturned. In November 2007, the Georgia Supreme Court overturned the state law that banned registered sexual offenders from residing within 1,000 feet of any location in which children gather, including schools, churches, day care centers, and bus stops. In a decision that was unanimous, the residency restriction was deemed unconstitutional because it placed a potentially undue burden on individuals, as they may be repeatedly uprooted in order to remain in compliance with the law. The case centered around a convicted child molester who purchased a house with his wife in 2003 that met the guidelines of the residency restriction law at the time. Later, two day care centers were built within the 1,000-foot buffer and the individual was told by his probation officer that he must move or risk arrest for being in violation, the penalty for which is up to ten years' imprisonment. He sued the department of corrections because theoretically this scenario could have replayed itself over and over in different locales throughout the state (*Mann v. Georgia Dept. of Corrections* [2007]).

In a similar ruling in New Jersey in July 2008, an appellate panel ruled that the state's Megan's Law was comprehensive enough to be the only law governing the restrictions placed on sexual offenders. As such, the panel rejected municipal laws that placed residency restrictions on sexual offenders that are in excess of those provided for in the Megan's Law legislation ("Sex Offenders Can Have More Freedom, Court Rules" 2008). This ruling impacts many municipalities that have residency restrictions so strict in a small area that the entire town is off limits to those convicted of a sexual offense. As a result, many municipalities have repealed their residency restrictions ("Eatontown to Repeal Its Sex Offender Law" 2008). While the American Civil Liberties Union applauds such rulings, victims' law centers and many victims' rights groups argue the importance of residency restrictions and are committed to appealing these rulings to the highest court. There are more than thirty states that have residency restriction legislation for sexual offenders who are on probation or parole that could be impacted by the ripple effect of this ruling.

Keep in mind that residency restriction laws restrict only where an offender sleeps, not one's movements or more general interactions with potential victims. One suggestion to replace residency restriction is the creation of "child safe zones," where offenders would be prohibited from entry. Such zones would prohibit any offender who has violated a child under the age of fourteen, regardless of whether that child was a stranger or a nonstranger. In a press release, the Iowa County Attorneys Association said, "Residency restrictions were intended to reduce sex crimes against children by strangers who seek access to children at the covered locations. Those crimes are tragic, but very rare. In fact, 80 to 90 percent of sex crimes against children are committed by a relative or acquaintance who has some prior" offense (Iowa County Attorneys Association 2006). The creation of "child safe zones" would seek to protect children more generally.

Residency restrictions also impact the family of the offender—many areas where offenders are permitted to live would not be ones where they would want to relocate their families. This has the potential to interfere with community reintegration, and may prevent an offender from living with supportive family members. An unintended consequence of residency restriction is that it displaces offenders, resulting in their absconding from registration requirements and thereby making it more difficult for law enforcement to keep track of registrants. Iowa officials estimate that prior to residency restrictions taking effect, law enforcement was able to keep track of approximately 90 percent of offenders, compared to just over half of offenders after the law was declared constitutional in 2005 (Human Rights Watch 2007). These restrictions put one more stressor on the offender, as described by a male offender convicted of sexually assaulting an adult female:

> You can't imagine everything these people [speaking of the criminal justice system] ask you to do. It is just too much. I mean, I understand about punishment to society and everything but I think all this stuff they ask of a guy might just backfire on 'em. Just for the fact it doesn't take a whole lot to go back to where you've been. It's harder to keep focused on where you're going than where you've been. And I think all this stuff they ask from you, the registration, all these appointments, all this money, the therapy, it just goes on and on. I sometimes do think it could be so much you just give up trying. (Meloy 2006: 92)

Another offender echoes similar sentiments:

> See, that's the part that the judicial system doesn't think about. What they do to sex offenders now, I mean, I understand the intentions behind it, but what it really does with all the reporting, the money, the PO's watching everything, the list [community notification], in many respects I think it is overkill and it has the potential to push people to that point where they reoffend. (Meloy 2006: 93)

Community management has to be about striking the delicate balance between protecting community safety from the high-risk offenders and permitting the lower-risk offenders to successfully reintegrate back into society. Patterns of recidivism illustrate that residency restriction laws do not prevent future sexual offenses but instead are an enormous drain on law enforcement because they encourage transience and have law enforcement tracking absconding offenders. If the goal is community protection, residency restriction laws, as some courts are realizing, are not the way to go.

CONTROL OF SEXUAL OFFENDERS THROUGH CIVIL COMMITMENT

Recall from chapter 4 the discussion of sexual psychopath legislation that was prevalent in the 1930s, 1940s, and 1950s and that fell out of favor as the public became concerned with the viability of treatment methods and due process issues surrounding commitment of sexual offenders. Recall from chapter 5 that Earl Shriner had an extensive history of repeated child sex offenses and was released from prison after serving the full length of a fixed sentence for sexual assault. Prior to his release, he expressed a continued desire to rape and torture children, encouraging attempts to commit him to a mental health facility involuntarily. These attempts, however, were not successful, and Earl Shriner committed another horrible sexual offense, resulting in the death of a child on his release from prison. The public was outraged, and within six months Washington State passed sweeping legislation to target sexual offenders, termed "special commitment laws" or "sexually violent predator laws." Similar laws have been passed in many states and take effect when an offender is about to be released from prison. It is believed that "experts" can identify which offenders have the potential to cause future harm, and the goal is therefore to confine these individuals until they are no longer a threat to society. Such laws permit the confinement of offenders who are believed to be "mentally abnormal and dangerous sex offenders" to a secure mental facility. Reading these laws, one would assume that the offender will be treated and released when no longer at risk of sexually reoffending.

Offenders, however, are offered treatment not in prison but only on commitment, making the primary purpose of such legislation incapacitation rather than therapeutic. Perhaps the major problem with sexually violent predator/civil commitment laws is that "experts" capable of identifying offenders who are potentially dangerous are not nearly as effective at identifying when these same offenders are rehabilitated and no longer a threat/danger to society. In addition, there have been cases where prosecutors will seek civil commitment for offenses that are noncontact crimes, such as public exposure ("Doubts Rise as States Hold Sex Offenders after Prison" 2007).

In a key Supreme Court decision (*Kansas v. Hendricks* [1997]), sexual predator laws were ruled constitutional. This case involved Leroy Hendricks, who had a history of sexual offenses, including indecent exposure (1955), lewdness against a child (1956), and sexual assault of children (1960, 1967, and 1984). Hendricks served time in prison for these offenses but was eventually released. The state of Kansas has a habitual criminal clause in which the state can petition the court to have an individual who has been convicted of three prior felonies designated as a habitual criminal, serving to dramatically increase the sentence on subsequent charges. In 1984, when Hendricks was charged with two counts of child molestation, the state did not seek to have him classified as a habitual criminal and instead permitted a plea agreement, resulting in a sentence of five to twenty years.

During the tenth year of Hendricks's sentence, the state petitioned the court to have him declared a sexually violent offender and indefinitely held to prevent future sexual offenses. After a psychological evaluation, it was determined that Hendricks was clinically a pedophile, and at trial he was found "mentally abnormal," which is one requirement of the sexually violent persons legislation in that state. Hendricks contested the finding, and his lawyer argued that the statute was unconstitutional, violated the provision against double jeopardy, and provided for ex post facto punishment. The Supreme Court, however, in a five-to-four decision, disagreed. The Court stated that

> a state statute providing for the involuntary civil commitment of sexually violent predators . . . does not violate the double jeopardy clause of the Federal Constitution's Fifth Amendment where, because the state did not enact the statute with punitive intent, the statute does not establish criminal proceedings, and involuntary commitment pursuant to the statute is not punitive; thus, for purposes of analysis under the double jeopardy clause, (1) initiation of commitment proceedings under the statute against a person upon his imminent release from prison after serving a sentence for the offenses which led to his being declared a violent sexual predator does not constitute a second prosecution, and (2) a person's involuntary detention under the statute does not violate the double jeopardy clause, even though that confinement follows a prison term (*Kansas v. Hendricks*, 521 U.S. 346 [1997]).

This case further established that treatment was not the constitutional justification for civil commitment by the state but that commitments were justified because they protected society from dangerous persons whose violence was a product of their mental disorder. Having a sex offender committed after serving a prison term, therefore, does not itself give rise to a constitutional right to treatment.

Of the approximately 4,500 individuals detained under civil commitment legislation, only three are women.

Kansas v. Hendricks (1997) clearly emphasized the power of the state to protect the community over individual liberty and the constitutional protections of this liberty. The Supreme Court in this case allowed statutes that permit the original offense that led to arrest to be a justification for continued confinement—even if the offense occurred ten to twenty years prior and no treatment has occurred as of yet. For some scholars, this essentially amounts to ex post facto punishment under the guise of treatment (Cornwell 2003). This decision has been upheld since the 1997 decision: these laws are constitutional because they are civil proceedings, not a second criminal punishment. Civil commitment requires proof of "serious difficulty controlling behavior," and the condition must be one that the psychiatric community considers a "serious mental disorder" (*Kansas v. Crane* [2002]). Leroy Hendricks, the man who challenged the constitutionality of civil commitment and lost, continues to be confined in Kansas, more than thirteen years after his prison term would have ended. He is seventy-two years old and has suffered a stroke and spends most days confined to a wheelchair because of diabetes.

As of 2007, there are twenty states with sexually violent predator statutes. These states are Arizona, California, Florida, Illinois, Iowa, Kansas, Massachusetts, Minnesota, Missouri, Nebraska, New Hampshire, New Jersey, New York, North Dakota, Pennsylvania, South Carolina, Texas, Virginia, Washington, and Wisconsin. Standards vary considerably by state regarding what would qualify an individual for civil commitment, but all involve some level of "dangerousness," a history of sexual offending, a "serious mental disorder," and "serious difficulty controlling" behavior. The language of the statute can vary considerably by state as well. For example, offenders in Minnesota must be "highly likely" to reoffend in order to be civilly committed, yet in Wisconsin the standard is "most likely to reoffend." By way of example, the following is the 1998 New Jersey Sexually Violent Predator Act:

Effective August 1999, The New Jersey Sexually Violent Predator Act (SVPA) "establishes an involuntary civil commitment procedure for a sexually violent predator, whom the bill defines as a person who: (1) has been convicted, adjudicated delinquent or found not guilty by reason of insanity for commission of a sexually violent offense, or has been charged with a sexually violent offense but found to be incompetent to stand trial; and (2) suffers from a mental abnormality or personality disorder that makes the person likely to engage in acts of sexual violence if not confined in a secure facility for control, care and treatment." "The Attorney General may initiate a court proceeding for involuntary commitment under this bill by submitting to the court a clinical certificate for a sexually violent predator, completed by a psychiatrist on the person's treatment team. . . . Upon receipt of these documents, the court shall immediately review them to determine whether there is probable cause to believe that the person is a sexually violent predator in need of involuntary commitment. If so, the court shall issue an order for a final hearing and temporarily authorize commitment to a secure facility designated for the custody, care and treatment of sexually violent predators. . . . The person's psychiatrist on the treatment team, who has examined the person no more than five calendar days prior to the court hearing, must testify to the clinical basis for the need for involuntary commitment as a sexually violent predator. Other treatment team members, relevant witnesses or next-of-kin are also permitted to testify. . . . At this hearing, and any subsequent review court hearing, the person has the following rights: The right to be represented by counsel or, if indigent, by appointed counsel; The right to be present at the court hearing unless the court determines that because of the person's conduct at the court hearing the proceeding cannot reasonably continue while the person is present; The right to present evidence; The right to cross-examine witnesses; and The right to a hearing in camera. The bill provides that if the court finds by clear and convincing evidence that the person is in need of involuntary commitment, it shall issue an order authorizing the involuntary commitment of the person to a facility designated for custody, care and treatment of sexually violent predators. Also, the court may order that the person be conditionally discharged in accordance with a plan to facilitate the person's adjustment and reintegration into the community, if the court finds that the person will not be likely to engage in acts of sexual violence because the person is amenable to and highly likely to comply with the plan. Additionally, the bill provides for annual court review hearings of the need for involuntary commitment as a sexually violent predator. The first hearing shall be conducted 12 months from the date of the first hearing, and subsequent hearings annually thereafter. In addition, at any time during involuntary commitment, if the person's treatment team determines that the person's mental condition has so changed that the person is not likely to engage in acts of sexual violence if released, the treatment team shall recommend that the Department of Human Services authorize the person to petition the court for discharge. Also, a person may petition the court for discharge without authorization from the department. In this case, the court shall review the petition to determine whether it is based on facts upon which a court could find that the person's condition had changed, or whether the petition is supported by a professional expert evaluation or report. If the petition fails to satisfy either of these requirements, the court shall deny the petition without a hearing." (Senate, No. 895, L.1998, c. 71)

Regardless of the state, the language is highly subjective and open to interpretation.

As mentioned at the beginning of this chapter, assessment of risk impacts a variety of aspects of an offender's life, including whether he will be released after a period of incarceration or considered for civil commitment. If the system works as it is intended to work, there should be a high degree of consensus regarding the type of individuals who are considered for commitment. Those considered for commitment should all be "dangerous," should have a serious history of sexual offending, should have a "serious mental disorder," and should exhibit a "serious difficulty controlling" their impulses. In a study of civil commitments of 116 sexual offenders in Minnesota between 1975 and 1996, there was significant variability among offenders civilly committed. Researchers suggested that while the commitment process targeted the most dangerous offenders, it was unclear whether evaluators were recommending the commitment of the individuals most likely to reoffend (Janus and Walbek 2000). More recently, however, studies have shown more consensus. In a study of 450 sexual offenders in Florida who met the first stage of commitment criterion and were referred forward for the second stage involving a clinical interview, Levenson (2004) found that the offenders recommended for civil commitment were those scoring higher on actuarial risk assessment instruments, and therefore this was consistent with the guidelines set forth in the state statute. In another study of 5,931 sexual offenders referred to the first stage of the civil commitment process in Florida between July 2000 and August 2003, researchers found that only 6.5 percent of offenders were referred to the second stage of assessment, which is the clinical interview. The fact that such a small percentage of offenders were referred forward in the commitment process illustrates that the procedure and actuarial assessments employed are reasonably effective in targeting those offenders who are high risk, have mental abnormalities, and will likely recidivate with sexually violent behavior (Lucken and Bales 2008).

Civil commitment is one of the most severe punishments a sex offender can face, so it is paradoxical that such legislation is unlikely to be used to indefinitely confine a family member or an offender close to the victim, despite overwhelming research demonstrating that most sex offenses are committed by someone known to or related to the victim.

A plea agreement in states with civil commitment statutes *cannot* preclude the possibility of seeking a civil commitment order once the offender has served his term and is ready for release.

The first stage of evaluation for civil commitment by a mental health professional usually involves a variety of processes completed by a psychiatrist. She ("she" to distinguish her from the offender) will gather outside information about the offender and his offenses from family and friends, gather any previous treatment records, gather department of corrections records, and compile victim statements. She will create a background history on the individual that will include a sexual history, involving any sexual deviations in which he has engaged or that he fantasizes about (though recall from an earlier discussion that much of the general population admits to engaging in sexual deviation). A mental status examination is conducted to evaluate for mental disorders, paraphilic behaviors, or personality disorders, and a variety of psychological tests and other assessment tools are frequently used. In addition, a physical exam and standard medical examination are performed (Lacoursiere 2003). In many states (as illustrated in the New Jersey statute provided previously), if the psychiatrist (on behalf of the department of corrections) determines that the offender meets the criterion for civil commitment, the case is referred to the attorney general's office. The decision to file a petition with the court is then left to the office of the attorney general. Should it be determined that a petition is going to be filed with the court, the offender is typically granted a variety of procedural protections that include counsel, the ability to procure expert witnesses, and the right to a jury hearing. The standard of proof in a civil commitment hearing is "beyond a reasonable doubt," the same standard that exists in a criminal trial. Should the offender be deemed a sexually violent predator, confinement is for an indeterminate length of time in order to treat the mental condition believed responsible for producing the sexual violence. Some state statutes provide a mandated period of reevaluation of the offender once committed, whereas other states do not. The court/jury must rule that the offender is safe and no longer a risk of sexual violence before he will be released to the community (Washington State Institute for Public Policy 2007b). Table 7.1 indicates, however, that the number of individuals released after receiving a term of civil commitment is very low.

Advocating a Preventive Approach

Keep in mind that sexually violent predator legislation, in order to avoid constitutional challenges, is not a criminal statute but a civil statute with the primary objective (theoretically) being the treatment of the offender. The goal is to protect the public through providing treatment for offenders who are likely to reoffend because of a mental abnormality that predisposes them to sexual violence. The focus is therefore not on continued punishment but on the prevention of future harm to women and children.

In a study examining public support for civil commitment legislation, researchers found that this policy was generally supported as an extension of the offender's punishment. The authors created various hypothetical situations in which a sexual offender received a lengthy sentence of twenty-five years versus a short sentence of three years and indicated a hypothetical risk of recidivating. The question was, then, Would you support civil commitment for this offender? As a general rule, the public seemed to support civil commitment in situations where the offender was perceived as receiving a lenient punishment for a serious offense (Carlsmith, Monahan, and Evans 2007). Critics of sexually violent predator legislation argue that this same effect could be accomplished without the appearance of constitutional violations with a policy similar to "three-strikes" laws for sexual offenders. Another suggestion would be the elimination or significant reduction of plea bargaining for serious, violent sexual offenses. This would satisfy both the public desire for a "just" (read: long) sentence for sexually violent offenders and one that does not appear to "sneak in the back door what would not fit through the front door."

Table 7.1. Synopsis of Sexually Violent Predator Laws by State, Including Confinement and Cost Information (as of 2007)

State in Which Sexually Violent Predator Law Was Effective	Persons Confined	Persons Released	Persons Who Had Their Release Revoked	Cost per Year for Sexually Violent Offender	Civil Commitment Budget per Year (in millions)	Cost per Year for Prison Inmate
Arizona	414	87	13	$110,000	$11.3	$20,564
California	558	96	2	$166,000	$147.3	$43,000
Florida	942	28	9	$41,845	$23.3	$19,000
Illinois	307	40	6	$88,000	$25.6	$21,700
Iowa	69	15	1	$71,000	$5.0	$23,002
Kansas	161	16	0	$69,070	$10.9	$22,630
Massachusetts	121	5	n/a	$73,197	$30.7	$43,026
Minnesota	342	43	27	$141,255	$54.9	$29,240
Missouri	143	10	0	$75,920	$8.3	$14,538
Nebraska	18	18	0	$93,325	$13.5	$26,031
New Jersey	342	30	2	$67,000	$21.9	$35,000
North Dakota	75	20	0	$94,728	$12.7	$27,391
Pennsylvania	12	n/a	n/a	$150,000	$1.8	$32,304
South Carolina	119	32	0	$41,176	$2.9	$15,156
Texas	69	n/a	n/a	$17,391	$1.2	$15,527
Virginia	37	5	2	$140,000	$8.2	$23,123
Washington	305	19	4	$149,904	$40.5	$29,055
Wisconsin	500	30	23	$102,500	$34.7	$27,600
Average	n/a	n/a	n/a	$92,017	$25.3	$25,994

Note: While there are many similarities by state, distinct differences exist in Texas because the law provides treatment on an outpatient-only basis and in Pennsylvania, which applies only to offenders as they come out of the juvenile system (Washington State Institute for Public Policy 2007a). n/a = not available.
Source: Adapted from information provided in Washington State Institute for Public Policy (2007a)

One concern with confinement is that for those offenders really wanting to openly and honestly participate in a treatment program, this could work against them negatively later. When it comes time to reassess an offender's risk, their score on at least four items will be impacted by revelations of additional victims, behaviors, or fantasies that they divulge while participating in therapy. In addition, the use of information revealed during therapy to assess an offender's risk of future offending has been upheld by the court. This information can also impact offenders who are participating in prison treatment and impact their assigned tier level and community notification requirements and registration length on their release (Corrigan 2006).

Concerns with a Preventive Approach

As alluded to previously, critics of sexually violent predator statutes argue that they violate the provision against double jeopardy and provide for ex post facto punishment despite the fact that the Supreme Court has disagreed. For many critical of this legislation, it would seem more "just" (read: fair) to sentence an offender to a long sentence from the beginning, that is, to change the laws so that sexual offenses garnered a reasonably long sentence at the outset, similar to mandatory minimum sentencing policies or three-strikes laws. And note that some of these changes have been made, for example, in the Adam Walsh Act. This "up-front" policy would be preferred to one of sending an offender to prison for three or four years and then seeking an indefinite (read: lifetime) sentence of commitment under the guise of treating him for a "mental disorder" that causes him "uncontrollable sexual desires." Another concern with this legislation is that the courts have failed to clarify whether this type of "prevention" can be used on other types of offenders. This type of approach is clearly a slippery slope; it is just that sex offenders are so socially hated and ostracized that they make for an easy first target. In addition, there is the touchy ethical subject of trying to assess/predict "future" behavior.

More practically, there is the financial concern. In 2007, New Hampshire and New York became, respectively, the nineteenth and twentieth states with civil commitment statutes, so these states are not represented in the analysis in Table 7.1. The financial investment in sexually violent predator laws is enormous. Table 7.1 shows, by state, the number of offenders confined, the number of persons released since confinement began, the number of commitments that have been revoked (for a subsequent sexual offense), the cost per year for each sexual offender, the budget per year for the state, and the comparable cost per year for a state prison inmate. By way of an overview, the average annual program cost is $97,000 per offender, and at the beginning of 2007, there were 4,534 sexual offenders confined nationally under sexually violent predator legislation in eighteen states. Under the most recent wave of sexually violent predator legislation (not counting sexual psychopath legislation of the 1930s through the 1950s), 495 offenders have been released (Washington State Institute for Public Policy 2007a).

Despite the notion of receiving treatment once civilly committed, many of these facilities are too underfunded to offer treatment at all or offer substandard levels of treatment with personnel who are not properly trained to treat sex offenders. Many of the existing treatment programs have not been empirically tested, and therefore the effectiveness of such programs is largely unknown. This begs the question: if you cannot empirically demonstrate the effectiveness of treatment programs, how do you determine who is "cured" and ready for release? In addition, some offenders committed do not attend treatment. "In California, three-quarters of civilly committed sex offenders do not attend therapy. Many say their lawyers tell them to avoid it because admission of past misdeeds during therapy could make getting out impossible, or worse, lead to new criminal charges" ("Doubts Rise as States Hold Sex Offenders after Prison" 2007). State-level oversight or monitoring of the facilities is lax, and like in many institutional settings, sexual contact between inmates is relatively common; however, this is more of a concern when you are dealing with a population of sexual offenders. This is a system that needs reworking, likely through the implementation of laws that result in longer prison sentences for violent and dangerous offenders and community treatment and supervision for lower-level offenders. While Minnesota spends approximately $20 million per year on civil commitment, the state spends only $1.1 million for treatment of sexual offenders in the community and $2.1 million to treat sexual offenders who are in prison (Janus 2003). Even though they have passed the muster of the Supreme Court, sexually violent predator statutes still have the appearance of a constitutional violation and a system of justice that is not really "just."

8

Considering the Victims

In a book discussing how legislation impacts sexual offenses and offenders, a section on how changes in legislation impact the victims of sexual offenses is also extremely important. Government has a duty to protect its citizens from violence, and the goal of sexual offending legislation must be to protect potential victims from sexual harm and to permit the successful reintegration of former offenders into society. This, however, requires a very delicate balance of interests and one that the United States clearly has not yet been able to strike. This chapter addresses the treatment of victims in the criminal justice system and how the laws view those impacted by sexual abuse and violence.

BARRIERS TO REPORTING

The ramifications of experiencing a sexual assault or an act of sexual violence can last a lifetime, and because of this, reporting of the crime is one major barrier for many victims. One woman who was sexually abused as a child by a family relative explains, "Being sexually assaulted as a child, for me, was like having my heart ripped to shreds. I am still trying to put it all back together" (Human Rights Watch 2007: 21). Although society has come a long way in dealing with sexual violence, statistics still show that less than 20 percent of adult women who are raped report it to the police (Human Rights Watch 2007). Because of the increased attention to the issues of child sexual abuse and sexual abuse of women by feminists and other advocacy groups, the stigma associated with sexual victimization is less today than it was thirty years ago, but a stigma remains, and this keeps many victims from reporting. Recall from chapter 6 that sexual abuse may not be reported for a variety of reasons, including shame or embarrassment resulting in the victim not wanting others to know. Victims may not understand that they were legally sexually assaulted, which may be especially true in the case of child sexual abuse or statutory rape but may also be the case for adult women. Victims may not want to allege abuse against someone they know, or they may fear that there is no "proof" of rape and therefore may be less willing to report it to the authorities. Victims may fear the response of police or the ordeal of an investigation by the criminal justice system or might fear retribution by the offender. Or an individual may not want the stigma associated with being labeled a rape victim or a victim of child sexual abuse because like an offender suffers ramifications from being labeled in society, so too do victims.

One barrier to reporting that many women learn from watching the media is how sexual assault is treated in the criminal justice system. In many cases in which a woman is forced to have sexual intercourse or relations against her will, the act is not treated by the criminal justice system as an offense to be prosecuted:

> In the[se] cases . . . , the man is not the armed stranger jumping from the bushes—nor the black man jumping the white woman, the case that was most likely to result in the death penalty prior to 1977, and the stereotype that may explain in part the seriousness with which a white male criminal justice system has addressed "stranger" rape. Instead the man is a neighbor, an acquaintance, or a date. The man and woman are both white, or both black, or both Hispanic. He is a respected bachelor, a student, a businessman, or a professional. He may have been offered a ride home or invited in. He does not have a weapon. He acted alone. It is, in short, a simple rape. (Estrich 1995: 183)

A major barrier to reporting sexual abuse is the circumstances of the offense: victims are more likely to report the "stereotypical" assault by a stranger, and these are the types of offenses most easily prosecuted by the criminal justice system. In talking to an educated, liberal, young prosecutor, Estrich revealed the "technical" rape case that is rarely prosecuted:

> The victim came to his office for the meeting dressed in a pair of tight blue jeans. Very tight. With a see-through blouse on top. Very revealing. . . . The man involved was her ex-boyfriend. And lover; well, ex-lover. They ran into each other on the street. He asked her to come [up to his apartment] and watch porno. They sat in the living room watching. Like they used to. He said, let's go in the bedroom where we'll be more comfortable. . . . They watched from the bed. Like they used to. He began rubbing her foot. Like he used to. Then he kissed her. She said no, she didn't want this, and got up to leave. He pulled her back on the bed and forced himself on her. He did not

beat her. She had no bruises. Afterward, she ran out. The first thing she did
was flag a police car. . . . The prosecutor pointed out to her that she was not
hurt, that she had no bruises, that she did not fight. She pointed out to the
prosecutor that her ex-boyfriend was a weightlifter. He told her it would be
nearly impossible to get a conviction. She could accept that, she said: even if
he didn't get convicted, at least he should be forced to go through the time
and expense of defending himself. That clinched it, said the DA. She was just
trying to use the system to harass her ex-boyfriend. He had no criminal
record. He was not a "bad guy." No charges were filed. (Estrich 1995: 183–84)

Estrich goes on to elaborate how this view is problematic for women
generally:

If only the aggravated cases are considered rape—if we limit our practical
definition to cases involving more than one man, or strangers, or weapons
and beatings—then "rape" is a relatively rare event, is reported to the police
more often than most crimes, and is addressed aggressively by the system. If
the simple cases are considered—the cases where a woman is forced to have
sex without consent by only one man, whom she knows, who does not beat
her or attack her with a gun—then rape emerges as a far more common,
vastly underreported, and dramatically ignored problem. (Estrich 1995: 184)

The "simple" rape—the "common" rape, the rape by a boyfriend, an acquaintance, or a date—is the type of assault that is infrequently reported
to law enforcement and is the type of assault that is the least likely to result in the conviction of the offender. This is problematic when this is the
most typical type of sexual assault committed against women and becomes a major barrier to reporting.

Barriers to reporting for children are somewhat different. Children may
not report their abuse because of shame or embarrassment, that is, because they do not want others to know. Children may not truly understand that anything "wrong" has happened, depending on their age and
the circumstances of the sexual abuse. For a child, telling a parent about
sexual abuse can cause great fear because threats of harm may be involved, especially if the offender is the other parent or a family member,
or it can mean fear of not being believed. The child may be dependent on
the adult for love, protection, nurturing, caregiving, and support. It is entirely possible that the abusive parent is the child's only source of emotional support, and the child's emotions of attachment may outweigh the
anger, humiliation, and self-blame. Often, a child simply hopes that the
situation will change, as expressed by one woman who had been sexually
victimized as a child:

Here is this wonderful man who is the most important person in your life,
whom you idolize and trust, and he's betraying your trust. Part of you is

angry, but another part is saying, maybe it'll stop, maybe it'll go away. I'd keep thinking, this is going to be the last time, praying that it was and that he'd look at me and say "you're my baby, I love you, let me hold you." My mother never held me, never loved me—when my father wasn't being sexual he'd love me the way I wanted to be loved, hold me right, and I must remember that when I was little he did this. He was all I had! How could I help but hope somehow he'd miraculously change? (Renvoize 1982: 18; emphasis in original)

Most frequently, the nonoffending parent (usually the mother) is not an active participant in the abuse, and she is normally not aware that the abuse is occurring. "As for the question of the mother's responsibility, maternal absence, literal or psychological, does seem to be a reality in many families where incest develops. The lack of a strong, competent, and protective mother does seem to render girls more vulnerable to sexual abuse" (Herman and Hirschman 1993: 49). The mother's "absence" from the family, however, does not make it any easier for the child to turn to her for help, as there may also be physical abuse in the family of the mother, the child, or both.

As children get older, they may not want to allege abuse against someone they know or may fear that there is no "proof" and therefore be less willing to report it to the authorities. Similar to an adult victim, an older child may fear the response of police or the ordeal of an investigation by the criminal justice system or may not want the stigma associated with being labeled a victim. For all minors, however, the challenge in reporting to the authorities is transferred to the parent(s), where, in the case of incest, this can become extremely traumatic.

CHALLENGES DURING INVESTIGATION

"Simple" rape cases are often "he said," "she said," without any other corroborating evidence. Police have the first level of discretion during initial investigation, meaning that a case of rape reported to the police may not ever come across the desk of a prosecutor. How the police respond to a report of abuse is a critical element in the recovery process for the victim. In reporting, many victims are hoping to increase their feelings of personal safety and security as well as to have the significance and seriousness of the offense validated (Jordan 2008). Instead, much research has found that the process of reporting can feel like a revictimization. How a victim responds to reporting has much to do with the sensitivity, effectiveness, and seriousness with which the police treat the allegation. Police response, however, can vary greatly, depending on the relationship between the victim and offender, obvious physical signs of an assault, and whether the victim is perceived as a "real" victim or someone who may be partially "blameworthy" in the assault (Jordan 2008). In assessing the victim's "blameworthiness," the rape myths of the past are revisited: What was she wearing? Was she alone? Had she been drinking? Did she make choices that may not have been very responsible? Is she a sexually "promiscuous" individual? These are the questions considered (consciously or unconsciously) in assessing the victim's role in the assault.

On the basis of their assessment, the police determine the extent to which they will investigate an alleged sexual assault, and this can have a dramatic influence on the strength of a prosecutor's case should it come to trial or the ability for a prosecutor to garner a reasonable plea agreement. An overwhelming percentage of police officers continue to be male, meaning that primarily men are responsible for assessing and evaluating the merit of a female's claim of sexual assault. Studies reveal that a significantly greater percentage of complaints of acquaintance rape are determined by police investigators to be unfounded, compared to the percentage of complaints of stranger rape (Estrich 1995). One longtime police officer and sex crimes investigator notes that

> motive is always a point. Generally speaking, I believe something happened, I believe what the lady is saying happened to her. But I'm also aware that someone else looking at the incident may see it a little differently, and that's what the jury's going to be doing—examining the whole picture. There are times, we joke, that the rape occurred *after* the sexual intercourse. (Beneke 1995a: 194–95; emphasis in original)

Rates of reporting remain significantly higher for individuals victimized by a stranger, and the experience of these victims with law enforcement seems to provide more validation than victims involved in a nonstranger offense.

CHALLENGES OF A LEGAL PROCEEDING

The challenges of a legal proceeding are inherently impacted by the constraints of the law; therefore, reforms in the law are important to discuss prior to elaborating the path through a legal proceeding. Male superiority has been reflected in historic laws regarding rape. For example, during slavery, the rape of black women by either black or white men was permissible; however, some jurisdictions permitted castration or the death penalty for the rape of a white woman by a black man. Historically, women were stereotyped as manipulative and seductive, and there existed the assumption that a woman would "cry rape" to explain away a variety of circumstances, including pregnancy and premarital sexual contact, or for the purposes of retaliation. In addition, in many jurisdictions, juries were instructed by the judge that rape was an allegation easily made but difficult to defend, and testimony regarding a woman's prior sexual contact and behavior was permitted to impeach her credibility in a rape trial. All these elements worked against the successful prosecution of rapists historically. As mentioned earlier, women's groups worked diligently for rape law reform beginning in the 1970s, and while there have been significant reforms, as practiced today the law continues to take more seriously the rape of white women by male members of a minority racial or ethnic group. This is one element of the law that has not changed over time.

With regard to child sexual abuse, historic laws were completely silent on this issue. Not until the late 1960s did this become an issue of concern, and it did not become a significant concern until the passage of the Child Abuse Prevention and Treatment Act in 1974, which was reauthorized in 2003 as the Keeping Children and Families Safe Act. Although some of the same issues arise in a legal proceeding for a child sexual abuse case as for an adult sexual assault case, there is the added issue of child competency. Each state has different provisions related to how a child is determined competent to provide testimony at trial, but generally the child must understand the difference between the truth and a lie, be able to understand the situation that occurred, and be able to recall and communicate to the court the events that occurred. Even if a child is declared competent, testifying can be extremely frightening and emotionally scarring, and the jury can have issues with child credibility, making it important for there to be a strong case against the offender aside from the child's testimony. To decrease the child's fear, the U.S. Supreme Court has ruled that children may testify via closed-circuit camera if they would be traumatized by a face-to-face confrontation (*Maryland v. Craig* [1990]).

Significant rape law reforms involved changing the term "rape" to "sexual assault" or "sexual battery" in order to draw attention to the violent nature of the offense as opposed to the sexual nature. This change in definition also broadened the crime from a traditional focus on sexual intercourse to other types of sexual acts occurring without consent that did not necessarily involve penetration. In addition, the category of individuals who can be held accountable for these offenses has broadened to include persons of either sex (in most states) as well as spouses (who were historically exempt). One of the major goals of rape law reform was to overcome the stereotype of the "black stranger" offender. Feminists wanted the criminal justice system and society generally to understand that rape could occur in a variety of situations and involve a diverse array of individuals and did not necessarily conform to the rape myths that had historically pervaded societal views. As such, reformers sought to expand the list of potential sex crimes to include incest offenders, acquaintance rape, marital rape, rape that did not involve serious physical harm, and assailants who did not fit the "stereotype" of a rapist (Corrigan 2006):

> Early antirape advocates believed that the extremely harsh penalties imposed for rape in many states discouraged prosecution and conviction. Revised sentencing was understood as key to more vigorous and effective prosecution and conviction of alleged rapists. Somewhat counterintuitively, advocates sought *lighter*, graduate sentences and the abolition of the death penalty for rape in order to encourage prosecutions and convictions for sex offenses. Feminist advocates believed that if penalties were seen as more proportionate and appropriate, cases against nonstereotypical offenders (those who were white, professionals, first-time offenders, or assaulted individuals known to them) would be taken more seriously by law enforcement, judges, and juries. (Corrigan 2006: 280; emphasis in original)

Another significant change was the removal of the legal requirement that the victim resist as much as possible. This reflected a change of focus to the behavior of the offender and no longer required the victim to put herself at increased risk of harm by resisting and angering the perpetrator. Evidentiary rules were also changed in order to remove proof that the victim resisted and special corroboration requirements. Prior to reform,

> the stringent New York rule produced distressing and even illogical results. Medical corroboration of intercourse obviously could not be required when a victim claimed that the rape attempt was foiled before penetration. But if the victim said penetration had occurred, the New York courts then insisted upon corroboration of that claim, regardless of whether the defendant was charged with completed rape or only the attempt. In the absence of medical evidence, a rape defendant could still be convicted of a sex crime, but only if the victim testified that penetration had *not* occurred. If she said she had been penetrated, then the defendant could not be convicted of any crime at all! New York's corroboration rule became so strict that in a typical year in the early 1970s, thousands of rape complaints were filed, but prosecutors obtained convictions in only eighteen cases. (Schulhofer 1998: 27; emphasis in original)

Other significant changes included the passage of rape shield laws. These laws placed restrictions on questioning a rape victim about her prior sexual encounters and were passed by forty-nine states by 1999. This reform, however, while it limits questioning regarding the victim's sexual history for the purposes of proving that she consented to the offense in question, does permit inclusion of sexual history to challenge the victim's credibility (Berger, Searles, and Neuman 1995). Two other legal reforms are that during a trial, judges are no longer permitted to provide cautionary instructions to jurors as they were in the past, and a defense of "mistaken age" has been eliminated that historically permitted men to assert that they "thought" the victim was older. It remains to be seen whether, in light of online chat rooms and social networking sites, this aspect of the law will be challenged. Moreover, it is problematic that the mistaken-age defense is no longer permissible despite the fact that American culture strongly encourages young girls to adorn themselves with makeup and clothing that makes them look sexually attractive and older than their chronological age to men and boys. Most recently, a woman now has the right to withdraw consent to sex in a handful of states *after* initial consent to sex has been given, and if the man continues with sexual intercourse, he can be charged with rape (Illinois was the first state to enact such legislation). In other states, however, once a woman consents to intercourse, she cannot then withdraw consent and allege rape. Legal reforms are not federal in scope and therefore vary dramatically by state. The outcomes of these reforms have yet to be widely studied, so it is unclear the extent to which they have been effective.

While the police have the first level of discretion during the initial investigation, once an alleged sexual offense case reaches the prosecutor's office, there exists another level of discretion, with prosecutors deciding to pursue or dismiss a case for a variety of reasons. Going forward with a case or choosing to dismiss it may depend on factors such as internal guidelines of the individual prosecutor's office; the perceived ability to successfully prosecute the offender; the believability of the victim; the perceived dangerousness of the offender to the larger community; extralegal factors, such as the age, race, and gender of both the victim and the offender; the presence or absence of violence by the offender and the level of resistance put forward by the victim; the presence or absence of corroborating evidence; and the relationship between the victim and the offender. A study conducted in the 1960s of juries revealed that they consider some of the same factors that prosecutors do during a trial (Kalven and Zeisel 1966). Juries in this study were initially biased against the prosecution and looked for any evidence that the victim may have contributed to or encouraged the offender's behavior (termed "contributory behavior"). Juries admitted to considering factors such as a prior relationship between the victim and the offender, the level of force used, and the amount of resistance put forward by the victim. Therefore, if juries consider such factors, it only makes sense that prosecutors consider them as well when evaluating whether to put a victim through the ordeal of a trial. When the prosecutor discussed earlier in this chapter was questioned about the factors that contribute to dismissing or taking a sexual offender to trial, he did mention the likely response of juries. And he leaned heavily on the "neutrality" of his decision. In considering force and resistance and prior relationship and lack of corroboration, factors he termed critical, he was, he claimed, treating this case just like the assaults and robberies and drug deals that he screens and dismisses every day. Feminists might claim that rape is treated uniquely, but not by him. He, and most prosecutors, consider the same factors every day in every crime. There, he concluded, he was beyond reproach. He was neutral. (Estrich 1995: 188)

However,

> because of the nature of the crime, rape is less likely to be supported by corroboration than these other crimes. Because of the sex and socialization of the victim, it may require less force and generate less resistance. To take into account prior relationship in rape in the same way as in other crimes communicates the message that women victims, particularly of simple rapes, are to blame for their victimization—precisely the sort of judgment that leads them to remain silent. Rape is different from assault or robbery or burglary. Ignoring these differences allow the exclusion of the simple "technical" rape from the working definition of the crime to appear neutral, when it is not. (Estrich 1995: 189)

Corroboration of a sexual offense is often extremely difficult to secure. Witnesses are usually not present, especially to nonstranger offenses, and women and children may be plagued by humiliation and fear, which may delay their reporting past the usefulness of any existing corroborating physical evidence. Physical corroboration can usually indicate only that sexual contact took place and does not reveal precisely the nature of the contact or whether the contact was consensual or forced. Indeed, not all victims forcefully resist an attack, as many fear further injury. The other factor strongly considered by juries and therefore prosecutors is the victim–offender relationship. When most victims are assaulted by someone known to them, placing large consideration for dismissing or pursuing a case on the relationship between victim and offender is unduly prejudicial for the victim. A recent rape victim called Susan Estrich for advice regarding a sexual assault by a former boyfriend:

> She had been raped by the man she used to date. The relationship had gone sour. This did not turn her into the vengeful female whom the law has so long feared. But it did, apparently, turn him into a vengeful attacker. He followed her and raped her brutally. She felt violated and betrayed. At first she did not know what to do. She talked to friends and relatives. She decided to report it to the police. She talked to the police and the assistant district attorney. She talked to the new victim-witness advocate. No one said that she was

a liar, exactly. No one laughed at her, or abused her. They just said that they would not arrest him, would not file charges. It was all explained thoroughly, the way things are done these days by good district attorneys. She had not gone immediately to the doctor. By the time she did, some of the bruises had healed and the evidence of sperm had not been preserved. She had not complained to the police right away. She knew the man. They'd had a prior relationship of intimacy. He was a respected businessman. He had no criminal record. She couldn't believe their response. She had been raped. She called to ask me what she could do to make the prosecutors do something. Nothing, said I, the supposed expert. But I didn't tell her that it was all "neutral" and therefore fair. She knew better. (Estrich 1995: 192–93)

Because of these many difficulties, at the levels of the police, the prosecutor's office, and the jury, cases of sexual assault are frequently plea-bargained.

If a case goes to trial, it is imperative to remember that the courtroom is an adversarial system that is designed to be contentious. In a quest for courtroom truth and in order to uphold the due process rights of the accused offender, victims are treated as witnesses to be questioned by both the prosecution and the defense, and this can make victims feel marginalized from the process and as though the system is working against them in favor of the offender. Many victims experience extreme levels of stress and anxiety prior to giving testimony in court. One victim revealed, "It's probably the biggest challenge I've ever had to give myself, to make myself do it" (Jordan 2008: 91). Another victim said, "I was totally scared, totally out of my tree, shaking, going to the toilet every two minutes before I went in the room, and it was sort of like, just get this over, I need it over" (Jordan 2008: 91).

Some have referred to the treatment of victims in the criminal justice system as state-sanctioned victimization (Taslitz 1999). One scholar argued, "Indeed, if one set out intentionally to design a system for provoking symptoms of traumatic stress, it might look very much like a court of law" (Herman 2005: 574). Yet, despite the flaws, some individuals are able to garner a sense of power from the experience: "I felt that it was kind of an ending, a closing. It was very much part of the healing process to actually physically get it out there and close the door on it" (Jordan 2008: 111). Another victim said, "It was a real challenge. When I came off the witness stand and walked out of that room, it was a real sense of achievement" (Jordan 2008: 112). And another victim reported, "Because it was brought up again for me, I really had to see it through. I was really torn between whether I should or shouldn't go through with it. . . . Going through the trial has helped me to end it. I'm pleased I did it. . . . I met the challenge and worked my way through it and I think because of that I'm a stronger person" (Jordan 2008: 112).

Of those cases taken to trial, only a small percentage of cases result in convictions. For those that do, the sentencing hearing can also be a place to regain some sense of control and power, especially if the offender is sentenced to a term of imprisonment deemed "just" by the victim. An interesting study (Berliner 2007) involved interviews with adolescent victims (ages thirteen to eighteen) and their parents involved in sexual offense cases in Washington State the offenders of whom were eligible for the Special Sex Offender Sentencing Alternative (SSOSA). There are a variety of factors that must be met for an offender to be considered eligible for SSOSA, including an established relationship between the victim and the offender, no violent crime within the past five years, no substantial bodily injury involved in the current offense, that the offender must be amenable to treatment, and that there should be some anticipated benefit to the community. Indeed, since SSOSAs have been in use in Washington State many benefits have been seen:

> Since SSOSA was enacted, significant changes in societal views toward victims and sex offenders have occurred. The social climate is now much more supportive of sexual assault victims. Most children are made aware of and educated about sexual assault, and services are widely available to victims. In Washington State, these changes are reflected in numerous social policy advances. There are state-supported sexual assault programs in every county that offer crisis response, legal advocacy, and counselling. (Berliner 2007: 3)

In this particular study, 18 percent of the cases involved an SSOSA sentence, which was fairly close to the state average of 23 percent. Most teen victims expressed a strong sense of support for the SSOSA (69 percent), whereas most parents were not in support of this option (71 percent were against this community-based sentencing option). The parents had this reaction despite the fact that the prosecutor included the family in the decision-making process in most cases (Berliner 2007). In order for the criminal justice system to work, the police, prosecutor's office, and victims need to understand their interconnected roles and work together in a system of understanding and respect. This is an experience that can be very difficult for a victim of sexual abuse yet one that can also be empowering.

PERSONAL AND FAMILY CHALLENGES

The *Diagnostic and Statistical Manual of Mental Disorders* (3rd ed., revised; American Psychiatric Association 1987) lists rape as a stressor that may precipitate posttraumatic stress disorder, and the term "rape trauma syndrome" began to be used in the mid-1970s to describe either an acute or a

long-term reaction to rape that can disrupt the psychological, social, physical, and sexual elements of a victim's life. Regardless of the label applied,
there are myriad negative consequences for women and children who
have experienced sexual victimization. The effects discussed here are general responses of victims to sexual assault. Not all of these symptoms are
experienced by all victims. There is no one "typical" way to respond to a
sexual assault, and it depends greatly on the circumstances of the offense,
the length of the offense, the relationship between the offender and the
victim, and the resolution of the offense (dismissal versus court trial, conviction of offender, offender never found and/or prosecuted, and so on).
There are many variables that influence the response an individual will
have to sexual abuse.

What research does show is that there may be both short- and longer-
term emotional and/or physical consequences of sexual abuse. These consequences include (but may not be limited to) anxiety; depression; a
heightened sense of helplessness; an increased sense of self-criticism,
guilt, or self-blame; a continual sense of fear or panic; dreams/nightmares
of the event(s); feelings of loss of control; anger; or an inability to concen-
trate. Victims may also experience eating disorders, lack of desire in sexual activity, or a hyperactive desire for sexual activity in an attempt to regain control, a desire to stop or limit involvement with the outside world
that may inhibit work function as well as interpersonal relationships with
family and friends, and a fear that a similar event may occur. Many victims self-medicate through the use of drugs and/or alcohol that may
serve to temporarily depress the emotional pain. Male victims of child
sexual abuse may fear growing up to be an offender. For children or
young adults who have never been sexually active, the association of sexual activity with abuse can be extremely scarring. It is often easier for
adults who are sexually victimized to resume a sexual lifestyle because
they have experienced the event without an associated trauma. For many,
the ability to trust in intimate relationships can be severely compromised;
conversely, other women feel the need for a relationship in order to feel
protected by someone (Finkelhor 1986). Many individuals who have been
victims also engage in a variety of "risk management" activities, including changing appearance; changing security at home, work, and travel
routes; having preprogrammed emergency numbers in phones, taking extra precautions when alone, not being alone at night or during other periods perceived as risky, and so on.

Most therapists recommend crisis intervention immediately following
a sexual assault. The goal is to return the victim to their previous state of
functioning (emotionally, psychologically, socially, and physically) as
soon as possible. It is believed that treatment has the best prognosis when
it immediately follows the incident and deals with issues of regaining a

sense of safety and security, reconnecting with a positive body image and sense of self-esteem, and overcoming a personal sense of powerlessness. The idea with treatment is to start the process back to "normal" as quickly as possible. The impact on the victim seems to have to do with individual characteristics, such as whether there was a prior history of sexual victimization, the emotional and psychological state at the time of the offense, and the extent of support received after the offense from friends, family, and a significant partner. Whether the offender was a stranger or an acquaintance appears to have no significant influence on the extent of emotional or psychological harm triggered in the victim. While some women experience many of the negative emotional and psychological effects discussed, some women experience very few if any of the side effects of a sexual assault and seek to regain control over their lives and their normal routines as quickly as possible. The individual nature of a victim's recovery journey cannot be overstated.

COMMUNITY RESOURCES

Each community usually has a variety of victims' service agencies that inform women and children of the resources to which they are entitled and how to access these services. These agencies provide referrals to other relevant agencies; provide assistance with any available restitution programs, including helping victims fill out paperwork; run programs that orient victims to the court process; and provide transportation for victims to and from the court. These services are invaluable to victims who either do not have a familial or friend-based network of support or choose not to rely on that support base. In addition, victim compensation programs are available. These programs first started in 1965 in California, and now every state has some type of compensation program for victims (Office of Victims of Crimes 1998). Compensation varies by significance of injury, but some monetary relief is provided to cover medical fees, counseling, and lost wages.

Rape law reforms have had a number of positive effects, including the improvement of attitudes toward victims of sexual abuse, which may result in less trauma experienced by the survivor both within the criminal justice system and within the larger community, and the decline in the prevalence of rape myths (Berger, Searles, and Neuman 1995). As such, there is less stigma associated with sexual abuse today than there was thirty years ago, making reporting of these crimes more likely. One anonymous place to report sexual violence is to a rape crisis hotline, funded in part by the 1994 Violence Against Women Act, which was reauthorized in 2005 to last through 2009. This act not only funds rape crisis hotlines but also funds grants to rural areas for the needs of sexual assault victims and child sexual abuse, allots funds to federal victims' counselors, and funds rape prevention and education.

The purpose of rape crisis hotlines is to provide information, counseling, and assertiveness training. These hotlines have helped many women after a sexual assault, such as one woman who did not want to be "just another victim":

> I had this terrible concern that they would put it into boxes and do a big study. They would try to psychoanalyse me and tell me I needed to break down, or tell me that I should be angry when I wasn't feeling that way. So I was really scared about contacting them. . . . I never wanted to be called a rape victim or a sexual abuse victim. I refuse to be associated with a label and I was very clear about that to the police too. . . . I just didn't want to be another woman to add to the list. (Jordan 2008: 129)

Community programs that consist of counseling can be enormously beneficial to women after an assault, as many women do not want to share intimate details of a rape with their family. One woman said, "It has been crucial to have someone I could offload my stuff to that isn't my family or friends. I didn't want them to have to hear what I was going through" (Jordan 2008: 130). Counselors help women feel like they are not alone and may help them find access to group programs or self-defense classes or other programs that will help the woman return to a place where she feels safe. Education is an important tool in community prevention of sexual violence: "As long as people have any sense of privacy about sexual acts and the human body, rape will, therefore, carry a stigma—not necessarily a stigma that blames the victim for what happened to her, but a stigma that links her name irrevocably with an act of intimate humiliation" (Benedict 1992: 254). We need to move to a place as a society that is past the stigma, a place where the structural roots of violence are understood, a place where society does not wonder what a woman was wearing or drinking or why she was alone, and a place where a woman will not need to call an anonymous rape crisis hotline to report rape because she will feel as open and free to report a rape to the police as she would a burglary—no questions asked.

III

LEARNING ALTERNATIVES

9

Can Treatment Work?

A common question is whether treatment for sex offenders is effective in preventing future sex crimes. Can treatment "cure" this type of behavior? This question cannot be answered easily, as there are as many types of sex offenses as there are people who commit sex crimes. Recall that men who pay for consensual adult sex may be classified as sex offenders, that some states still outlaw consensual oral sex between adults, and that, in a select few states, public urination qualifies as a sexual offense. A sex offender is not the strange old man wandering aimlessly around town as the stereotype suggests. Sex offenders are politicians soliciting sex in washrooms and frequenting prostitutes, fathers who rape their daughters, husbands who rape their wives, and strangers who assault children. Consequently, it is not beneficial to paint all offenders with the same brush. Although traits exist that are similar among various types of offenders, treatment success varies. As elaborated on in chapter 6, research reveals that recidivism rates for sex offenders are lower than for nonsexual offenders, with treatment a significant variable decreasing the likelihood of reoffense. The challenge is identifying the types of treatment that are most successful and finding talented and educated individuals to provide treatment. Treatment success is dependent on a number of factors, including therapist ability, treatment composition, familial support, and type of offense. This chapter elaborates on the various treatment options and discusses research findings regarding which types of treatment are most successful.

AVAILABLE TREATMENT OPTIONS

Currently, there are three broad treatment options used for sexual offenders: surgery, psychotherapy, and pharmacotherapy. The vast array of treatment options available likely stems from the fact that the etiology of sexual offending is not fully understood. Hypothesized etiologies include interpersonal deficits, difficulty attaining and maintaining intimacy, loneliness, social processing deficits and cognitive distortions (Wood, Grossman, and Fichtner 2000). The most common treatment option is psychotherapy, but the form it takes can vary widely. However, the preferred method of treatment, especially in correctional institutions, is pharmacotherapy, and this form of treatment is mandated in several states, including Georgia, Louisiana, and Florida.

Surgical Treatment

A popular knee-jerk reaction to sexual offenders is, "Just castrate him!" Surgery is definitely one treatment option available in the United States but is rarely used, as its therapeutic value is highly questionable. Surgery, or castration, involves the removal of the testicles. The underlying assumption is that removing the testicles will dramatically decrease testosterone levels to the point that an erection will not be possible and sexual desire will be virtually eliminated. The procedure is rarely performed, so statistics on its success or failure are limited. However, a small study in the United States found that 40 percent of castrated men continued to have sexual intercourse three to seven years postsurgery (Sheldon et al. 1985). An additional study found that 50 percent of castrated men were capable of sustaining a full erection while watching sexually explicit movies three to five years post surgery (Wille and Beier 1989). In contrast, a study of 104 castrated men found that sexual activity was virtually eliminated within six months of surgery for more than 75 percent of offenders, and only 15 percent of men were capable of sexual activity after prolonged and intensive sexual stimulation (Stone, Winslade, and Klugman 2000). Florida is an example of a state that gives the option of castration to convicted sex offenders instead of partaking in lifelong pharmacotherapy.

There are some obvious issues concerning castration as a treatment option. First, the effects of the surgery are fully reversible by taking oral or injectable testosterone. Acquiring such medication is fairly simple if one is computer savvy or knows a local drug dealer (as "street" testosterone is used by do-it-yourself transsexuals/transgendered individuals in their transformation from female to male). Second, having a surgery to ostensibly correct what amounts to a sociosexual issue can be regarded as unethical and unwarranted. Other, noninvasive treatment options have proven to be highly successful, so to resort to the permanent removal of body parts is excessive. Third and most important, without changing the sexual attitudes and behaviors that resulted in the offense in the first place, sexual offending is still possible for a castrated male. Oral assault by an offender or assaulting an individual with an object that can be much more physically damaging to the victim is a possible alternative for a surgically altered offender.

Psychotherapy

Psychotherapy is an extremely broad term used to describe virtually any type of talk therapy. The term is unregulated in many states, with no set standards for education, training, or certification of providers. For the purposes of this discussion, psychotherapy is divided into four categories: sexological, polygraph, plethysmography, and cognitive-behavioral. The most well-known and universally accepted psychotherapy is cognitive-behavioral, which encompasses varying degrees of behavioral modification.

Sexological Treatment

Sexological treatment, in the form of intensive therapy, has a long but relatively unknown history. The paraphilias were originally identified and defined by leading sexologists Krafft-Ebing and Freud, who compiled extensive information about the nature and extent of numerous sexual "deviances." Currently, sexologists strenuously object to any mention of deviancy or abnormality in relation to sex or sexuality and focus instead on providing education and counseling directed to help individuals become fully functioning sexual beings. In terms of the treatment of sexual offenders, sexologists utilize a sex-positive perspective, meaning that the focus is on the positives of sex and sexuality and on helping offenders realize their full sexual potential within society's legal limits. Respect for oneself and others and consent are key areas of sexological treatment. One of the cornerstones of this treatment is a program called Sexual Attitudes Restructuring (SAR), which is designed to challenge the perceptions and opinions that people hold in relation to a wide variety of sexual activities and promote sexual education. Topics addressed include sexual orientation, offending behaviors, communication, establishing boundaries, and sexual self-esteem.

William Seabloom, a sexologist and reverend, conducted one of the first and most comprehensive longitudinal studies of sexual offenders in therapy. Seabloom and his team modified the traditional SAR to be appropriate for adolescent sex offenders. He called his program the Family Journey

Seminar, which focused on providing sexual education to teen offenders and their family members and sought to challenge sexual stereotypes and misconceptions. The Family Journey Seminar was one of four components of the Personal/Socio Awareness treatment program offered through the Lutheran Social Service of Minnesota for teens with sexual behavior that was deemed troubling to the community. The emphasis was on sexual enrichment, over a two-day, sixteen-hour experience involving both large- and small-group sessions in which participants and facilitators shared reactions to various topics and sexually explicit media (Seabloom 1983). This was followed with bimonthly twenty-seven-hour group therapy marathons and biannual family education/sexual awareness seminars (Tokheim 2005). The program was designed to overcome the negative attitudes impacting good communication about sexuality and to provide a supportive community environment for teens and their families (Seabloom 1983). Seabloom and his team contend that children are born sexual and desperately require continual affirmation of their sexuality throughout childhood and adolescence in order to develop into healthy adults.

To assess the efficacy of this program, Seabloom followed the 122 youth participants and more than 400 family members for a period of between fourteen and twenty-four years and found that recidivism was zero for program completers (Seabloom et al. 2003). This recidivism rate is better than all other forms of psychotherapy, surgery, and pharmacotherapy combined and demonstrates that utilizing a sex-positive, education-based approach that focuses on the underlying causes of sexual offending—attitudes and behaviors related to sex and sexuality—are keys to eliminating this problem. Moreover, Seabloom confirmed what other researchers have suggested: that the involvement of the offender's family in treatment is key to virtually eliminating recidivism (Mann 2004; Marshall 1988; Seabloom et al. 2003; Wakeling, Webster, and Mann 2005). This demonstrates that social networks are extremely important and should be fostered as part of any treatment modality. Also noteworthy is that the cost of the program annually is $9,165 per participant (Tokheim 2005). Seabloom raises an interesting question: "But, one might ask if the state chooses to ignore the facts, to abandon proven treatment methods, and to ignore the evidence, based on solid data available for years, that sex offenders are treatable, isn't the state then choosing to be complicit in criminal sexual behavior?" (Tokheim 2005).

Polygraph

Although not traditionally considered a form of psychotherapy, the polygraph is included in this discussion, as it may be incorporated into psychotherapy mandated to offenders on probation or parole. The polygraph is almost always accompanied by talk therapy of some sort and is used as part of the community safety model. The reliability of the polygraph has yet to be established throughout the law enforcement community and is admissible only in some federal circuits and some states, such as New Mexico. Limited research has been conducted regarding the effectiveness of the polygraph as part of the treatment arsenal for sex offenders. A recent five-year study demonstrated that there was no difference in sexual recidivism rates between those offenders who were polygraphed and those who were not, but there was a significant variance in non–sexually violent offenses between the two groups. In this study, 2.9 percent of polygraphed offenders committed a subsequent non–sexually violent offense versus 11.5 percent for nonpolygraphed offenders (McGrath et al. 2007). Whether this speaks to the usefulness of the polygraph as a treatment option or whether offenders are benefiting predominantly from the talk therapy they are required to partake in is unknown. Moreover, the fact that recidivism rates are lower for non–sexually violent crimes may suggest that its benefits rest in reducing overall crime as opposed to sexually based offenses.

Penile Plethysmography

Penile plethysmography is an instrument that measures changes in the circumference of the penis when a male is exposed to various types of sexually explicit material. Any changes in penis size, even those not physically felt by the male, are recorded, and computer software generates graphs that illustrate the degree of arousal the male is experiencing for each sexually explicit image he is shown. Degree of arousal is determined by the speed at which the circumference of the penis increases as well as the extent of engorgement. Treatment may include some form of aversion therapy whereby when the males become aroused at "deviant" sexual materials, they receive an electric shock or are submitted to a foul odor to help redirect their arousal to more appropriate images. However, penile engorgement is not necessarily equated with sexual arousal and can be associated with feelings of anxiety, like those experienced when taking a plethysmography test. Moreover, the plethysmography's design is based on the assumption that sexual arousal is linked to sexual "deviancy," and this has not been empirically proven. Additionally, there are no universal methods, equipment, or analytical standards for the plethysmography, thus resulting in further doubts as to its validity and reliability (Wood et al. 2000). Studies regarding the effectiveness of the device are contradictory, with most research leaning toward a negative assessment of penile plethysmography as a treatment option.

Cognitive-Behavioral Therapy

Cognitive-behavioral therapy (CBT) is a general term used to encompass a wide array of therapies, including emotive behavior therapy, rational behavior therapy, rational living therapy, and dialectic behavior therapy. The overarching principle of CBT is that thoughts cause feelings and behaviors. External factors, such as socioeconomic status or stress, do not cause feelings and behaviors. The underlying basis of this type of therapy is that thoughts can be changed and that people can change their behavior regardless of the situations they encounter. CBT grew out of behavior modification techniques whereby behaviors and reactions to certain stimuli are altered through positive and/or negative reinforcement or punishment. In the area of sexual offending, CBT has come to incorporate a vast amount of key areas, including but not limited to cognitive distortions, denial, victim empathy, and offender motivation.

Since the 1970s, CBT has focused predominantly on behavior modification to change the sexual fantasies of offenders. By the 1980s, this therapy was supplemented with the introduction of cognitive distortions, the identification and elimination of beliefs that excused or justified offending behaviors, and a shift to confrontational methods of therapy.

Prison-based programs are not offered at every correctional institution, and the content of the program varies between and within states. Extensive research has been undertaken on sexual offenders within the prison population, and best practice has been identified. For instance, it has been suggested that four-month open-ended treatment is ideal and that supportive therapists promote better treatment results. (For more information on current best standards for institutional treatment, see Marshall et al. [2006], who conducted a research study on Canadian inmates.)

Currently, most CBT focuses on "deviant" sexual arousal and the elimination of cognitive distortions (Mann 2004). "Deviant" is defined as those behaviors listed in the *Diagnostic and Statistical Manual of Mental Disorders* (*DSM*) of the American Psychiatric Association (for a discussion surrounding the controversy of the *DSM*, see chapter 2). In 1999, Ward and Keenan elaborated on five cognitive distortions present in child sexual offenders. These distortions, albeit unsubstantiated by the research of others, are being used to treat all types of sex offenders. The five hypothesized distortions include the following:

- The child (or victim) is a sexual being who needs and desires the sexual pleasure of the offense.
- The offender is entitled to take what he wants sexually from others because they feel superior.

- The child (or a particular victim) is more trustworthy than adults.
- The offense was committed as a result of uncontrollable behavior (e.g., because of alcohol or drug use).
- The harm caused by the act could have been much worse (Marziano et al. 2006).

Sometimes, CBT-trained therapists will also include maladaptive beliefs and distorted thinking into their treatment modalities (Auburn and Lea 2003). CBT contends that sex offenders have an animated, exaggerated recollection of their offenses that encompasses bias, minimization of harm caused, and outright denial of wrongdoing. However, there are limited empirical studies that have analyzed offenders' descriptions of their offenses, and thus this form of therapy is based mostly on unsubstantiated assumptions (Auburn and Lea 2003).

Other forms of CBT incorporate psychoeducation, elaborate how sexual fantasy contributes to offending, and discuss relapse prevention (Wood et al. 2000). A major element of CBT is journaling and analyzing how offenders' narratives fit within the context of their social practice (Auburn and Lea 2003). The incorporation of relapse prevention into treatment gained increasing popularity in the late 1980s and early 1990s, especially by the criminal justice system and the public. Basically, relapse prevention looks at the factors that potentially cause offending behavior and how an offender can avoid or address those factors in a positive manner. Some of the dynamic, or changeable, risk factors of offending include "deviant" sexual arousal, sexual preoccupation, pervasive anger or hostility, emotional management difficulties, impulsivity, cognitive distortions, and intimacy deficits (Center for Sex Offender Management [CSOM] 2006). These are the behaviors and characteristics that are commonly targeted in the development of relapse prevention plans.

The relapse prevention plan is a self-management strategy that CBT practitioners contend works regardless of the type of offense pathway the offender employs. There is no empirical evidence to suggest that relapse prevention is more advantageous than other elements contained within CBT; however, it tends to be a more positive approach to treatment by focusing on the good aspects of change and how that can enhance an offender's life.

There are four offense pathways proposed by sex offender researchers. The avoidant-passive pathway describes an individual who no longer wants to offend but lacks the necessary coping strategies for a nonoffending lifestyle. Avoidant-active is the pathway describing a person who does not want to offend but uses ineffective coping strategies that actually increase the risk of recidivism. The third pathway is termed approach-automatic, wherein the offender is motivated by situational factors and lacks self-management strategies. Finally, the approach-explicit pathway describes a person who actively plans all of one's offenses and works to ensure that one's offending behavior can continue (CSOM 2006). These models were designed to take into account biological, cultural, environmental, and behavioral factors as well as dynamic risk factors that can, in turn, be utilized to help the offender develop a relapse prevention plan.

CBT also attempts to incorporate and analyze the impacts of denial, attachment, schema, and heterosocial skills on sexual offenders. Outside the offender management community, denial is considered by therapists to be a natural coping strategy, but for sexual offenders, denial is wholly negative. It is hypothesized that three factors influence an offender's decision to deny: motivation (e.g., unwillingness to stop offending or poor perspective skills), threats to self-esteem and image (e.g., fear of being negatively regarded by others), and fear of negative extrinsic factors (e.g., being assaulted) (Lord and Willmot 2004). As addressed in chapter 2, William Marshall has done extensive research on the role of attachment to sexual offending and hypothesizes that sexual offenders often possess insecure attachment styles, such as having emotionally distant parents, and that this impacts their offending behavior (Marshall et al. 2006). A schema is used in CBT to suggest that sex offenders may perceive hostile rejections by adult females and hold misogynistic attitudes about women that ultimately result in offending (Mann 2004). The CBT practitioner then attempts to find the cognitive distortions present and works with the offender to overcome these issues. Finally, CBT may include training in heterosocial skills, as sex offenders have been found to generally lack the ability to function in heterosexual social situations (Dreznick 2003).

CBT is a fairly convoluted type of treatment that encompasses a wide array of topics and considerations. Research on the effectiveness of CBT has been mixed: although the impact of certain social factors has been shown to influence offending behavior, it is unclear how all the factors covered in CBT work together. In other words, how does an offender who had a bad childhood, is poor and uneducated, and has self-esteem issues differ from an offender who comes from a loving and secure family but who holds misogynistic attitudes that promote rape? Is the same type of treatment appropriate for both? Or would it be more advantageous to develop more individualistic treatment plans as opposed to the one-size-fits-all approach? Moreover, most CBT treatment modalities evaluated in research have been conducted in correctional institutions. Relying on this minority group of sex offenders for the development of treatment options is dubious at best, as we know that most sexual offenders go unreported and untreated. Additionally, sex and sexuality are completely absent from CBT, leaving one to wonder how a crime based on sex and sexuality can have a treatment modality that ignores these components.

Pharmacotherapy

Pharmacotherapy is the ingestion of drugs to treat the symptoms of sexual offending and in some circumstances is mandated by the court as part of sentencing. Generally, two types of medications are used in this form of treatment: antiandrogens and psychotropic drugs. Antiandrogens decrease the normal production of testosterone or perform an antagonizing action to testosterone at the level of the receptor (Rosler and Witztum 2000). In other words, it prevents testosterone from being produced and is thus believed to decrease both sexual desire and the ability to sustain an erection. Psychotropic drugs are used to control conditions believed to be associated with sexual offending, such as obsessive-compulsive disorder or manic depression. The most commonly prescribed medications of this type are antidepressants.

Studies have demonstrated that the testosterone concentrations in sexual offenders are identical to those found in the general male population. Medical researchers hypothesize that sexual offenders have naturally enhanced receptors or abnormal responses to androgens by the receptors that cause them to offend. Consequently, pharmacotherapy with antiandrogens is designed to completely reduce testosterone and/or result in the total suppression of androgen action at the level of the receptor (Rosler and Witztum 2000).

Two of the most commonly used antiandrogen medications are medroxyprogestrone acetate (MPA) and cyproterone acetate (CPA). Cyproterone acetate was the first commercially available antiandrogen and has been used in the treatment of sexual offenders since 1970. Doses can vary between 50 and 100 milligrams per day, and the average patient realizes a 150-milligram-per-day decrease in testosterone production (Rosler and Witztum 2000). Patients also report decreases in "deviant" sexual fantasies and "abnormal" sexual behavior, but to what extent is unclear. Recidivism while on the drug varies widely, depending on the study, with the mean at 6 percent, and the effects of treatment are reversible within one to two months after termination of the medication (Rosler and Witztum 2000). Lifetime treatment is recommended for patients considered to have severe or recurrent offending behaviors, although the definitions of severe or recurrent are debatable. Side effects of CPA include breast enlargement, bodily weakness, weight gain, blood clots, depression, potentially fatal cancers, and decreased bone density (Rosler and Witztum 2000).

Medroxyprogesterone acetate results in the inhibition of gonadotropin secretion, and therefore secretion of testosterone by the testicles is significantly reduced. Doses of MPA range from 500 to 1,000 milligrams weekly, with the most common dosage being between 300 and 500 milligrams

weekly by injection. This type of drug was first used by a highly controversial sexologist in the 1960s for the treatment of transgendered patients
and reduces testosterone levels to castration concentrations within one to
two weeks (Rosler and Witztum 2000). It is used most commonly for the
treatment of pedophilia, exhibitionism, and voyeurism. As with CPA, recidivism rates vary dramatically, depending on the study, with a mean of
27 percent (Rosler and Witztum 2000). Unlike CPA, the vast majority of patients taking MPA develop side effects that may include weight gain,
malaise, intense nightmares, gallstones, decreased bone density,
headaches, muscular cramps, constant pain in the upper middle part of the
stomach, diabetes, and pulmonary embolism (Rosler and Witztum 2000).

Medroxyprogesterone acetate is the treatment choice in many American correctional institutions. In Georgia, conviction of aggravated child
molestation results in the mandatory ingestion of MPA either in lieu of
prison or just prior to release from prison. In Louisiana, multiple convictions of offenses against persons under twelve years of age results in
mandatory MPA treatment, with the offender being responsible for the
full cost of the drugs as well as accompanying evaluations. Florida requires certain classes of sex offenders to be treated with MPA for the entirety of their lives or submit to castration as part of the punishment
(Stone, Winslade, and Klugman 2000).

Psychotropic drugs are most commonly known to treat disorders related to depression, compulsivity, and impulsivity. Frequently, however,
sex offenders are being prescribed these drugs because they are being co-
diagnosed as having a paraphilia and other mental health disorders. Generally, selective serotonin reuptake inhibitors (SSRIs) are given to offenders identified as sexually "addicted," compulsive, impulsive, or sexually
excessive or with variants of obsessive-compulsive disorder (Marshall
and Marshall 2001). Despite the fact that there is no empirical evidence to
support comorbidity between sexual offending and sexual "addiction,"
often offenders are prescribed both SSRIs and antiandrogens in combination (Marshall and Marshall 2001).

As with other treatment options, there are significant drawbacks to
pharmacotherapy. Drug therapy often involves the provision of lifelong
treatment. This commitment would be challenging for the average citizen,
let alone a person who has diagnosed behavioral issues. Moreover, the
side effects of the medications may also be lifelong, and no longitudinal
studies have been conducted to identify what, if any, risks are associated
with such medications. Although researchers can borrow information and
make hypotheses from literature on male-to-female transgenderism (as
this process involves complete chemical castration), it is challenging to
understand the long-term full effects of the drugs on nontransgendered
persons. The related cost to the health care system could easily be more

than providing lifelong psychotherapy or incarceration, as patients of pharmacotherapy are forced to contend with cancer, diabetes, and other serious medical concerns that result in a significant financial burden.

Additionally, pharmacotherapy may lull the public and correctional and medical establishments into a false sense of security, believing that offending is virtually impossible while an offender is medicated. Quite the contrary: humans are very adaptable, and when behaviors are as engrained as sexuality and offending, such individuals will inevitably locate another venue to release their stress and anxiety, such as viewing illegal materials (e.g., child pornography) or employing objects in their assaults as substitutes for their nonfunctioning genitalia. Most important, like surgery, pharmacotherapy does not treat the underlying attitudes or behaviors that result in offending in the first place and instead focuses only on the symptoms. Without changing how a person thinks about sex and sexuality and the role of women and children, the offending thoughts will remain and present themselves in other, equally destructive ways. This is not to say that pharmacotherapy does not have benefits. In fact, when used in conjunction with appropriate psychotherapy, it can have dramatic results. However, the goal should be not lifelong dependency on drugs but, rather, utilizing medication in the early stages of treatment to help remove the anxiety and nervousness that accompany entering intensive counseling. Drugs can often help offenders refocus their thinking so that counseling can begin in a more productive manner.

RESEARCH ON TREATMENT SUCCESS

Research on sexual offenders is seriously flawed for a variety of reasons. First, outside of limited sexological data collected through sexual history taking (see Gebhard et al. 1965; Kinsey et al. 1948, 1953), research includes only studies of individuals charged with and convicted of sexual offenses. Consequently, those who were able to plead their crimes down to nonsexual offenses and those whose crimes have not been reported to the police (i.e., the vast majority of incest offenses) do not form part of the sex crimes statistics. Moreover, the individuals studied are often serving jail or prison sentences and were therefore less likely to be able to afford adequate legal representation to have their charges reduced or dropped and are predominantly from lower socioeconomic backgrounds. Basing research and ultimately public policy on such a limited sample of offenders has significant repercussions. Focusing on the minority of sexual offending behavior like "stranger danger" as opposed to the more frequent intrafamilial assaults leads to public policy that erroneously targets extrafamilial perpetrators and does not provide for punishments suitable to the vast majority of offenses in which the offender is known to the victim, such as a husband or father.

Second, there is no consistent methodology regarding the study of sexual offending or the creation of treatment methods based on studies of sexual offenders. Researchers cannot agree on the definition of a sexual offense, on the measures of recidivism, or on the creation of treatment modalities. Some research defines sexual offenses as those listed explicitly in legislation, while other research defines sexual offenses as those conditions outlined in the *DSM*. In addition, research is often conducted by scholars with little or no clinical experience. Clinicians working with sex offenders are often trained to analyze verbal and nonverbal communication in order to probe more deeply into the underlying psychological issues that resulted in the person offending. For these reasons, research on sexual offenders has been highly contradictory and controversial. Yet review of studies with solid methodologies and theoretical frameworks that support validation and replication reveal general trends of significance.

To date, not one scientifically sound research study has concluded that sex offenders are incurable and have an insatiable desire to commit more offenses (Webster, Gartner, and Doob 2006). In fact, studies repeatedly demonstrate that offenders have low rates of recidivism compared to other offenders, as discussed in chapter 6. Researchers have been unable to consistently uncover associations between traditional criminological factors and recidivism. There is no link between recidivism of sexual offenders and marital status, prior nonsexual offenses, prior nonviolent offenses, a history of juvenile delinquency, "deviant" sexual preferences, a developmental history of family problems, poor relationships with parents, or having experienced sexual abuse as a child (Campbell 2000). Some studies have also found no correlation between substance abuse, psychological problems, lack of appropriate social skills, victim empathy, denial of the offense, limited or lack of motivation for treatment, length of treatment, antisocial personality disorder, "deviant" sexual attitudes or anger problems, and recidivism (Campbell 2000). Other researchers found that both institutional and community-based treatments were associated with decreased recidivism rates for sexual offenders (Hanson et al. 2002). Thus, sexual offending may not follow the same trends as nonsexual offending, meaning that prior offenses and behaviors are not positively correlated with reoffending (State of Ohio Department of Rehabilitation and Corrections 2001).

Although sexual offenders may be at greater risk of reoffending based on such actuarial measures as prior offenses and types of victims, not all studies support this finding. Such conclusions can have significant implications for public policy and the criminal justice system. Sexual offending does not pose the same risk to society as nonsexual crimes in terms of recidivism, and the false belief that "once a sex offender, always a sex offender" is negatively guiding the actions of police in terms of charging practices, the development of presentence reports, the sentences handed down by the judiciary, and conditions given to sexual offenders for probation and parole (Webster et al. 2006).

Recidivism rates do vary by type of offense. Generally, rapists tend to have the highest recidivism rates, followed by extrafamilial child molesters and then incest offenders (Seto and Barbaree 1999). Moreover, rapists tend to score higher on the psychopathy scale than other sexual offenders, although these scores are strongly related to the offender's age, level of education, and socioeconomic status at the time of arrest (Seto and Barbaree 1999). This essentially means that young, poorly educated, low-income males are most likely to score high on psychopathy scales used by medical professionals. The consequence is that young, uneducated males tend to be overrepresented in prisons as sexual offenders compared to older, more educated, and economically successful males. In addition, when incest offenders are imprisoned (in substantially lower numbers than extrafamilial offenders), such individuals are more likely to be granted parole (Seto and Barbaree 1999). The manner in which the criminal justice system is designed can effectively impact access to and the effectiveness of treatment. Throughout the criminal process, defendants are encouraged by their attorneys to resist treatment or blatantly deny culpability. Those accused of sex crimes generally do not provide statements or testimony at trial, and the sentencing may not reflect the actual level of criminality involved in the act (Birgden and Vincent 2000). In this sense, the law contributes to the dysfunctional thinking of the offender.

Treatment design has traditionally been based on the notion of a one-size-fits-all approach. The basic elements of treatment include informed consent (knowing the type of intervention and its risks and benefits), which is driven by formal assessment mechanisms. Additional elements are the maintenance of a positive rapport between therapist and client, the identification of specific and measurable goals, and the movement toward documented progress (CSOM 2006). Treatment has been broadly defined as promoting goal attainment and managing "crime producing factors" (CSOM 2006: 2). However, goals of sex offender treatment tend to be predetermined with little opportunity for the individual to modify one's treatment regimen. This stems from the belief that sex offenders are not motivated or insightful enough to identify the areas in which they need assistance (CSOM 2006). Consequently, most government-sanctioned treatment is based on CBT and relapse prevention. Providing treatment based solely on what the government is willing to fund is problematic for obvious reasons. Other therapies, such as SAR, although proven to be highly successful, will not receive government monies because they fail to subscribe to the traditional medical model of treatment. Recent research suggests that sexual offenders may feel inadequate as sexual beings and seek to redefine their victims' response to their sexual advances as an expression of love and mutuality as opposed to abuse (Lawson 2003). Thus, treatment would need to focus on appropriate sexual expression, identifying and working through feelings of isolation, and redefining sexuality by helping the offender move beyond sexualized affection to equality, mutuality, and respect. This type of treatment would involve delving into the highly controversial topic of sexuality and has therefore remained elusive in treatment modalities provided to offenders.

Studies demonstrate that treatment has proven successful in keeping recidivism rates low for sexual offenders. The effects of other variables on recidivism, such as social networks, employment, the response of the criminal justice system, and socioeconomic status, have not been fully evaluated. Research has demonstrated that sexual offenders recidivate less often than nonsexual offenders, but why this is the case is not yet fully understood. This represents a huge gap in the literature and has serious repercussions for any treatment programs developed. If sex offenders simply mature out of their crimes, as do most nonsexual offenders, it would have implications for the types of treatments offered. However, it is likely that the answer is much more complex: sexuality is fluid over the course of a lifetime, meaning that desire and sexual orientation are not static. Biochemical, social, and environmental elements vary greatly over the life span; hormone levels fluctuate; and social circles change, as do sexual attitudes and behaviors. People begin their sexual existence as infants with a focus on oneself (e.g., masturbation and self-exploration) and then become asexual (e.g., uninterested in self or others), and then the majority develop heterosexual attractions, while others develop same-sex attractions. The development of one's sexual orientation does not necessarily terminate in adolescence and is not linear for everyone. In adulthood, sexual experimentation may continue as individuals discover that sexual attraction is based on attraction to the personality or character of an individual as opposed to the genitalia. What this means for the study and treatment of sex offenders has not yet been illuminated, but the consequences could be significant. Sexual offending is not merely a result of opportunity or so-called deviant sexual desire but goes to the heart of how people regard themselves as sexual beings.

It is troublesome that treatment programs do not focus on sex (biological aspects) and sexuality (sociocultural aspects). As discussed in chapters 2 and 4, the focus has shifted from sex crimes being defined by religion to medicine in the form of psychiatrists and psychologists defining, measuring, and treating the problem. Sex is still a highly taboo topic and one that many people, including psychiatrists and psychologists, are very uncomfortable discussing. The belief has generally been that sex offenders have underlying mental disorders that require medical intervention. However, as society changes, so too does the framework by which we define sex crimes. Recall that it was only a few decades ago that society insisted that homosexuality was a deviant behavior and forced individuals to undergo intrusive behavior modification therapies (e.g., electric shock). Currently, we use similar although less barbaric treatments for transgendered persons. Would it not be more beneficial to approach treatment from a more cautious perspective, with a "do-no-harm" model as a guide? Using a sexological treatment framework, whereby sexuality education forms the foundation of therapy, is significantly more beneficial, as it addresses the underlying issues of sex and sexuality. The literature on treatment modalities clearly illustrates that sex and sexuality are lacking components in current treatments. There is a long way to go in the treatment of sexual offending, and it is vital for policymakers and the public to view this highly charged issue through a more objective lens. Through research, we will continue to learn that the repression of sexuality within society, our families, and our religions is a key reason for sexual offending. Until and unless we, as a society, openly and honestly discuss sex and sexuality from a positive perspective and not focus solely on the negatives, we will continue to have to deal with the consequences in the very real form of victims and offenders.

10

Looking beyond U.S. Policies

If it does not increase safety and instead promotes a false sense of security we need to find more effective, less dangerous ways of achieving
the paramount goal of protecting [women and] children. (Steinbock
1995: 8)

In order to understand where the United States is on the continuum of
sexual control, it is necessary to learn the types of legislation and controls that exist in other countries. This chapter explores how sex-positive,
sex-neutral, and sex-negative countries manage sexual expression and
what lessons may be learned for the United States. America is a sex-
negative country in which sexual expression is heavily legislated and controlled, although this may seem counterintuitive, as sex is talked about
and viewed virtually everywhere via television, radio, and an array of ad-
vertising media. Despite the fact that Americans are inundated with sex
messages, accurate information is severely lacking, and society is quick to
label individuals negatively who participate in certain sexual activities.
American society controls sex and thereby controls the behaviors of its citizens. Interestingly, America is not alone as a sex-negative culture; its
neighbor to the north, Canada, also severely restricts various sexual outlets and imposes harsh penalties on citizens who break sexual taboos.
Conversely, Thailand is a sex-positive country in which minimal behaviors are considered illegal and consent is emphasized. Thailand has taken
the approach that citizens are capable of managing their own behavior
within social boundaries, and thus few activities warrant criminalization.
An example of a sex-neutral country is Japan. In Japan, if citizens are ful-
filling their social obligations, such as marriage and procreation, then

177

other sexual outlets are accepted, provided that they are not flaunted publicly. The key in Japan is discretion; if behaviors are made public that are contrary to custom, such as homosexuality, then the law intervenes.

A SEX-POSITIVE COUNTRY—THAILAND

Thailand for many is associated with media coverage of male American tourists traveling abroad to have sexual relations with children. Although this occurs, it is not because Thailand devalues its children. Severe poverty has resulted in families making extraordinarily difficult choices, and race and class hierarchies have resulted in structural inequalities and abuse. Many of the child sex workers are bought from their families in rural areas because of extreme economic hardship. Most parents believe that their children will be working low-paying jobs in the cities and sending home much-needed money for the family to survive. In Thailand, 1.7 percent of females under eighteen years of age are involved in the child commercial sex trade (Taywaditep, Coleman, and Dumronggittigule 2004). Many child sex workers return home after reaching the age of majority and marry with little stigmatization attached to their activities. Although the American press has covered this issue, Thailand does not have a national policy that supports or endorses child exploitation, abuse, or neglect. On the contrary, Thailand can be viewed as an example of a sex-positive country whereby sex is decriminalized as opposed to being a nation of high regulation, such as the United States. Basic customs and social mores are generally understood by all citizens, and thus there is no need to criminalize a vast array of sexual activities.

Thailand is a Buddhist country. Buddhism associates sex with good karma and generally has no prohibitions surrounding sex and sexuality. Thailand regards the body spiritually; the head is sacred, the feet are the base, and the genitalia are neutral, meaning that there are no overt taboos about sexuality (Collins 1989). Contrary to Western culture, Thailand considers sex a religious act that gains a person merit, and there are no concepts of shame or guilt linked with sexuality. Importantly, Thailand has few proscribed sexual behaviors, meaning that most sex is not criminalized. The activities that are forbidden socially, although not necessarily legally, include those that go against the Buddhist faith of sexual misconduct: adultery, rape, sexual abuse of children, and activities that result in the sorrow of others (Taywaditep et al. 2004). In Thailand, there is no age-of-consent law related to sexual conduct, which reverts to the religious belief that sex is good and good for you thus that it need not be regulated or controlled by government. However, Thailand is a male-dominated, patriarchal society that recognizes women mainly as mothers. Although sex and sexuality are expressed positively, women find honor in being conservative and feminine (Taywaditep et al. 2004).

Rape is a criminal offense in Thailand, although the law is rarely enforced. Media coverage of rape is more titillating than condemning. The government does not keep statistics on the incidence of sexual crimes, but a 1990 study of soldiers reported that 5 percent of the twenty-one-year-old male respondents had admitting to forcing a woman to have sex (Taywaditep et al. 2004). Studies reveal that Thai men rationalized coercive sex by stating that a woman would get them sexually excited and then not be receptive to sex. At this point, the man believed he could not control himself. The social belief among Thai men asserts that once sexual arousal of a man is initiated, it cannot be controlled (Taywaditep et al. 2004). No data currently exist about incest in Thailand.

The country has very different social mores surrounding touch. Touching others is extremely common in Thailand and frequently does not have any sexual connotations attached. Commenting on the good looks of others and smiling and flirting are encouraged as a way to positively reinforce one's sexuality and self-esteem (Collins 1989). Touching is done for the pure enjoyment of the act and the positive feelings it engenders and not for sexual satisfaction per se. Because of the sex positive attitude in Thailand, pornography and fantasy tend to be very romantic and "soft" core in comparison to what is available in the United States. Nudity, especially among children, is considered natural. Thai people are comfortable with their bodies and thus have no taboos against nudity. Contrastingly, in America, nudity—especially among children—has a sexual connotation. Americans have come to link nudity with sex and promiscuity and thus regard child nudity as abusive. It is important to remember that these are cultural attitudes that are not universal.

For the Thai, sexuality and sex are forms of interpersonal communication: an exchange whose meaning is defined based on what is being given (Collins 1989). Sex is not restricted to marriage, for procreation, or for committed relationships, although women are still expected to be more virtuous than men and less sexually experienced. Sex can be an expression of friendship or for pure pleasure or enjoyment (Collins 1989). Interestingly, Thai people use vaginal intercourse as their main sexual outlet, with minimal occurrence or participation in oral or anal sex. In Thailand, money has just recently replaced the barter system, so exchanging sex for gifts, food, or money does not have the negative connotations it has in America. Research into the sexual attitudes and behaviors of Thai people began by the government in the 1990s as a result of increasing HIV/AIDS infections. Because of the AIDS epidemic sweeping the globe, commercial sex has started to become stigmatized. Men are expected to learn some social restraint, whereas women are more expected to be chaste and less sexual.

A SEX-NEUTRAL COUNTRY—JAPAN

Japan is a sex neutral country, meaning that sex is handled with discretion, and only when socially unacceptable behaviors are publicly flaunted does the legal system become involved. In size, Japan is slightly larger than the state of California, but close to 90 percent of the country is mountainous, meaning that local communities are often isolated from each other and have consequently developed their own cultures, customs, religions, and mores. Despite the increasing Western influence in Japan, many of the various cultures have yet to be assimilated into a common, urban culture (Hatano and Shimazaki 2004). The vast majority of citizens reside in urban centers and practice either the Shinto or Buddhist faiths. Japan is a society of strict social classes and gender codes of conduct that are rooted in millennia of history. Gender roles are defined traditionally and stereotypically, and in direct contrast fantasy and pornography are replete with themes of sadism and violence. In light of the country's polite and formal exterior, there are laws proscribing certain forms of sexual expression, including pornography (Collins 1989).

Although the role of women is publicly devalued in Japan, roles in the home are often reversed, and women have complete control over family finances. This may leave men with a sense of emasculation that is indirectly compensated for through legislation that severely restricts female autonomy. For example, women can rarely keep their maiden names after marriage, and few receive financial supports (including for children) after divorce (Hatano and Shimazaki 2004). The religious faiths of the Japanese do not recognize good or evil, and thus any guilt or shame traditionally associated with sex found in Western countries is absent. In the 1950s and 1960s, there was a social separation of reproduction from other sexual behaviors. The result was that many young people lost their sexual self-identity and turned to their parents and politicians for cues on appropriate sexual morality, as there was no other source of guidance (Hatano and Shimazaki 2004).

Historically, Japan has strictly controlled the sexuality of certain classes, such as soldiers and commanders, limiting the expression of their passion and sexual desires. Consequently, romantic love, behaviors deemed immoral, and adultery were forbidden. If these rules of social conduct were broken, the penalty was often death (Hatano and Shimazaki 2004). Conversely, the average Japanese citizen was allowed to partake in romantic love and was extremely frank and uninhibited about sex and sexuality. Over time, as Japan's influence in the world increased, so did its prohibitive sexual mores. The reliance on stereotypes used to define social roles amplified, and women were increasingly expected to be modest and passive sexual beings. Psychosexual development shifted to gathering knowledge through television, comics, and computers, resulting in a lack of social skills and an inability to succeed in interpersonal relationships (Hatano and Shimazaki 2004). Japan's increasing influence globally coincided with a significant slowing in the sexual development of its citizens. Currently, it is not uncommon for women in their twenties to never have masturbated or for teenagers to lack any interest in sex or dating until in mid-adolescence. The age of consent in Japan is sixteen in large urban centers and thirteen in the provinces, which coincides with the age at which people can work in bars and sell liquor in the cities and with the age of puberty in the provinces (Collins 1989). Contrast that with the average age of coitus, which is twenty-one years for males and twenty-two years for females (Hatano and Shimazaki 2004).

In Japan, sex is generally repressed and is regarded as an embarrassing topic. Statistics on oral and anal sex, frequency of coitus, positions used, and the levels of sexual satisfaction are not publicly reported (Hatano and Shimazaki 2004). Moreover, Japanese culture is highly focused on the family, and thus sexual acts can cause shame to be placed on the family name. Thus, specific behaviors are discouraged from becoming public, such as homosexuality. However, there is no sexual sin in Japan per se, so activities socially frowned on in America, such as extramarital sex, are common.

In terms of sex crimes, Japan, like many countries around the world, considers intergenerational sex a learning experience for the younger partner, especially in male homosexual relations. Although rape is against the law, there is no definition as to what constitutes rape, and the victim or his or her parents are required to file a complaint against the accused and produce evidence of force or the threat of violence (Hatano and Shimazaki 2004). However, in recent years there has been an increase in the reports of rape: 5,009 in 1992 compared to 12,501 in 2003 (Sudo et al. 2006). Public concern regarding rape has increased in recent years as a result of an incident in October 2004 in which an eight-year-old child was abducted and killed by a repeat sexual offender. Until that time, Japan disregarded the possibility of recidivism in the release decisions of sexual offenders (Sudo et al. 2006). Understanding sexual offenses and sexual offenders is very much a new phenomenon in Japan.

A SEX-NEGATIVE COUNTRY—CANADA

Like the United States, Canada can be considered a sex-negative country wherein sexual expression is heavily legislated. Although Canada currently follows a hybrid model of justice, the focus tends to be on the punitive aspects of the model. Dangerous offender legislation has been introduced and is regularly used against persons who have committed sexual crimes, especially nonincest child offenders. National databases have been created to monitor the movements of those convicted of sexual crimes. In addition, persons who have committed sexual crimes report being harassed by the police: police will unexpectedly show up at an offender's workplace or home and offenders are followed by the police and stopped for traffic offenses, and many have been "convinced" by police to provide a DNA sample for inclusion in the national database despite not being charged or convicted of a crime that requires DNA registration. This level of control is counterproductive, as it has the effect of limiting an offender's social networks and thereby his means for not reoffending. A small number of high-profile cases of stranger assaults against both women and children prompted lawmakers to "get tough on crime" and enact various pieces of legislation. As in the United States, such legislation is rarely applied to family or acquaintance offenders, as the social view is that families should not be torn apart as a result of sexual abuse when treatment is available.

In 1947, Canada witnessed its first legislation to deal with repeat offenders, the Habitual Offender Act. This act was not intended to deal exclusively with sexual crimes, so in 1948 the government introduced the Criminal Sexual Psychopath Act, requiring mental health experts to diagnose and treat "dangerous" sexual offenders. But what constituted a "dangerous" offender? At this point in history, "dangerous" referred mostly to homosexual men. Sentences under the Criminal Sexual Psychopath Act were a minimum of two years to a maximum of indeterminate imprisonment, which would be reviewed every three years to ascertain eligibility for parole. This act was replaced in 1960 by the Sexual Offender Act, which more clearly articulated the concept of dangerousness. Dangerousness was now based on a person's criminal record and the circumstances of one's most recent crime. Thus, if a person's most recent offense involved violence, it was likely that they would have strict conditions for release.

In 1977, at the recommendation of a correctional committee and a desire to move away from a reliance on the medical model, both the Habitual Offender Act and the Sexual Offender Act were rescinded and replaced with amendments to the Criminal Code of Canada. These amendments applied equally to violent offenders regardless of whether their crime was sexually motivated (John Howard Society of Alberta 1999). It was around this time that Canadian law mandated the release of all offenders after serving two-thirds of their sentences, primarily as a result of prison overcrowding. This laissez-faire criminal justice response, however, ended as the 1980s began.

In the 1980s, public opinion became more conservative, and laws were changed so that sex offenders could be detained for their full sentences if they were considered by the National Parole Board to be dangerous offenders (John Howard Society of Alberta 1999). This coincided with a resurgence of the feminist movement, in which rape and violence against women became metaphors of women's oppression. The women's movement lobbied for the passage of new sexual assault legislation in 1983 that sought to protect victims' privacy rights as well as expand the scope of the type of offender who could be charged with rape (to include a husband, date, or acquaintance). The Canadian media covered this lobbying in depth, drawing attention to sexual aggression, and often questioned the motives of the women's movement for not wanting the victim's past sexual experiences to be a reflection of her character. Unfortunately, the sensationalization of the media attention came to trivialize women's experiences with sexual violence, and this permeated the criminal justice system (Los and Chamard 1997). The goal of the 1983 legislation was to shift the focus to the notion that rape was a crime of power and violence as opposed to sex. The goal was to give women more protection under the law; however, many continued to perceive acquaintance assault as less serious, and offenders often received lesser sentences, as women were regarded as somehow complicit in the offense (Los and Chamard 1997).

Later in the 1980s, the high-profile case of Joseph Fredericks captured the media's attention. In late winter of 1988, Joseph Fredericks was released from prison with mandatory supervision after serving two-thirds (the mandatory release time) of a five-year sentence for raping a child. Three months after his release, Fredericks abducted an eleven-year-old from a shopping mall. He held and raped the child for two days before strangling him, slitting his throat, and leaving him to die in the woods. Fredericks had a history of both mental illness and perpetration of sexual assaults against male children. His case occurred during a period of institutional reform and fell between the ever-growing gap between the criminal justice and the mental health systems (Petrunik 2003).

After a thorough examination of America's response to sexual violence, the Canadian government drafted civil commitment legislation five years after the Frederick case. This legislation was also in response to the 1993 arrest of serial rapist and murderer Paul Bernardo for the kidnapping, rape, sodomy, and murder of two teenage girls. However, the legislation was deemed a violation of the Charter of Rights and Freedoms and was revoked. Instead of postsentence detention, new legislation was created to eliminate maximum sentencing for dangerous offenders, extend the application deadline for dangerous offender status, provide intensive long-term postprison supervision orders, and provide judicial restraint/recognizance orders to restrict the movement of sex offenders in the community (Petrunik 2003).

In responding to the Fredericks and Bernardo cases, Canada created a task force to study potential reform of sex offender legislation. It was not until 1995 that the National Flagging System was introduced to track offenders considered to be high risk and/or dangerous. This system provides officials with information about an offender's likelihood of being a high and/or continuous risk of future violent conduct. Candidates are placed into this system if records indicate that there is a reasonable prospect that the government will seek a dangerous or long-term offender designation and there is a high likelihood of reoffense. Placement on this list is a result of risk assessment of the offender, based on psychological evaluation. The major problem with this system is that it penalizes a person for crimes one might commit in the future. Such laws appear to be a clear violation of a person's civil liberties and a draconian measure of control.

The Canadian government espoused incapacitation, as opposed to punishment, as the goal of sexual predator laws. The introduction of dangerous offender legislation in 1997, Bill C-55, changed the manner in which sex offenders could apply for and receive parole (John Howard Society of Alberta 1999). It allowed the government to keep an offender institutionalized for longer than justified by the criminal act and the offender's criminal record by creating two categories of dangerousness: dangerous offender and long-term offender. According to the Criminal Code of Canada, there are a number of conditions that must be met for a dangerous offender designation. The offense must have caused personal injury, and the offender must be a threat to the well-being of others, as demonstrated through a pattern of behavior that is aggressive or fails to show restraint or a demonstration that shows lack of control over sexual impulses. In addition, in order to be considered for a dangerous offender designation, an individual must have been subject to a minimum of ten years in prison. To be designated a long-term offender, an individual must have received a sentence of at least two years, show a pattern of repetitive behavior, be at risk of recidivism, or have committed a sexual offense. With changes in the laws, those deemed dangerous were now required to spend seven, as opposed to three, years in prison before being eligible to contest the finding of dangerousness, and their sentence was considered indeterminate. If the government is unsuccessful in designating an offender as dangerous or long term, the option exists of pursuing an 810.1 warrant. This warrant is reserved for offenders who have served their full sentence in prison (because they were denied early release) and after leaving prison are rearrested and brought to court to have restrictions similar to parole invoked. At this moment, it is uncertain whether Bill C-55 will withstand a Charter of Rights and Freedoms challenge, as it potentially violates the offender's right to life, liberty, and security of person.

In 2000, the DNA Identification Act was passed, governing the establishment and administration of the National DNA Databank, which allows judges to make postconviction orders requiring DNA samples. The act also applies retroactively so that offenders convicted prior to the law may be required to submit DNA samples on the order of a judge; this retroactive provision applies to offenders convicted of two or more sex crimes or those who were under sentence at the time an application was made to the court for a DNA sample. The retroactive provision applies to more than 4,700 offenders. By March 2005, there were almost 100,000 profiles in the DNA Databank of either convicted offenders or samples from crime scenes. Later in 2005, the law was strengthened, resulting in an increase of offenses for which a DNA sample is required.

The media's attention is a powerful tool that often forces governments into action, and this is precisely what happened with sex offenders in Canada. Media reports of sexual attacks escalated, causing the government to place blame for the allegedly increasing crime problem onto persons who have committed sexual crimes. The result was a "get-tough" approach to legislation and a throwback to the justice model. Another such example is the Sex Offender Information Registration Act passed in 2004. This act gave police unprecedented rapid access to information in real time and resulted in the creation of the National Sex Offender Registry. Unlike U.S. sex offender registration legislation, this registry is accessible only to the police and contains the offender's name, date of birth, address, photograph, identifying marks, and the crimes for which he was convicted (Royal Canadian Mounted Police 2005). Public notification of sex offender information is governed by the Privacy Act and is at the discretion of each province or territory. While historically it was rare for police to notify the public of the whereabouts of a sexual offender in Canada, this is becoming more and more common. The model of preventive incarceration, although in existence in Canada, has not occurred to nearly the extent it has in the United States despite the fact that in both countries legislation was encouraged by the media representation of and public reaction to high-profile sex offenses. The United States has experienced a due process counterrevolution that contrasts sharply with Canadian court decisions that have protected the due process rights, at least in part, of sexual offenders. It remains to be seen when and if there will be a Charter of Rights and Freedoms challenge to the dangerous and long-term offender laws as well as the 810.1 legislation. The best approach to reducing recidivism, albeit not the most commonly used one, has proven to be the reintegration of sex offenders into the community.

This multidisciplinary approach involves intensive monitoring of sex offenders on parole or probation to prevent them from committing new offenses, with the primary goal being "no more victims." In an approach varied for each offender, a case management team closely cooperates to reduce the risk of future offenses with the aim being to eliminate opportunity and access. Through in-depth knowledge of the offender (including history, potential victims, high-risk behaviors, and polygraph tests), the team works to compile a modus operandi for each offender that provides the foundation for surveillance and supervision plans to lower risk by denying the access and privacy that is required to reoffend (English, Jones, and Patrick 2003). Such a model is used in Canada by the Mennonite Central Committee, which offers support to recently released high risk offenders and seeks to hold the offender accountable. The Mennonites call this program a Circle of Support and Accountability. It involves members of the faith community and other volunteers meeting collectively and individually with persons deemed high-risk offenders. The purpose is to provide a social safety net and social supports. Many of the offenders who have Circles have been incarcerated for more than ten years and are completely unfamiliar with how society currently operates. The Circle volunteers work with the offender and teach him basic skills, such as getting a health card, shopping for groceries, taking public transit, and arranging accommodation. Although this group is not found nationally, it is present in many provinces and works collaboratively with the police to ensure that community safety is a top priority. This group boasts a high success rate and is supported by many victims of sexual crimes. However, the statistics kept by the Mennonite Central Committee are related to rearrests for sexual crimes and are not inclusive of rearrests for other crimes and technical violations of probation, parole, or 810.1 warrants.

Some faith groups have developed programs to deal with sexual offending that incorporate surrender to a higher power. One of the most innovative and recently publicized is the restorative justice movement of the Mennonite community. The basic tenets of restorative justice are that it is vital to understand that sexual violence is generational and requires support of victim and offender, the belief that people can change for the better when given the tools to do so, and that genuine forgiveness and healing are possible. (For more information about this movement, refer to Yantzi 1998.)

LEARNING FROM OTHER COUNTRIES

What can the United States learn from the experiences of Thailand, Japan, and Canada? Culture plays a significant role in the establishment of sexual crimes, and as the United States becomes increasingly mosaic in terms of culture, the current laws will likely be challenged as irrelevant or overly restrictive. The experiences in Thailand and Japan, although certainly not ideal in all respects, demonstrate that decriminalization and demedicalization of most sexual activity is effective and does not necessarily promote "deviancy." Perhaps America needs to reevaluate its age of consent and the supposed harms of intergenerational sexual activity, where there are few years between the two parties (e.g., a male who is nineteen and a female who is fifteen). Further, having more laws restricting sexual expression has proven to be ineffective in dealing with sexual crimes and recidivism. Truly sadistic and violent sexual offenders are rare, and the laws should reflect the common, not the atypical. Canada, like the United States, has created laws in response to high-profile cases, and these laws have been applied to nonviolent sexual offenders in ways that are inappropriate. The United States, unlike any country in the world, has taken legislation regarding sexual offenders to the extreme. Once offenders are released from prison, the government continues to regulate every aspect of their movement, from where they live, to the type of job they can have, to the associates they can keep, to when they can begin a consensual adult relationship, to whether they can use a computer. The restrictions have become overwhelmingly excessive and apply to offenders who are not at a high risk of reoffense. Such stringent regulations that interfere with their social networks, their employment, and their reintegration into the community—indeed, with their basic existence—ostracize these men to the point where the laws themselves may increase stress and loneliness and thereby increase the likelihood of recidivism. Society has become so caught up in the rhetoric and fear surrounding sexual offenders and offenses that we have lost sight of the fact that these men are human beings, with parents and siblings and, many times, children of their own. We have reached the point where we define these men by the very worst act in their life, and it becomes their defining moment—how society sees them—for the rest of their lives. Recall that only in rare cases are these men the violent predators we read about in the newspaper and see on television. American society has evolved to the point where we treat sexual offenders worse than we treat murderers, and an overwhelmingly percentage of Americans do not even think twice about these policies. We cannot continue to treat all sex offenders like this, regardless of seriousness, without expecting this to become a self-fulfilling prophecy.

A phenomenon termed "governing through crime" occurs in many nations, specifically in sex-negative countries, such as Canada and the United States. "Governing through crime . . . is attractive to people because it permits popular fears and experiences to be valorized in the strongest and most public terms . . . [to create] a sense of renewed solidarity with fellow citizens" (Simon 2000: 1119–20) in the name of public safety. Thus, despite the fact that sound public policy is not a "get-tough-on-crime" approach, politicians play on the fears of citizens to secure votes. The result quickly becomes a broken system in which harsh laws "protect" the public against certain classes of offenders, such as stranger attackers, and ultimately divert attention away from the real causes of sexual abuse and violence: structural inequalities between genders and classes and a lack of basic sexuality education and sexual communication skills. To prevent sexual violence at its roots, we must understand that sexual offenders are not monsters spawned but humans beings created by forces within our society, forces that can be changed if we are willing to learn the lessons other nations have to teach and not succumb to the false promises of political and legislative rhetoric. A human being is worth more to us as a society than the worst thing they do in their lives.

References

Adkins, Geneva, Huff, David, and Stageberg, Paul. (2000). *The Iowa sex offender registry and recidivism*. Des Moines: Iowa Department of Human Rights, Division of Criminal and Juvenile Justice Planning and Statistical Analysis Center.

Administration on Children, Youth, and Families. (2007). *Child maltreatment 2005*. Washington, DC: U.S. Department of Health and Human Services.

American Psychiatric Association. (1987). *Diagnostic and statistical manual of mental disorders* (3rd ed., revised). Washington, DC: American Psychiatric Association.

American Psychiatric Association. (1994). *Diagnostic and statistical manual of mental disorders* (4th ed.). Washington, DC: American Psychiatric Association.

American Psychiatric Association. (2008). *Diagnostic and statistical manual*. Available: http://psych.org/MainMenu/Research/DSMIV.aspx

Auburn, Timothy, and Lea, Susan. (2003). Doing cognitive distortions: A discursive psychology analysis of sex offender treatment talk. *British Journal of Social Psychology*, 42, 281–98.

Avrahamian, K. (1998). A critical perspective: Do "Megan's Laws" really shield children from sex predators? *Journal of Juvenile Law*, 19, 1–18.

Barbaree, Howard E., Seto, Michael, Langton, Clavin M., and Peacock, Edward J. (2001). Evaluating the predictive accuracy of six risk assessment instruments for adult sex offenders. *Criminal Justice and Behavior*, 28(4), 490–521.

Barnoski, Robert. (2005). *Sex offender sentencing in Washington state: Has community notification reduced recidivism?* Olympia: Washington State Institute for Public Policy.

Bass, Ellen. (1995). Child sexual abuse. In Patricia Searles and Ronald J. Berger (Eds.), *Rape and society: Readings on the problem of sexual assault* (pp. 115–18). Boulder, CO: Westview Press.

Bass, E., and Thornton, L. (Eds.). (1983). *I never told anyone: Writings by women survivors of child sexual abuse*. New York: Harper and Row.

Bedarf, A. (1995). Examining sex offender community notification laws. *California Law Review*, 83, 885–939.

Benedict, Helen. (1992). *Virgin or vamp: How the press covers sex crimes*. New York: Oxford University Press.

Beneke, Timothy. (1995a). Jack and Ken. In Patricia Searles and Ronald J. Berger (Eds.), *Rape and society: Readings on the problem of sexual assault* (pp. 194–98). Boulder, CO: Westview Press.

Beneke, Timothy. (1995b). Jay: An "armchair" rapist. In Patricia Searles and Ronald J. Berger (Eds.), *Rape and society: Readings on the problem of sexual assault* (pp. 55–57). Boulder, CO: Westview Press.

Berger, Ronald J., Searles, Patricia, and Neuman, W. Lawrence. (1995). Rape-law reform: Its nature, origins, and impact. In Patricia Searles and Ronald J. Berger (Eds.), *Rape and society: Readings on the problem of sexual assault* (pp. 223–32). Boulder, CO: Westview Press.

Berliner, Lucy. (2007). *Sex offender sentencing options: Views of child victims and their parents* (Document No. 07-08-1201). Olympia: Washington State Institute for Public Policy.

Best, Joel. (1990). *Threatened children: Rhetoric and concern about child-victims*. Chicago: University of Chicago Press.

Best, Joel. (2001). *Damned lies and statistics: Untangling numbers from the media, politicians, and activists*. Berkeley: University of California Press.

Best, Joel. (2004). *More damned lies and statistics: How numbers confuse public issues*. Berkeley, CA: University of California Press.

Bible, King James Version. (1986). Oklahoma: Rainbow Studies Inc.

Birgden, Astrid M., and Vincent, Frank. (2000). Maximizing therapeutic effects in treating sexual offenders in an Australian correctional system. *Behavioral Sciences and the Law*, 18, 479-488.

Bloch, Iwan. (1930). *The sexual life of our time in its relations to modern civilization*. London: William Heinemann (Medical Books).

Brecher, Edward, M. (2000). *The sex researchers*. San Francisco: Specific Press.

Briere, J. (1989). University males' sexual interest in children: Predicting potential indices of "pedophilia" in a nonforensic sample. *Child Abuse and Neglect*, 13, 65–75.

Brownmiller, Susan. (1975). *Against our will: Men, women, and rape*. New York: Bantam Books.

Bryant, Clifton. (1982). *Sexual deviancy and social proscription: The social context of carnal behavior*. New York: Human Sciences Press.

Buchwald, Emilie, Fletcher, Pamela R., and Roth, Martha (Eds.). (2005). *Transforming a rape culture* (rev. ed.). Minneapolis: Milkweed Editions.

Bullough, Vern L. (1994). *Science in the bedroom: A history of sex research*. New York: Basic Books.

Bullough, Vern L. (1998). Alfred Kinsey and the Kinsey report: Historical overview and lasting contributions. *Journal of Sex Research*, 35(2), 127–31.

Bunting, Lisa. (2007). Dealing with a problem that doesn't exist? Professional responses to female perpetrated child sexual abuse. *Child Abuse Review*, 16, 252–67.

Bureau of Justice Statistics. (1997). *Sex offenses and offenders: An analysis of data on rape and sexual assault* (NCJ 163392). Washington, DC: U.S. Department of Justice.

Bureau of Justice Statistics. (2000). *Sexual assault of young children as reported to law enforcement: Victim, incident, and offender characteristics* (NCJ 182990). Washington, DC: U.S. Department of Justice.

Bureau of Justice Statistics. (2002). *Summary of state sex offender registries, 2001* (NCJ 192265). Washington, DC: U.S. Department of Justice.

Bureau of Justice Statistics. (2003). *Recidivism of sex offenders released from prison in 1994* (NCJ 198281). Washington, DC: U.S. Department of Justice.

Bureau of Justice Statistics. (2005). *Criminal victimization 2004* (NCJ 210674). Washington, DC: U.S. Department of Justice.

Bureau of Justice Statistics. (2006). *Criminal victimization in the United States 2005: Statistical tables* (NCJ 215244). Washington, DC: U.S. Department of Justice.

Bureau of Justice Statistics. (2007). *Prisoners in 2006* (NCJ 219416). Washington, DC: U.S. Department of Justice.

Burgress, Ann Wolbert. (1995). Rape trauma syndrome. In Patricia Searles and Ronald J. Berger (Eds.), *Rape and society: Readings on the problem of sexual assault* (pp. 239–45). Boulder, CO: Westview Press.

Burick, Lawrence T. (1968). An analysis of the Illinois Sexually Dangerous Persons Act. *Journal of Criminal Law, Criminology, and Political Science*, 59(2), 254–66.

Campbell, Ference W. (2000). Sexual predator evaluations and phrenology: Considering issues of evidentiary reliability. *Behavioral Sciences and the Law*, 18, 111–30.

Carlsmith, Kevin J., Monahan, John, and Evans, Alison. (2007). The function of punishment in the "civil" commitment of sexual violent predators. *Behavioural Sciences and the Law*, 25, 437–48.

Carringella-MacDonald, S. (1998). The relative visibility of rape cases in national popular magazines. *Violence Against Women*, 4(1), 62–80.

Cavanagh, Sheila L. (2005). Sexing the teacher: Voyeuristic pleasure in the Amy Gehring sex panic. *Social Text*, 23(1), 111–34.

Center for Sex Offender Management. (2000). *Community supervision of the sex offender: An overview of current and promising practices*. Washington, DC: U.S. Department of Justice.

Center for Sex Offender Management. (2002). *Managing sex offenders in the community: A handbook to guide policymakers and practitioners through a planning and implementation process*. Washington, DC: U.S. Department of Justice.

Center for Sex Offender Management. (2006). *Understanding treatment for adults and juveniles who have committed sex offenses*. Washington, DC: U.S. Department of Justice.

Chenier, Elise. (2003). The criminal sexual psychopath in Canada: Sex, psychiatry and the law at mid-century. *Canadian Bulletin of Medical History*, 20(1), 75–101.

Child Welfare Information Gateway. (2006). *Child abuse and neglect fatalities: Statistics and interventions*. Washington, DC: U.S. Department of Health and Human Services.

Cleary, Shawna. (2004). *Sex offenders and self-control: Explaining sexual violence*. El Paso, TX: LFB Scholarly Publishers.

Cohen, S. (1972). *Folk devils and moral panics: The creation of the mods and rockers.* London: MacGibbon and Kee.

Cole, Simon A. (2000). From the sexual psychopath statute to "Megan's Law": Psychiatric knowledge in the diagnosis, treatment, and adjudication of sex criminals in New Jersey, 1949–1999. *Journal of the History of Medicine*, 55, 292–314.

Collins, John. (1989). Sexuality and culture: Views from Thailand, Japan and the United States [Video transcript]. San Francisco: Exodus Trust.

Connell, R. W. (2005). Growing up masculine: Rethinking the significance of adolescence in the making of masculinities. *Irish Journal of Sociology*, 12(2), 11–28.

Conte, J., Wolf, S., and Smith, T. (1989). What sexual offenders tell us about prevention strategies. *Child Abuse and Neglect*, 13, 293–301.

Cooper, Susan. (2005). Understanding, treating and managing sex offenders who deny their offense. *Journal of Sexual Aggression*, 11(1), 85–94.

Cornwell, John Kip. (2003). Sex offenders and the Supreme Court: The significance and limits of *Kansas v. Hendricks*. In Bruce J. Winick and John Q. LaFond (Eds.), *Protecting society from sexually dangerous offenders: Law, justice, and therapy* (pp. 197–210). Washington, DC: American Psychological Association.

Correctional Service of Canada. (1996). *Case studies of female sex offenders*. Ottawa: Correctional Service of Canada.

Corrigan, Rose. (2006). Making meaning of Megan's Law. *Law and Social Inquiry*, 31(2), 267–312.

Cowburn, Malcolm. (2005). Hegemony and discourse: Reconstructing the male sex offender and sexual coercion by men. *Sexualities, Evolution and Gender*, 7(3), 215–31.

Craig, Leam A., Browne, Kevin D., Stringer, Ian, and Beech, Anthony. (2005). Sexual recidivism: A review of static, dynamic and actuarial predictors. *Journal of Sexual Aggression*, 11(1), 65–84.

Davenport, W. H. (1977). Sex in cross-cultural perspective. In F. A. Beach (Ed.), *Human sexuality in four perspectives* (pp. 115–63). Baltimore: Johns Hopkins University Press.

Deirmenjian, J. (1999). Stalking in cyberspace. *Journal of the American Academy of Psychiatry and the Law*, 27(3), 407–13.

DeKeseredy, Walter, and Schwartz, Martin. (1998). *Women abuse on campus: Results from the Canadian national survey*. Thousand Oaks, CA: Sage Publications.

Denov, M. S. (2004). *Perspectives of denial on female sex offending: A culture of denial.* Aldershot: Ashgate Publications.

Dorn, Lorah D., Dahl, Ronald E., Woodward, Hermi Rojahn, and Biro, Frank. (2006). Defining the boundaries of early adolescence: A user's guide to assessing pubertal status and pubertal timing in research with adolescents. *Applied Developmental Science*, 10(1), 30–56.

Doubts Rise as States Hold Sex Offenders after Prison. (2007, March 4). *New York Times*. Retrieved July 20, 2008, from http://www.nytimes.com

Dowler, Kenneth. (2006). Sex, lies, and videotape: The presentation of sex crime in local television news. *Journal of Criminal Justice*, 34, 383–92.

Dreznick, Michael T. (2003). Heterosexual competence of rapists and child molesters: A meta-analysis. *Journal of Sex Research*, 40(2), 170–78.

Duwe, Grant, and Donnay, William. (2008). The impact of Megan's Law on sex offender recidivism: The Minnesota experience. *Criminology*, 46(2), 411–46.

Earl-Hubbard, Michele L. (1996). The child offender registration laws: The punishment, liberty deprivation, and unintended results associated with the scarlet letter laws of the 1990s. *Northwestern University Law Review*, 90, 788–862.

Eatontown to Repeal Its Sex Offender Law. (2008, August 8). *Asbury Park Press*. Retrieved August 13, 2008, from http://www.asburyparkpress.com

Elliot, M., Browne, K., and Kilcoyne, J. (1995). Child sexual abuse prevention: What offenders tell us. *Child Abuse and Neglect*, 19, 579–94.

Ellis, Havelock. (1942). *Studies in the psychology of sex: Volumes I, II, III, IV*. New York: Random House.

English, Kim, Jones, Linda, and Patrick, Diane. (2003). Community containment of sex offender risk: A promising approach. In Bruce J. Winick and John Q. LaFond (Eds.), *Protecting society from sexually dangerous offenders: Law, justice, and therapy* (pp. 256–69). Washington, DC: American Psychological Association.

Epps, K. J. (1999). Causal explanations: Filling the theoretical reservoir. In M. C. Calder (Ed.), *Working with young people who sexually abuse: New pieces of the jigsaw puzzle* (pp. 7–26). Dorset: Russell House.

Epstein, J., and Langenbahn, S. (1994). *The criminal justice and community response to rape*. Washington, DC: U.S. Department of Justice.

Ericksen, Julia A. (1998). With enough cases, why do you need statistics? Revisiting Kinsey's methodology. *Journal of Sex Research*, 35(2), 132–40.

Estrich, Susan. (1995). Is it rape? In Patricia Searles and Ronald J. Berger (Eds.), *Rape and society: Readings on the problem of sexual assault* (pp. 183–193). Boulder, CO: Westview Press.

Fehrenbach, P. A., and Monastersky, C. (1988). Characteristics of female adolescent sexual offenders. *American Journal of Orthopsychiatry*, 58, 148–51.

Ferguson, Christopher J., and Meehan, D. Cricket. (2005). An analysis of females convicted of sex crimes in the state of Florida. *Journal of Child Sexual Abuse*, 14(1), 75–89.

Finkelhor, D. (1980). Sex among siblings: A survey report on its prevalence, its variety, and its effect. *Archives of Sexual Behavior*, 9, 171–194.

Finkelhor, D. (1984). *Child sexual abuse: New theory and research*. New York: Free Press.

Finkelhor, D. (1986). *A sourcebook of child sexual abuse*. London: Sage Publications.

Finn, P. (1997). *Sex offender community notification: Research in action*. Washington, DC: U.S. Department of Justice.

Florida Executes Child Killer. (2008, July 1). *CNN*. Retrieved July 1, 2008, from http://www.cnn.com

Foucault, Michel. (1978). *The history of sexuality: An introduction volume I*. New York: Random House.

Freud, Sigmund. (1962). *Three essays on the theory of sexuality*. New York: Basic Book Publishers.

Furby, L., Weinrott, M. R., and Blackshaw, L. (1989). Sex offender recidivism: A review. *Psychological Bulletin*, 105, 3–30.

Galliher, John F., and Tyree, Cheryl. (1985). Edwin Sutherland's research on the origins of sexual psychopath laws: An early case study of the medicalization of deviance. *Social Problems*, 33(2), 100–113.

Gebhard, Paul H., Gagnon, John H., Pomeroy, Wardell B., and Christenson, Cornelia V. (1965). *Sex offenders: An analysis of types*. New York: Bantam Books.

Geffner, Robert, Franey, Kristina Crumptom, Arnold, Teri Geffner, and Falconer, Robert (Eds.). (2003). *Identifying and treating sex offenders: Current approaches, research, and technologies.* New York: Haworth Press.

Georgia: Sex Offenders Sue over Church Ban. (2008, June 25). *CNN.* Retrieved August 12, 2008, from http://www.cnn.com

Gillin, J. L. (1935). Social backgrounds of sex offenders and murderers. *Social Forces*, 14(2), 232–39.

Gottfredson, Michael, and Hirschi, Travis. (1990). *A general theory of crime.* Stanford, CA: Stanford University Press.

Graber, Julia A., and Sontag, Lisa M. (2006). Puberty and girls' sexuality: Why hormones are not the complete answer. *New Directions for Child and Adolescent Development*, 112, 23–38.

Grayston, A. D., and DeLuca, R. V. (1999). Female perpetrators of child sexual abuse: A review of the clinical and empirical literature. *Aggression and Violent Behaviour*, 4, 93–106.

Group for the Advancement of Psychiatry. (1977). *Psychiatry and sex psychopath legislation: The 30s to the 80s.* New York: Group for the Advancement of Psychiatry.

Haas, L., and Haas, J. (1990). *Understanding sexuality.* Boston: Mosby.

Hacker, Frederick J., and Frym, Marcel. (1955). The Sexual Psychopath Act in practice: A critical discussion. *California Law Review*, 43(5), 766–80.

Haeberle, Erwin, J. (1983). Introduction in *The birth of sexology: A brief history in documents.* Washington, DC: World Congress of Sexology. www.indiana.edu/~Kinsey/resouces/sexology.html (not paginated).

Haeberle, Erwin J. (no date.) Iwan Block. *Archive of sexology.* Humboldt-Universitat zu Berlin. http://www2.hu-berlin.de/sexology/GESUND/ARCHIV/COLLBL01.HTM (not paginated).

Haeberle, Erwin J (no date.) Albert Moll. *Archive of sexology.* Humboldt-Universitat zu Berlin. http://www2.hu-berlin.de/sexology/GESUND/ARCHIV/MOLL1.HTM (not paginated).

Hall, Rayan, and Hall, Richard C. W. (2007). A profile of pedophilia: Definitions, characteristics of offenders, recidivism, treatment outcomes, and forensic issues. *Mayo Clinic Proceedings*, 82(4), 457–71.

Halpern, Carolyn Tucker. (2006). Integrating hormones and other biological factors into a developmental systems model of adolescent female sexuality. *New Directions for Child and Adolescent Development*, 112, 9–22.

Hanson, R. Karl. (2003). Empathy deficits of sex offenders: A conceptual model. *Journal of Sexual Aggression*, 9(1), 13–23.

Hanson, R. Karl, Gordon, Arthur, Harris, Andrew J. R., Marques, Janice K., Murphy, William, Quinsey, Vernon L., and Seto, Michael C. (2002). First report of the collaborative outcome data project on the effectiveness of psychological treatment for sex offenders. *Sexual Abuse: A Journal of Research and Treatment*, 14(2), 169–94.

Haroain, Loretta. (1994) Sexual development in children and adolescents [Unpublished manuscript]. San Francisco: Institute for Advanced Study of Human Sexuality.

Harris, Charles. (1946, August). Sex crimes: Their cause and cure. *Coronet*, 20(4), 3–9.

Harry, B., Pierson, T., and Kuznetsov, A. (1993). Correlates of sex offender and offense traits by victim age. *Journal of Forensic Science*, 38, 1068–74.

Hatano, Yoshiro, and Shimazaki, Tsuguo. (2004). Japan (Nippon). In Robert T. Francoeur and Raymond J. Noonan (Eds.), *The continuum complete international encyclopedia of sexuality updated with more countries* (pp. 636–78). New York: Continuum Publishing.

Health Canada. (2001). *Child maltreatment in Canada: Canadian incidence study of reported child abuse and neglect, selected results*. Ottawa: Minister of Health.

Herman, J. (2005). Justice from the victim's perspective. *Violence Against Women*, 11(5), 571–602.

Herman, Judith, and Hirschman, Lisa. (1993). Father-daughter incest. In Pauline B. Bart and Eileen Geil Moran (Eds.), *Violence against women: The bloody footprints* (pp. 47–56). Newbury Park, CA: Sage Publications.

Hirschi, Travis. (1969). *Causes of delinquency*. Berkeley, CA: University of California Press.

Holmes, Stephen T., and Holmes, Ronald M. (2009). *Sex crimes: Patterns and behavior* (3rd ed.). Thousand Oaks, CA: Sage Publications.

Human Rights Watch. (2007). *No easy answers: Sex offender laws in the U.S.* New York: Human Rights Watch.

Illinois Measure Would Move Some from Sex Offender List. (2006, June 24). *Associated Press*. Retrieved June 24, 2006, from http://www.ap.org

Iowa County Attorneys Association. (2006, December 11). Statement on sex offender residency restrictions in Iowa [Press release]. Des Moines: Iowa County Attorneys Association.

Jackson, Stevi. (1995). The social context of rape: Sexual scripts and motivation. In Patricia Searles and Ronald J. Berger (Eds.), *Rape and society: Readings on the problem of sexual assault* (pp. 16–27). Boulder, CO: Westview Press.

Janus, Eric S. (2000). Sexual predator commitment laws: Lessons for law and the behavioral sciences. *Behavioral Sciences and the Law*, 18, 5–21.

Janus, Eric S. (2003). Examining our approaches to sex offenders and the law, Minnesota's sex offender commitment program: Would an empirically-based prevention policy be more effective? *William Mitchell Law Review*, 29, 1–37.

Janus, Eric S. (2006). *Failure to protect: America's sexual predator laws and the rise of the preventive state*. Ithaca, NY: Cornell University Press.

Janus, E. S., and Walbek, N. H. (2000). Sex offender commitments in Minnesota: A descriptive study of second generation commitments. *Behavior Sciences and the Law*, 18, 343–74.

Jenkins, Philip. (1998). *Moral panic: Changing concepts of the child molester in modern America*. New Haven, CT: Yale University Press.

Jenkins, Philip. (2001). *Beyond tolerance: Child pornography on the internet*. New York: New York University Press.

John Howard Society of Alberta. (1999). *Dangerous offender legislation around the world*. Alberta: John Howard Society.

Johnson, Holly. (1996). *Dangerous domains: Violence against women in Canada*. Toronto: Nelson Canada.

Jordan, Jan. (2008). *Serial survivors: Women's narratives of surviving rape*. Sydney: Federation Press.

Kalven, H., and Zeisel, H., (1966). *The American jury.* Chicago, IL: University Press.

Kansas v. Hendricks, 521 U.S. 346 (1997).

Kinsey, Alfred C., Pomeroy, Wardell B., Martin, Clyde E., and Gebhard, Paul H. (1948). *Sexual behavior in the human male.* Philadelphia: W. B. Saunders Company.

Kinsey, Alfred C., Pomeroy, Wardell B., Martin, Clyde E., and Gebhard, Paul H. (1953). *Sexual behavior in the human female.* Philadelphia: W. B. Saunders Company.

Kitzinger, Jenny. (2007). *Framing abuse: Media influence and public understandings of sexual violence against children.* London: Pluto Press.

Koss, M. P. (1990). The women's mental health research agenda: Violence against women. *American Psychologist,* 45(3), 374–80.

Krafft-Ebing, R. V. (1922). *Psychopathia Sexualis.* New York: Rebman Company.

Kruttschnitt, C., Uggen, C., and Shelton, K. (2000). Predictors of desistance among sex offenders: The interaction of formal and informal social controls. *Justice Quarterly,* 17, 62–87.

Lacoursiere, Roy B. (2003). Evaluating offenders under a sexually violent predator law: The practical practice. In Bruce J. Winick and John Q. LaFond (Eds.), *Protecting society from sexually dangerous offenders: Law, justice, and therapy* (pp. 75–97). Washington, DC: American Psychological Association.

La Fond, John Q. (1998). The costs of enacting a sexual predator law. *Psychology, Public Policy and Law,* 4, 468–504.

La Fond, John Q. (2000). The future of involuntary civil commitment in the U.S.A. after *Kansas v. Hendricks. Behavioral Sciences and the Law,* 18, 153–67.

Larson, N., and Maison, S. 1987. *Psychosexual treatment program for female sex offenders, Minnesota Correctional Facility-Shakopee.* St. Paul, MN: Meta Resources.

Lawson, Louanne. (2003). Isolation, gratification, justification: Offenders' explanations of child molesting. *Mental Health Nursing,* 24, 695–705.

Levenson, Jill. (2004). Sexual predator civil commitment: A comparison of selected and released offenders. *International Journal of Offender Therapy and Comparative Criminology,* 48(6), 638–48.

Levenson, Jill S., Brannon, Yolanda N., Fortney, Timothy, and Baker, Juanita. (2007). Public perceptions about sex offenders and community protection policies. *Analysis of Social Issues and Public Policy,* 7(1), 1–25.

Levenson, Jill S., and Cotter, Leo P. (2005). The impact of sex offender residence restrictions: 1,000 feet from danger or one step from absurd? *International Journal of Offender Therapy and Comparative Criminology,* 49(2), 168–78.

Levenson, Jill S., D'Amora, David A., and Hern, Andrea L. (2007). Megan's Law and its impact on community re-entry for sex offenders. *Behavioural Sciences and the Law,* 25, 587–602.

Lewandowski, Herbert. (1984–1985). *The history of sexology.* Humboldt-Universitat zu Berlin. http://www2.hu-berlin.de/sexology/GESUND/ARCHIV/LHIST .HTM (not paginated).

Lewis, Catherine F., and Stanley, Charlotte R. (2000). Women accused of sexual offenses. *Behavioral Sciences and the Law,* 18, 73–81.

Lewis, R. (1988). *Effectiveness of statutory requirements for the registration of sex offenders: A report to the California state legislature.* Sacramento: California Department of Justice.

Lieb, Roxanne, and Nunlist, Corey. (2008). *Community notification as viewed by Washington's citizens: A 10-year follow-up* (Document No. 08-03-1101). Olympia: Washington State Institute for Public Policy.

Lieb, R., Quinsey, V., and Berliner, L. (1998). Sexual predators and social policy. *Crime and Justice*, 23, 2–49.

Lord, Alex, and Willmot, Phil. (2004). The process of overcoming denial in sexual offenders. *Journal of Sexual Aggression*, 10(1), 51–61.

Los, Maria, and Chamard, Sharon E. (1997). Selling newspapers or educating the public? Sexual violence in the media. *Canadian Journal of Criminology*, 39(3), 293–328.

Lucken, Karol, and Bales, William. (2008). Florida's sexually violent predator program: An examination of risk and civil commitment eligibility. *Crime and Delinquency*, 54(1), 95–127.

Lucken, K., and Latina, J. (2002). Sex offender civil commitment laws: Medicalizing deviant sexual behavior. *Barry Law Review*, 15, 1–19.

Lussier, P., LeBlanc, M., and Proulx, J. (2005). The generality of criminal behavior: A confirmatory factor analysis of the criminal activity of sex offenders in adulthood. *Journal of Criminal Justice*, 33(2), 177–89.

Lyn, Tamara, S., and Burton, David L. (2005). Attachment, anger and anxiety of male sexual offenders. *Journal of Sexual Aggression*, 11(2), 127–37.

Mann, Ruth E. (2004). Innovation in sex offender treatment. *Journal of Sexual Aggression*, 10(2), 141–52.

Marshall, W. L. (1988). The use of sexually explicit stimuli by rapists, child molesters, and nonoffenders. *The Journal of Sex Research*, 125(2), 267-288.

Marshall, L. E., and Marshall, William L. (2001). Excessive sexual desire disorder among sex offenders: The development of a research project. *Sexual Addiction and Compulsivity*, 8, 301–7.

Marshall, William L., Marshall, Liam E., Serran, Geris A., and Fernandez, Yolanda M. (2006). *Treating sexual offenders: An integrated approach.* New York, NY: Routledge Press.

Marshall, W. L., Serran, G. A., Fernandez, Y. M., Mulloy, R., Mann, R. E., and Thorton, D. (2003). Therapist characteristics in the treatment of sexual offenders: Tentative data on their relationship with indices of behavior change. *Journal of Sexual Aggression*, 9(1), 25–30.

Marziano, Vincent, Ward, Tony, Beech, Anthony R., and Pattison, Philippa. (2006). Identification of five fundamental implicit theories underlying cognitive distortions in child abusers: A preliminary study. *Psychology, Crime and Law*, 12(1), 97–105.

Mayer, A. (1992). *Women sex offenders: Treatment and dynamics.* Holmes Beach, FL: Learning Publications.

McGrath, Robert, Cumming, Georgia, Hoke, Stephen, and Bonn-Miller, Marcel. (2007). Outcomes in a community sex offender treatment program: A comparison between polygraphed and matched non-polygraphed offenders. *Sexual Abuse: A Journal of Research and Treatment*, 19(4), 381–93.

McIlvenna, Ted. (2007, February). Lecture on the Socio-Sexual Response Cycle. Basic Lecture Series. Institute for Advanced Study of Human Sexuality, San Francisco.

Meloy, Michelle L. (2005). The sex offender next door: An analysis of recidivism, risk factors, and deterrence of sex offenders on probation. *Criminal Justice Policy Review*, 16, 211–36.

Meloy, Michelle L. (2006). *Sex offenses and the men who commit them: An assessment of sex offenders on probation*. Boston: Northeastern University Press.

Meyenburg, Bernd, and Sigusch, Volkar. (1977). Sexology in West Germany. *Journal of Sex Research*, 13(3), 197–209.

Michels, Tricia M., Kropp, Rhonda Y., Eyre, Stephen L., and Halpern-Relsher, Bonnie L. (2005). Initiating sexual experiences: How do young adolescents make decisions regarding early sexual activity? *Journal of Research on Adolescence*, 15(4), 583–607.

Miller, Robert D. (2003). Chemical castration of sex offenders: Treatment or punishment? In Bruce J. Winick and John Q. LaFond (Eds.), *Protecting society from sexually dangerous offenders: Law, justice, and therapy* (pp. 249–64). Washington, DC: American Psychological Association.

Morrison, Steven R. (2008). *Creating sex offender registries: The religious right and the failure to protect society's vulnerable*. Boston: Steven R. Morrison.

Mother Knew Best. (1947, March 17). *Time*. Retrieved July 2, 2008, from http://www.time.com/time/magazine/article/0,9171,793391,00.html

Moulden, H. M., and Marshall, W. L. (2005). Hope in the treatment of sex offenders: The potential application of hope theory. *Psychology, Crime and Law*, 11(3), 329–42.

Murray, J. (2000). Psychological profile of pedophiles and child molesters. *Journal of Psychology and Human Sexuality*, 134(2), 221–24.

MySpace Deletes 146 Profiles of NE Sex Offenders. (2008, August 15). *KPTM Fox 42 News*. Retrieved August 18, 2008, from http://www.kptm.com

National Adolescent Perpetrator Network. (1993). The revised report from the National Task Force on Juvenile Sexual Offending. *Juvenile and Family Court Journal*, 44, 1–120.

New Jersey Court Says 12-Year-Old Must Register as a Sexual Offender. (1996, April 12). *New York Times*. Retrieved July 17, 2008, from http://www.nytimes.com

No Internet for Some Sex Offenders in New Jersey. (2007, December 27). *CNN*. Retrieved December 27, 2007, from http://www.cnn.com

Office of Juvenile Justice and Delinquency Prevention. (2001). *The decline in child sexual abuse cases* (NCJ 184741). Washington, DC: U.S. Department of Justice.

Office of Juvenile Justice and Delinquency Prevention. (2004). *Explanations for the decline in child sexual abuse cases* (NCJ 199298). Washington, DC: U.S. Department of Justice.

Office of Victims of Crimes. (1998). *New directions from the field: Victims' rights and services for the 21st century* (No. 172829). Washington, DC: Office of Justice Programs.

On the Web, Pedophiles Extend Their Reach. (2006, August 21). *New York Times*. Retrieved July 20, 2008, from http://www.nytimes.com

Pallone, Nathaniel J. (2003). Without plea-bargaining, Megan Kanka would be alive today. *Criminology and Public Policy*, 3(1), 83–96.

Palmer, Timothy, and Haffner, Rev. Debra W. (2007). *A time to seek study guide on sexual and gender diversity*. Westport, CT: Religious Institute on Sexual Morality, Justice, and Healing.

Payne, Brian K., and Gainey, Randy R. (2005). *Family violence and criminal justice: A life-course approach* (2nd ed.). Dayton, OH: LexisNexis.

Petrosino, A.J. and C. Petrosino. (1999). The public safety potential of Megan's law in Massachusetts: An assessment from a sample of criminal sexual psychopaths. *Crime and delinquency* 45(1), 140-158.

Petrunik, Michael. (1994). *Models of dangerousness: A cross jurisdictional review of dangerousness legislation and practice.* Ottawa: Ministry of the Solicitor General of Canada.

Petrunik, Michael. (2003). The hare and the tortoise: Dangerousness and sex offender policy in the United States and Canada. *Canadian Journal of Criminology and Criminal Justice,* 45, 51–53.

Pithers, W. (1990). Relapse prevention with sexual aggression: A method for maintaining therapeutic gain and enhancing external supervision. In W. L. Marshall, D. R. Laws, and H. E. Barbaree (Eds.), *Handbook of sexual assault: Issues, theories, and treatment of the offender* (pp. 343–61). New York: Plenum.

Ploscowe, M. (1960). Sex offences and the American legal context. *Law and Contemporary Problems,* 15(3), 217–24.

Prentky, R. A., Lee, A. F., Knight, R., and Cerce, D. (1997). Recidivism rates among child molesters and rapists: A methodological analysis. *Law and Human Behavior,* 21(6), 635–59.

Pryor, Douglas W. (1996). *Unspeakable acts: Why men sexually abuse children.* New York: New York University Press.

Puglia, Michelle L., Stough, Con, Carter, James D., and Joseph, Megan. (2005). The emotional intelligence of adult sex offenders: Ability based EI assessment. *Journal of Sexual Aggression,* 11(3), 249–58.

Quayle, E., Vaughn, M., and Taylor, M. (2006). Sex offenders: Internet child abuse images and emotional avoidance: The importance of values. *Aggression and Violent Behavior,* 11(1), 1–11.

Quinsey, V., and Earls, C. (1990). The modification of sexual preferences. In W. L. Marshall, D. R. Laws, and H. E. Barbaree (Eds.), *Handbook of sexual assault: Issues, theories, and treatment of the offender* (pp. 279–95). New York: Plenum.

Quinsey, V. L., Rice, M. E., and Harris, G. T. (1995). Actuarial prediction of sexual recidivism. *Journal of Interpersonal Violence,* 10, 85–105.

Raby, Rebecca C. (2002). A tangle of discourses: Girls negotiating adolescence. *Journal of Youth Studies,* 5(4), 425–48.

Rape a Child, Pay with Your Life, Louisiana Argues. (2008, April 15). *CNN.* Retrieved April 15, 2008, from http://www.cnn.com

Reinhardt, James M., and Fisher, Edward C. (1949). The sexual psychopath and the law. *Journal of Criminal Law and Criminology,* 39(6), 734–42.

Remer, R., and Ferguson, R. A. (1995). Becoming a secondary survivor of sexual assault. *Journal of Counselling and Development,* 73(4), 407–13.

Renvoize, Jean. (1982). *Incest: A family pattern.* London: Routledge and Kegan Paul.

Rind, Bruce, Tromovitch, Philip, and Bauserman, Robert. (1998). A meta-analytic examination of assumed properties of child sexual abuse using college samples. *Psychological Bulletin.* 124 (1), 22-32.

Rosler, Ariel, and Witztum, Eliezer. (2000). Pharmaco-therapy of paraphilias in the next millennium. *Behavioral Sciences and the Law,* 18, 43–56.

Royal Canadian Mounted Police. (2005). National sex offender registry, Retrieved June 12, 2006, from http://www.rcmp-grc.gc.ca/techops/nsor/nsor_brochuree .pdf

Russell, Diana E. H. (1974). *The politics of rape: The victim's perspective.* New York: Stein and Day Publishers.

Sample, Lisa L., and Bray, Timothy M. (2003). Are sex offenders dangerous? *Criminology and Public Policy,* 3(1), 59–82.

Sampson, Robert J., and Laub, John H. (1993). *Crime in the making: Pathways and turning points through life.* Cambridge, MA: Harvard University Press.

Sarrel, Lorna J., and Sarrel, Philip M. (1979). *Sexual unfolding sexual development and sex therapies in late adolescence.* Boston: Little, Brown and Company.

Schram, D., and Milloy, C. (1995). *Community notification: A study of offender characteristics and recidivism.* Seattle: Urban Policy Research.

Schulhofer, Stephen J. (1998). *Unwanted sex: The culture of intimidation and the failure of law.* Cambridge, MA: Harvard University Press.

Scully, Diana. (1994). *Understanding sexual violence: A study of convicted rapists.* New York: Routledge.

Scully, Diana, and Marolla, Joseph. (1995). Riding the bull at Gilley's: Convicted rapists describe the rewards of rape. In Patricia Searles and Ronald J. Berger (Eds.), *Rape and society: Readings on the problem of sexual assault* (pp. 58–73). Boulder, CO: Westview Press.

Seabloom, William. (1983). The family journey: A multigenerational sex education experience for families. Paper presented at the Sixth World Congress of Sexology, Washington, DC.

Seabloom, William, Seabloom, Mary E., Seabloom, Eric, Barron, Robert, and Hendrickson, Sharon. (2003). A 14- to 24-year longitudinal study of a comprehensive sexual health model treatment program for adolescent sex offenders: Predictors of successful completion and subsequent criminal recidivism. *International Journal of Offender Therapy and Comparative Criminology,* 47(4), 468–581.

Searles, Patricia, and Berger, Ronald J. (Eds.). (1995). *Rape and society: Readings on the problem of sexual assault.* Boulder, CO: Westview Press.

Sentencing Guidelines Commission. (2004). *Sex offender sentencing: Sentencing guidelines commission 2004.* Seattle: State of Washington.

Seto, Michael C. (2005). Is more better? Combining actuarial risk scales to predict recidivism among adult sex offenders. *Psychological Assessment,* 17(2), 156–167.

Seto, Michael C., and Barbaree, Howard E. (1999). Psychopathy treatment behavior and sex offender recidivism. *Journal of Interpersonal Violence,* 14(12), 1235–48.

Sex Offenders Can Have More Freedom, Court Rules. (2008, July 15). *South Jersey News.* Retrieved August 12, 2008, from http://www.nj.com

Sex Offenders Locked Down in the Dark for Halloween. (2007, October 31). *CNN.* Retrieved October 31, 2007, from http://www.cnn.com

Shanahan, Michael J., Erickson, Lance D., and Bauer, Daniel J. (2005). One hundred years of knowing: The changing science of adolescence, 1904 and 2004. *Journal of Research on Adolescence.* 15(4), 383-394.

Sheldon, Travin, Bluestone, Harvey, Coleman, Emily, Cullen, Ken, and Melella, John. (1985). Pedophilia: An update on theory and practice. *Psychiatric Quarterly,* 57(2), 89–103.

Sieving, Renee E., Eisenberg, Marla E., Pettingell, Sandra, and Skay, Carol. (2006). Friends' influence on adolescents' first sexual intercourse. *Perspectives on Sexual and Reproductive Health*, 38(1), 13–19.

Simon, Jonathan. (2000). Megan's law: Crime and democracy in late modern America. *Law and Social Inquiry*, 25, 1111–50.

Simon, L. (1997). The myth of sex offender specialization: An empirical analysis. *New England Journal on Criminal and Civil Confinement*, 23(2), 387–403.

Simon, Leonore M. J., and Zgoba, Kristen. (2006). Sex crimes against children: Legislation, prevention and investigation. *Crime Prevention Studies*, 19, 65–100.

Sjostedt, Gabrielle, and Langstrom, Niklas. (2002). Assessment of risk for criminal recidivism among rapists: A comparison of four different measures. *Psychology, Crime and Law*, 8, 25–40.

Snyder, H. (2000). *Sexual assault of young children as reported to law enforcement: Victim, incident, and offender characteristics*. Washington, DC: Bureau of Justice Statistics, U.S. Department of Justice.

Song, Lin, Lieb, Roxanne, and Donnelly, Shiela. (1993). *Female sex offenders in Washington state*. Olympia: Washington State Institute for Public Policy.

Stadtland, Cornelis, Hollweg, Matthias, Kleindienst, Nikolaus, Dietl, Julia, Reich, Ursula, and Nedopil, Norbet. (2005). Risk assessment and prediction of violent and sexual recidivism in sex offenders: Long-term predictive validity of four risk assessment instruments. *Journal of Forensic Psychiatry and Psychology*, 16(1), 92–108.

State of Louisiana. (2008, June 25). Governor signs chemical castration bill, authorizing the castration of sex offenders in Louisiana [Press release]. Baton Rouge: Office of the Governor. Retrieved July 18, 2008, from http://gov .louisiana.gov

State of Ohio, Department of Rehabilitation and Corrections. (2001, April). Ten-year recidivism follow-up of 1989 sex offender releases. Department of Rehabilitation and Corrections. Office of Policy and Bureau of Planning and Evaluation. Available: http://www.drc.state.oh.us/WEB/Reports/Ten_Year_ Recidivism.pdf

Statistics Canada. (2006). *Measuring violence against women: Statistical trends 2006* (Catalog no. 85-570-XIW). Ottawa: Statistics Canada.

Steinbock, B. (1995). A policy perspective, Megan's Law: Community notification of the release of sex offenders. *Criminal Justice Ethics*, 14, 4–9.

Stone, Howard T., Winslade, William J. and Klugman, Craig M. (2000). Sex offenders, sentencing laws, and pharmaceutical treatment: A prescription for failure. *Behavioral Sciences and the Law*, 19, 83–110.

Sudo, Junya, Sato, Makoto, Obata, Shugo, and Yamagami, Obata. (2006). Exploring the possibility of risk assessment of Japanese sexual offenders using Static-99. *Criminal Behaviour and Mental Health*, 116, 146–54.

Sutherland, Edwin. (1950). The diffusion of sexual psychopath laws. *American Journal of Sociology*, 56(2), 142–48.

Taslitz, Andrew E. (1999). *Rape and the culture of the courtroom*. New York: New York University Press.

Taylor, C. L. (1975). Mexican gay life in historical perspective. *Gay Sunshine Journal*, 26/27, 75–76.

Taylor, C. L. (1978). How Mexicans define male homosexuality: Labeling and the *Buga* view. *Kroeber Anthropological Society Papers, 53 and 54*, 106–28.

Taywaditep, KittiwutJod, Coleman, Eli, and Dumronggittigule, Pacharin. (2004). Thailand (Prathet Thai). In Robert T. Francoeur and Raymond J. Noonan (Eds.), *The continuum complete international encyclopedia of sexuality updated with more countries* (pp. 1021–53). New York: Continuum Publishing.

Terry, Karen. (2006). *Sexual offenses and offenders: Theory, practice, and policy*. Belmont, CA: Wadsworth Publishers.

Tewksbury, Richard. (2005). Sex offender registries as a tool for public safety: Views from registered sex offenders. *Western Criminology Review, 7*, 1–8.

Texas Office of the Attorney General. (2001). Cybercrimes. *Criminal Law Update, 8*(3), 4–11.

Theodosi, Eleni, and McMurran, Mary. (2006). Motivating convicted sex offenders into treatment: A pilot study. *British Journal of Forensic Practice, 8*(3), 28–35.

Tokheim, Russell. (2005, June). Juvenile sex offenders can be changed, counselor contends. *Metro Lutheran*. Available: http://www.metrolutheran.org

Torah. (1998). JPS Electronic Edition. Available: http://www.jewishvirtuallibrary.org/jsource/Judaism/Torah.html

The Toxic Offender. (2007, March 4). *New York Times*. Retrieved March 4, 2007, from http://www.nytimes.com

Trailer Park Becomes Paradise for Sex Offenders. (2007, October 18). *CNN*. Retrieved October 18, 2007, from http://www.cnn.com

Travin, S., Cullen, K., and Protter, B. (1990). Female sexual offenders: Severe victims and victimizers. *Journal of Forensic Sciences, 35*, 140–50.

Uniform Crime Report. (2007). *Crime in the United States, 2006*. Washington, DC: U.S. Department of Justice.

The Unknown Sex Fiend. (1950, February 13). Time. Retrieved December 1, 2008, from http://www.time.com/time/magazine/article/0,9171,811945,00.html?iid=digg_share

Unusual Sentence Stirs Legal Dispute. (1987, August 27). *New York Times*. Retrieved July 17, 2008, from http://www.nytimes.com

U.S. Department of Justice. (2005, July 20). Department of Justice activates National Sex Offender Public Registry website [Press release]. Washington, DC: Department of Justice.

U.S. Department of Justice. (2007, October 16). DOJ announces ICAC task forces in all 50 states [Press release]. Washington, DC: Department of Justice.

Vandiver, D. M., and Walker, J. T. (2002). Female sex offenders: An overview and analysis of 40 cases. *Criminal Justice Review, 27*(2), 284–300.

Vasquez, Bob Edward, Maddan, Sean, and Walker, Jeffery T. (2008). The influence of sex offender registration and notification laws in the United States: A time-series analysis. *Crime and Delinquency, 54*, 175–92.

Wakeling, Helen C., Webster, Stephen D., and Mann, Ruth E. (2005). Sexual offenders' treatment experience: A qualitative and quantitative investigation. *Journal of Sexual Aggression, 11*(2), 171–86.

Wakeling, Helen C., Webster, Stephen, Moulden, Heather M., and Marshall, William L. (2007). Decisions to offend in men who sexually abuse their daughters. *Journal of Sexual Aggression, 13*(2), 81–99.

Wallmyr, Gudrun, and Welin, Catherine. (2006). Young people, pornography, and sexuality: Sources and attitudes. *Journal of School Nursing*, 22(5), 290–95.

Ward, Tony, Hudson, Stephen M., and Marshall, William L. (1996). Attachment style in sex offenders: A preliminary study. *Journal of Sex Research*, 33(1), 17–26.

Warren, J., Reboussin, R., and Hazelwood, R. (1998). Crime scene and distance correlates of serial rape. *Journal of Quantitative Criminology*, 14, 35–39.

Washington State Institute for Public Policy. (2007a). *Comparison of state laws authorizing involuntary commitment of sexually violent predators: 2006 update, revised* (No. 05-03-1101). Olympia: Washington State Institute for Public Policy.

Washington State Institute for Public Policy. (2007b). *Six-year follow-up of 135 released sex offenders recommended for commitment under Washington's sexually violent predator law, where no petition was filed* (No. 03-12-1101). Olympia: Washington State Institute for Public Policy.

Webster, Cheryl Marie, Gartner, Rosemary, and Doob, Anthony N. (2006). Results by design: The artefactual construction of high recidivism rates for sex offenders. *Canadian Journal of Criminology and Criminal Justice*, 48(1), 79–93.

Weeks, J. (1986). *Sexuality*. New York: Routledge.

Wertham, Frederic. (1938). Psychiatry and the prevention of sex crimes. *Journal of Criminal Law and Criminology*, 28(6), 847–53.

Wille, Reinhard, and Beier, Klaus M. (1989). Castration in Germany. *Sexual Abuse: A Journal of Research and Treatment*, 2(2), 103–33.

Wilson, Robin J., Picheca, Janice E., and Prinzo, Michelle. (2005). *Circles of support and accountability: An evaluation of the pilot project in south-central Ontario*. Ottawa: Correctional Service of Canada.

Wood, Raymond M., Grossman, Linda S., and Fichtner, Christopher G. (2000). Psychological assessment, treatment and outcome with sex offenders. *Behavioural Sciences and the Law*, 18, 23–44.

World Health Organization. (2002). *World report on violence and health*. Geneva: World Health Organization.

Yantzi, Mark. (1998). *Sexual offending and restoration*. Waterloo, Canada: Herald Press.

Yessine, Annie K., and Bonta, James. (2006). Tracking high-risk, violent offenders: An examination of the national flagging system. *Canadian Journal of Criminology and Criminal Justice*, 48(4), 573–607.

Zevitz, Richard G., and Farkas, Mary Ann. (2000a). *Sex offender community notification: Assessing the impact in Wisconsin*. Washington, DC: U.S. Department of Justice, National Institute of Justice.

Zevitz, Richard G., and Farkas, Mary Ann. (2000b). Sex offender community notification: Managing high risk criminals or exacting further vengeance? *Behavioural Sciences and the Law*, 18, 375–91.

Zgoba, Kristen J., and Simon, Leonore, M. J. (2005). Recidivism rates of sexual offenders up to 7 years later. *Criminal Justice Review*, 30(2), 155–173.

Zilney, Lisa Anne, and Zilney, Laura Joan. (2008). Sex offender laws. In Gregg Barak (Ed.). *Battleground: Criminal justice* (pp. 671–81). Westport, CT: Greenwood Press.

Zimring, Franklin E., Piquero, Alex R., and Jennings, Wesley G. (2007). Sexual delinquency in Racine: Does early sex offending predict later sex offending in youth and young adulthood. *Criminology and Public Policy*, 6(3), 507–34.

Zonana, Howard V., Bonnie, Richard J., and Hoge, Steven K. (2003). In the wake of *Hendricks:* The treatment and restraint of sexually dangerous offenders viewed from the perspective of American psychiatry. In Bruce J. Winick and John Q. LaFond (Eds.), *Protecting society from sexually dangerous offenders: Law, justice, and therapy* (pp. 131–45). Washington, DC: American Psychological Association.

Index

About the Authors

Laura J. Zilney is a sexologist in private practice in Toronto.

Lisa A. Zilney is assistant professor in the Department of Justice Studies at Montclair State University in New Jersey.